GAY CHILDREN GROWN UP

Gender Culture and Gender Deviance

Joseph Harry

PRAEGER SPECIAL STUDIES • PRAEGER SCIENTIFIC

Library of Congress Cataloging in Publication Data

Harry, Joseph.
    Gay Children Grown Up .

    Bibliography: p.
    Includes index.
    1. Homosexuality, Male. 2. Sex role.
3. Sex differences (Psychology) 4. Children
--Sexual behavior. 5. Youth--Sexual behavior.
I. Title.
HQ76.H353   306.7'662   82-5259
ISBN 0-03-060551-2   AACR2

Published in 1982 by Praeger Publishers
CBS Educational and Professional Publishing
a Division of CBS Inc.
521 Fifth Avenue, New York, New York 10175, U.S.A.

© 1982 by Praeger Publishers

23456789   145   987654321

Printed in the United States of America

PREFACE

This is the story of the ugly duckling who grows up to be a beautiful gay swan. It is a description of virtues acquired through adversity in pre-adulthood. It describes how many gay men were loners, alienated from their childhood and adolescent peers, and averse to male gender culture during that period of their lives. Out of that early differentness they devised varying solutions to their problems of alienation, some of which proved highly useful during adulthood for educational and occupational advancement. Often they adopted a generally social conformist solution which made them model citizens who rarely commit the more serious crimes. Through being alienated from conventional male gender culture they were freed to devise or invent modified gender roles which contain varying mixtures of masculine and feminine culture and which were closer to their individual needs.

The findings and analyses of the present work will probably be objected to by that, still large, segment of the psychiatric profession and their fellow travelers who believe that homosexuality is a psychopathology. This segment includes psychiatrists such as Socarides and Bieber who still maintain that position despite the fact that in 1973 the American Psychiatric Association repudiated their views. Actually, many of the data of the present work are quite similar to the observations of gay men and their childhoods which psychiatrists have noted for many years. However, there is a huge difference between the way in which those data are interpreted in the present work and the way in which they were interpreted by psychiatry. Informed by an unquestioning adoration of gender roles, psychiatrists observed that most gay men were cross-gendered during childhood, e.g., their massive disinterest in sports, and then proceeded to infer that departures from gender-conformist behaviors must be psychopathological. However, such an inference requires several (alternative) assumptions. It may require the sexist assumption that any rational person would choose to be a male if they were given the option. It may require the equally sexist assumption that the feminine gender is inherently inferior. It certainly requires the assumption that it is better for males to be masculine and females to be feminine than alternative possibilities. If one abandons the assumption that gender conventionality is inherently superior to non-conventionality then any link between gender non-conventionality and psychopathology is broken.

Past psychiatric writings on the topic of homosexuality may best be seen as an unrelenting exercise in the apotheosis of gender. Psychiatrists accurately observed some of the ways in which gay men were different, even better, than non-gay men and then proceeded to transform gay virtues into vices according to the conventional rules for gender-appropriate behavior. For example, the present data show that there is a major difference between gay and non-gay males in their propensities toward violent behaviors with the non-gays being much more violent. Psychiatrists have also observed the gentleness of gay men but viewed it as weakness. Psychiatric fellow traveler Karlen (1978, p. 231) observed among gays a "meticulous Peter Pan manner and grooming and an absence of displays of male aggressiveness." In so describing gay men he transforms gay virtues into vices and makes manifest his gender-adoring view of the importance of being a macho man. Similarly, the present work shows that many gays find flair and theatricality more appealing than the drab and rigid costumery in which conventional gender roles have been clothed. Again Karlen (1978, p. 31) does a transvaluation of this flair: "One feels it in the self-consciously exotic atmosphere of many gay restaurants and the melodramatic decor of many gay apartments, certainly in some gay clothing styles which seem a bit like flamboyant costumes. I believe that much of the hostility to the gay scene comes from the hostility to these masks and dramatizations, which leave outsiders feeling that they are talking to actors who hold to their scripts no matter what is said to them." Apparently, Karlen feels gays should "butch up" their apartments and appurtenances.

The great emphasis given in the present work to childhood cross-gendering will be taken by some psychologists and some gays as inconsistent with the position that there are no or few notable differences between gay and non-gay males except in their sexual preference. It is. That position, stemming from the seminal work of Hooker done during the late 1950s, arose during the 1960s and early 1970s from a long series of studies, mostly by psychologists, which found no or minimal differences between gays and non-gays on a variety of psychological measures. The present work also finds no or minimal differences between gays and non-gays on such measures. However, that there may be no gay/non-gay differences on psychological measures does not mean that there are no differences. The differences dealt with in the present work are largely cultural rather than psychological ones. For example, correlates of commitment to the feminine gender role among gay men are explored at length and role femininity is not the same thing as psychological femininity. As the present work shows, the position of no differences has been much overstated. There are many and large differences between gay and non-gay men and these differences are largely in the area of culture rather than psychology.

I would like to acknowledge the methodological and statistical assistance of my colleague, Robert Suchner. Thanks are also due to the publication Gay Life of Chicago for their assistance in the fieldwork phase of the present research and to the organization Maturity for permission to gather data from their members and thereby increase the numbers of truly older respondents in the Chicago sample. Special acknowledgements are due to William Simon who criticized earlier versions of the present work. I am also indebted to Simon for a number of concepts and ideas which have been, variously, borrowed, changed, or distorted to inform the present research. Needless to say, he is not responsible for the fate of his ideas in the hands of others. Thanks are also extended to Ann James, Rich Rice, and John Calimee who assisted in the clerical aspects of the study and to the respondents, gay and non-gay, who took the time to respond to the questionnaires.

CONTENTS

1

THE COMPONENTS
OF GENDER

GENDER AND GENDER DEVIANCE

All societies appear to use the physical fact of sex differences around which they construct the social statuses of gender--men and women. The attribution of gender labels to individuals is immensely consequential for them since it defines in the eyes of others, and usually for themselves, their "essential" and "normal" natures (Kessler and McKenna 1978, p. 2). For example, males are attributed to be normally - intrinsically - more aggressive than females and normally attracted to the opposite sex. Such attributions are usually elaborated in cultural ideologies interpreting the intrinsic natures of men and women, those ideologies variously being formulated in religious or biological or cosmological modes (Herdt 1981, pp. 255-260).

The attribution of gender labels to individuals serves as the basis of an immense number of further attributions of roles, interests, activities, motivations, sexual orientations, skills, and identities. All societies appear to have used gender labels as bases around which to organize and allocate work and authority roles (Linton 1936, p. 116). Such further attributions are made with varying degrees of force, varying from the gender-mandatory to the gender-preferred to the completely optional. We conceive of gender-attributions as being of three principal types: intrinsic mandatory components of gender, derivative aspects of gender, and sex-typed options.

Sex-Typed Options are cultural activities, or, if sufficiently crystallized and elaborated, roles which are usually thought of as being more consistent with one gender or the other but which both genders may engage in without appearing markedly gender-deviant. Examples are sports for males and artistic activities for females. Often, however, if a person of the "wrong" gender engages in the activity some justification may be needed. Derivative Aspects of Gender consist of activities or roles which, while not intrinsic or defining aspects of gender, are based on having a particular gender. For example, while the role of mother is not a defining aspect of gender it is based upon a prior attribution of gender. Sometimes these derivative activities may also be mandatory. Depending on the culture mothering and work roles may be mandatory or optional. One may also have options within such mandatory activities. Intrinsic Mandatory Components of Gender are conceived of as being at least three in number and as always being attributed with a gender. They are variables on which a human must have an attributed score or state and without which he does not have a gender. These components are gender identity, gender role, and sexual orientation.

Gender identity is a self-applied label which a person uses to organize and categorize other attributions and gender-significant phenomena. While Green and Money (1969, p. xv) have defined gender identity as "an individual's sense of maleness or femaleness" we find a definition in terms of self-applied labeling a more precise way of defining this phenomenon and considerably easier to measure than a "sense." In the research done on the gender identities of children or transexuals the usual practice has been to elicit from respondents their own gender labels. The ability to correctly apply gender labels to one's self seems to be established by about age three, although some children may need to be five in order to always correctly place themselves (Thompson 1975). It is interesting to note that before approximately age five or six children do not usually use genitalia as the basis upon which they attribute gender labels. A wide variety of characteristics such as hair length, size, and clothes are viewed as defining characteristics (Kessler and McKenna 1978, pp. 105-109).

Gender role is the set of activities routinely expected of a particular gender. The learning of gender roles starts very early in childhood but, unlike gender labels, continues for many years and throughout life. The continuous learning and reformulation of gender roles appears to derive from two sources. First, gender roles are somewhat age-specific with some activities, e.g., the wearing of cosmetics and various adornments, being expected only of persons of a particular gender and age. Secondly, given the vast number of activities which have been gender-typed, the learning of these normative structures takes more effort and time than the simple learning of a dichotomous set of gender labels.

Sexual orientations are eroticized attractions for a particular gender. So defined, sexual orientations are not exhaustive of all eroticized attractions since there are individuals who eroticize objects other than humans. However, they may be exhaustive of normatively prescribed attractions. This definition of sexual orientations is explicitly not formulated in terms of actual sexual behaviors of an individual since there are a variety of motives other than erotic attractions for which an individual may engage in sexual behaviors. It seems that sexual orientations are always attributed to persons as an intrinsic part of gender attribution, even in those cases where individuals are expected to be sexually inactive. For example, Vestal Virgins, Catholic Priests, and the old are expected to be heterosexually asexual and not simply asexual.

The attribution of a sexual orientation may be to a person's past, as in the case of the old, to a person's present, as for most adults, or to a person's future, as with children. In the case of children, it seems that sexual orientations are attributed to their futures and children are early made aware of those futures through such comments as "when you begin to date boys" or "when you grow up and marry a nice man." Although there appear to be a few societies (Herdt 1981) in which individuals are expected to behave homosexually during one phase of their lives and heterosexually during a later phase, constancy of sexual orientation across the life-span is the much more common case. Also, knowledge of one's attributed future sexual orientation often seems an important part of one's present and may partially organize that present. The "effects" of such future attributions on one's present is seen in children's preoccupations with who and what kind of person they plan to marry.

Empirically the components of gender are highly correlated across persons. Males usually have a male gender identity, play a male gender role, and eroticize females. However, there are many exceptions. Figure 1.1 illustrates the logically possible combinations of the three components of gender for males. For simplicity we present these three components as being dichotomous although in reality some may be continua. Of the eight possible combinations of the three components only one is viewed as normative in western cultures. The other seven constitute various forms of gender deviance. An inspection of these categories reveals that a sizable minority of the general population is gender-deviant in some way with the homosexuals constituting the largest groups.

It should be noted that what is gender deviance in one culture may not be in another. Herdt (1981) has recently reported that in the Sambia tribe of Papua homosexual behaviors are mandatory for all males between the approximate ages of seven and 19. Prepubescent males are expected and coerced into fellating adolescent males on a daily basis. The Sambian rationales for this practice are the beliefs that boys will not grow into masculine adults unless they acquire semen from other males and that males are incapable of producing semen. They only pass it down from one cohort to the next. During late adolescence they marry and become exclusively, and normatively, heterosexual. In this culture it appears that male homosexual activity occurs in the service of the masculine gender role rather than, as in western and many other cultures, being attributed to some aspect of the feminine gender role (Carrier 1977).

Figure 1.1

Possible Combinations Among Men of Gender Identity,
Gender Role Preference, and Sexual Orientation

	Gender Identity							
	Male				**Female**			
	Gender-Role Preference				Gender-Role Preference			
	Masculine		Feminine		Masculine		Feminine	
Sexual Orientation	Sexual Orientation		Sexual Orientation		Sexual Orientation		Sexual Orientation	
	Heterosexual	Homosexual	Heterosexual	Homosexual	Heterosexual	Homosexual	Heterosexual	Homosexual
Heterosexual	(1) Conventional Heterosexuals		(3) Effeminate Heterosexuals, Heterosexual Transvestites		(5) ?		(7) Heterosexual Transsexuals ("Lesbians")	
Homosexual		(2) Masculine Gays		(4) Effeminate Gays		(6) ?		(8) Most Transsexuals

4

The existence of sizable numbers of gender deviants shows that the gender attribution process is not a mechanical completely predictable sequence of events in which what is attributed to individuals is also internalized by them. While the attribution of gender seems highly predictable the recipient individual may misperceive the attributions or may not like them and resist. Until approximately age five or six, not all children are completely convinced that one cannot change one's gender by changing one's activities or clothes (Kohlberg 1966). Green (1976) has reported many cases of boys who, while knowing that they are males, prefer the feminine gender role and resist efforts to involve them in the masculine gender role. Hence, the gender role attributed need not result in a corresponding gender-role preference.

The existence of sizable numbers of gender-deviant persons shows that the process of gender ascription, and perhaps all ascribed roles, involve a societal mystification of gender. Gender ascription involves teaching individuals that the components of gender are necessary and natural. It involves teaching them what is not possible. However, since gender deviants clearly are possible their existence shows that gender ascription is a mystificatory denial of the possible. It may be this denial of the possible which makes gender deviants so "abnormal" and incomprehensible to gender non-deviants. As one woman said of a gay man of the author's acquaintance, "people like that aren't supposed to exist." This mystification may also give rise to the "hide the children" phenomenon in which the impossible is hidden from those exploring possibilities.

We are not here suggesting that gender-conventional persons typically believe that gender-deviant ones do not exist. Rather, it seems that conventional persons attempt to hide the incomprehensible reality of gender-deviant persons from themselves and, on those occasions on which gender deviance is discussed, it is used to support the naturalness and credibility of gender conventionality. While the gender-conventional are able to discuss quite seriously non-gender-deviant forms of deviance with psychological comfort, e.g., rape or homicide, many experience considerable uneasiness in entertaining gender deviance. This uneasiness seems to lie behind the quite conscious efforts of the gender-conventional to deny visibility to such persons as gays, lesbians, and transexuals. As Levitt and Klassen (1974) reported from a national survey, 81 percent of the population agreed to the item "I won't associate with these people (homosexuals) if I can help it."

Gender-ascription involves teaching persons that each component of gender inevitably implies and requires the others. It involves teaching individuals of the "fact" of gender constancy. It involves teaching them that anatomy is destiny and that in some sense the components of gender have a natural link to that anatomy. Individuals so convinced can then be reliably trusted not to deviate far from gender norms. Although they may become involved in sexual deviance, e.g., prostitution or rape, they will not become involved in gender deviance.

It seems that the major step in this mystification process is in inducing the child to believe in gender labels. This involves teaching him that persons are, in fact, either of one gender or the other. After the establishment of such gender identities their role content is filled in over the years. However, the teaching of the reality of gender-labels is instruction in the reification of gender. It involves not simply instruction that the components of gender are sufficiently highly correlated that they may be treated as if they were a single entity, but that they are a single entity. Individuals so convinced are then unlikely to question the reality of genders. Among such individuals the components of gender are unlikely to become unglued and thereby unpredictable.

But what happens when they do become unglued? Does their behavior become unpredictable and vary widely across the components of gender and other gender-typed activities? Since few cultures prepare normatively acceptable alternative scripts for individuals inclined to gender deviance there is a consequent lack of mechanisms for the control of gender-deviance. While several primitive cultures have provided alternative roles for persons who may want to play the cross-gender role, e.g., the berdache in some Indian tribes , such alternatives are not normatively available in modern societies (Tripp 1975, pp. 65-66). Given the lack of institutional support for gender-deviant alternatives and the only employed means of their control being repression, one might anticipate considerable variability in the gender-significant behaviors of the gender deviant.

At first glance there does appear to be considerable varia- tion over time among the gender-deviant in the nature of their sexual behaviors. Saghir and Robins (1975, pp. 88, 246) have reported that 46 percent of their gay male respondents and 79 percent of their lesbian respondents have had heterosexual inter- course. Similarly, Bell and Weinberg (1978, p. 286) reported that two-thirds of their gay men and five-sixths of their lesbians had had heterosexual intercourse. These percentages seem considerably higher than the 37 percent of the total male population which "has had at least some overt homosexual experience to the point of orgasm between adolescence and old age" (Kinsey et al. 1948, p. 650). Do these data suggest that once the individual has departed from conventional conceptions of gender-appropriate behavior he then is freed to drift from one form of erotic behavior to another without the constraints of gender mystification.

In dealing with this question, one must note that when examining erotic behaviors, and most others, it is necessary to determine the gender significance or meaning of that behavior to the individual. Individuals can engage in sexual behaviors for such a wide variety of reasons other than erotic interest that sexual behaviors seem almost intrinsically meaningless. As any prostitute knows, sexual intercourse does not necessarily imply erotic attraction on her part. Similarly, a considerable percentage of those gay men who have engaged in heterosexual intercourse did so, not out of feelings of heterosexual attraction, but in order to conform to societal expectations that they should be or become heterosexual. Similarly, I have talked to heterosexually married gay men who, while engaging in intercourse with their wives, fantasized about males in order to be able to complete the act. The lack of strongly erotic motivations for engaging in heterosexual acts was reported by Saghir and Robins (1973, p. 92) who said that "None of the homosexual males was adequately satisfied with his heterosexual experiences" while "All of the heterosexual controls reported adequate and positive satisfaction."

It is also possible for gender-conventional individuals to engage in homosexual behaviors without those behaviors being expressive of homosexual erotic interests, i.e., without eroticization of the sexual partner. Reiss (1961) has reported cases of adolescent males who engaged in homosexual acts for money with adult homosexuals while denying any homoerotic feelings and representing themselves as completely gender-conventional. They viewed their behaviors, apparently, as sexually deviant rather than gender-deviant. In order to assess the gender significance of the homosexual behaviors of youthful male prostitutes providing sexual services to males Freund (1974) administered phallometric tests to them in which pictures of nude persons of varying sexes were shown to the subjects while a phallometer measured their physical responses. He found that none of them showed any responsiveness to pictures of males. All proved thoroughly heterosexual. In broadening the scope of his subjects for his phallometric tests Freund (1974) has reported an inability to find any truly bisexual males who respond approximately equally to both sexes. However, Masters and Johnson (1979, pp. 144-173) may have found some true bisexuals in their "ambisexuals." We need not here take any position on the question of whether true bisexuals exist but rather observe that a large amount of sexual behavior, both conventional and non-conventional, seems motivated by other than erotic interests.

That objectively conventional or nonconventional sexual behaviors are often not expressions of corresponding conventional and nonconventional erotic interests means that we must distinguish between subjective versus behavioral gender deviance and gender conventionality. Persons classified as deviant by a behavioral criterion need not be also so classified by a subjective criterion and conversely. This distinction seems somewhat accepted in popular views of gender-deviant sexual behaviors. A number of rationalizations for engaging in homosexual behaviors under certain circumstances seem to have popular acceptance since the rationalizations for these behaviors call upon temporary motivations and situational influences other than truly homoerotic feelings. Examples of such justifications are "I was drunk," "I was in prison," "I was just a kid." Tripp (1975, pp. 125-131) has also described several additional justifications. Such justifications seem to be classic "techniques of neutralization" for defending against an accusation of truly gender-deviant motivations (Sykes and Matza 1957). It is the truly - subjectively-gender-deviant motivations which remain incomprehensible and abhorrent to the gender conventional.

It is important to note that some of the accounts given for engaging in gender-deviant sexual behaviors call upon quite gender-conventional motives. This is shown in studies of homosexual behaviors in prisons where younger prisoners destined by circumstances to play the role of sexual insertees are also cast into an approximation of the feminine gender role by their older insertors (Lockwood 1980, pp. 124-126). Through casting the sexual partner into the feminine role, at least subjectively, homosexual behavior becomes psychologically possible for the insertors without staining their own self images as masculine. (We recognize the presence of other motivations of dominance and aggression toward their sexual partners who are typically of a different race.) The reasons for the insertees engaging in these behaviors appear to be combinations of being coerced, sometimes being truly homosexual, and profit. Such cases of prison homosexuality seem to be ones where the insertor engages in objectively gender-deviant sexual behaviors through informing the acts with gender-conventional meanings such that they, in their own eyes, are gender conformists.

Many gender deviants, and particularly the categories of gender deviance which are the most common, seem to also inform their nonconformist sexual behaviors with meanings taken from conventional gender-roles. However, in these cases it is the self which is cast into the cross-gender role rather than, as in the case of insertor prisoners, the sexual partner. The cases in which the gender role is concordant with sexual preference are homosexual male transexuals and effeminate homosexuals or those homosexuals who had childhood histories of a cross-gender role-preference. These two categories are by far more common than those of male-to-female heterosexual transexuals, effeminate heterosexuals, heterosexual transvestites, and somewhat more common than homosexuals with no histories of a cross-gender role-preference (see Figure 1).

That gender-role seems to inform sexual behaviors in a probable majority of gender-deviant persons suggests that such gender deviants are only departing in certain specific ways from gender conventionality and that, given their commitment to a particular role, they are rather culturally gender conservative. The case best illustrative of this point is that of homosexual transexuals. The latter have been found to be extremely conservative in their interpretation of their adopted feminine gender-role (Kando 1974, 1973). They often have an occupational ideal of housewife, are only interested in highly traditional sex-typed erotic activities in bed, and agree more than either heterosexual males or females to such items as "In the final analysis men should lead and women should follow" or "cooking and sewing are women's skills" (Kando 1974). The evidence on transexuals seems to say that they, rather than being gender-revolutionaries, appear to be counter-revolutionaries. Effeminate homosexuals are a case which may also be manifesting a considerable measure of cultural role conservatism.

The case of masculine gay men is the most common one where sexual object choice does not conform to role-preference. These individuals seem to be true departures from both male and female gender roles in that they have not cast themselves into a feminine gender-role in order to engage in homosexual behaviors. There, of course, remains the question of whether they, like heterosexual insertor prisoners, tend to feminize the sexual partner in order to engage in homosexual acts. Such feminization of the sexual partner, however, need not conform to the role preference of the partner since the erotic desires of sexual partners do not always result in a close match of those desires. If masculine gays do not tend to feminize the partner, they would then seem to be reasonable examples of gender revolutionaries who have departed from gender roles and organized their erotic interests around other visions.

The cases of heterosexual male-to-female transexuals, heterosexuals transvestites, and effeminate heterosexuals also seem to be instances where gender-roles are not concordant with sexual orientation. It should be noted that the boundaries or distinguishing criteria between these three categories of men are less than clear. Raymond (1979, p. 104) has raised the question of deception by heterosexual transexuals in order to obtain sex-reassignment operations. Candidates for sex-reassignment must pass a number of tests of their femininity and prove to the attending physicians that they do, in fact, have a cross-gender identity. One of the major such tests is a desire to have sexual relations with persons of the same sex. If there was, in fact, deception on the part of many such transexuals, it would seem they should more reasonably be classified as heterosexual transvestities rather than heterosexual transexuals (Column 4 rather than Column 7 in Figure 1). It is also possible that they changed their minds about their sexual interests after the sex-reassignments.

Classificatory problems also arise with heterosexual transvestite men since it is often not clear just what objects they are eroticizing (Barr et al. 1974; Feinbloom et al. 1976). While many appear to engage in heterosexual relations, it is not clear whether they are simply enamored of the feminine gender-role and enjoy cross-dressing, often in explicitly sexual settings such as the marital bedroom, but may be rather asexual persons. Alternatively, some may have eroticized, not women, but the feminine gender-role and like to masturbate while cross-dressing. They do not seem to have homosexual fantasies in which they relate sexually to another man as a man. Rather, they seem to fantasize either relating sexually to another man as a woman or to a woman as a man. Some such men seem to have a measure of bisexuality or, alternatively, alternative gender-typed erotic scripts into which they can cast themselves and their partners. To the extent this is so, they strain our dichotomous classifications of gender-role, gender-identity, and sexual orientation. Their gender-visions may be so multiple, or chaotic and confused, that an analysis of them which does not take into account considerable idiosyncratic experiences and biographies may not be possible.

The other case which does not conform to the notion that gender-roles often provide meanings around which erotic behaviors are formed is that of effeminate heterosexual men. However, one may question the extent to which effeminacy in heterosexual nontransvestite men is an indicator of a cross-gender role preference. While personal styles of self presentation and sex-typed cultural interests are aspects of a gender-role preference, there is considerable variability within both males and females in the manifestation of such styles and interests which is not indicative of a cross-gender role-preference. To be indicative of role preference they should be behaviorally clustered or organized to a sufficient extent that one may speak of a role, rather than of interests, or alternatively, they must be sufficiently blatant, e.g., cross-dressing, that their role significance is difficult to mistake. More importantly, there is the question of whether the effeminate heterosexual man perceives his cross-gender manifestations as indicative of a feminine gender-role preference or as simply gender nonsignificant, even though statistically uncommon for a male. Since behavioral gender deviance need not entail self-perceived gender deviance, the case of effeminate heterosexual men as it bears on the relationship between gender role and sexual orientation remains an empirical question.

The very common, although not unexceptional, influence of gender-roles in informing both the erotic and non-erotic behaviors of persons both gender-conventional and unconventional seems to attest to the power of gender-roles in guiding behavior in often very gender-conservative directions. Sex-typed cultural interests and activities, once crystallized to the organizational levels of roles and thereby given gender-significance, appear to lead persons into inhabiting rather different cultural worlds. This cultural gender segregation, not sex segregation, appears to occur to an even greater extent for those individuals who have proceeded to make the inferential leap from gender-role preference to a concordant gender identity. The great gender-conservatism of male transexuals has already been noted. Such cultural conservatism and segregation also seems to occur in the case of female-to-male transexuals. McCauley and Ehrhardt (1977), comparing female transexuals and lesbians, found the former to be more often found in traditionally masculine manual jobs. Conventional heterosexuals are also a case where gender role has become linked to gender identity. Hence, we would expect a fairly high degree of gender conservatism among them, as compared with effeminate homosexuals where a cross-gender role-preference has not been accompanied by a corresponding inference of identity.

It should be noted that there are reasons for expecting the effects of gender-role preference to be greater among males than among females, particularly in the allocation of work-roles and domestic chores. Women are disproportionately found in those jobs sex typed for women, e.g., clerical, sales, service, and selected professions such as nursing (Sewell et al. 1980). These occupations have considerably lower status and pay than those occupied by men. Hence, there are substantial material inducements for women to want to depart from traditional gender roles but lesser inducements for men. Consistent with this, a variety of sources indicate that men are more self-confined to their gender role than women. A 1970 Gallup Poll reported that 16 percent of women versus 4 percent of men said they had "ever wished (they) belonged to the opposite sex" (The Gallup Poll 1972). Similarly, Kohlberg and Zigler (1967, p. 141) in studying children of ages four to seven found that "girls are less feminine in their (play) choices than boys are masculine and that this difference between the sexes becomes increasingly large as the children get older".

That conventional males are more restricted to their own gender-role and express less interest in the cross-gender role than do females seems partially inconsistent with other data that most forms of role-significant gender deviance are much more common among the former than the latter. There appears to be fairly general agreement that male homosexuals are more common than female homosexuals and that male transexuals are more common than female transexuals by ratios varying from 2:1 to 4:1 (Kinsey et al. 1953, pp. 474-475; Pauly 1969; Money and Ehrhardt 1972). Several explanations for this are possible. First, when girls engage in "tomboyish" behavior they are less likely to be negatively sanctioned than are boys engaging in feminine behaviors. Hence, more girls may be tomboyish without being perceived as significantly departing from their gender-role. Thus, there may be more cross-gender behavior among females than has been acknowledged. Saghir and Robins (1973, p. 193) found that 3 percent of their heterosexual males exhibited a "sissy" syndrome in childhood--Zuger (1966) found 5 percent among grade school boys--versus 16 percent being tomboyish among their heterosexual females. Secondly, the lower rate of homosexuality among females than among males may be partially due to the latter's options being more socially narrowly controlled such that they are impelled into marriages by their relatives and friends more than are men. In this case, a number of potentially homosexual women have become submerged in the world of heterosexual marriages. Consistent with this, Bell and Weinberg (1978, p. 374) and Saghir and Robins (1973, p. 255) found that a higher percentage of homosexual women than of homosexual men had been married. Thirdly, it may be that gender-role preferences are more causative of sexual preferences among males than females.

Whitam (1977) has reported that a childhood cross-gender role preference is more common in the childhoods of homosexual males than of homosexual females. [However, Saghir and Robins (1973, pp. 78, 193) found no corresponding difference.] Blumstein and Schwartz (1977) have found that lesbians seem to be a more heterogeneous group than gay men in their motivational accounts for engaging in homosexual behaviors. For example, a number became lesbians substantially due to feminist ideologies rather than the impulsions of erotic scripts. The probable greater heterogeneity of motivations leading to female homosexual behaviors implies a looser link between role preference and sexual preferences among women. This interpretation may partly account for the fact that there are fewer female than male homosexuals, but not for the "fact" that there are fewer women with a cross-gender role preference than there are men.

We are led from the above to offer that departures from the conventional triple attribution of identity, role, and sexual orientation are infrequently complete departures. Many aspects of conventional gender roles continue to be employed by the gender deviant to give meaning to unconventional behaviors. For example, Gagnon and Simon (1973, pp. 197-209) have observed that lesbians often use highly feminine romanticized conceptions of love to inform their relationships. Such conceptions could almost have been taken from teenage romance magazines. Other types of gender deviants seem to cling to some of the most conservative elements of gender roles, e.g., transexuals, so that, aside from their unconventional combinations of identity and sexual behaviors, they would be culturally presentable to anyone's mother. It seems that, in the world of gender-deviance, there is much more cultural conservatism than is often believed. Still, some, such as always masculine homosexual males, seem to be true gender revolutionaries.

THE LINKS AMONG GENDER ROLE, GENDER IDENTITY, AND SEXUAL ORIENTATION

It is apparent from Figure 1.1 that a cross-gender role preference is neither necessary nor sufficient for a homosexual orientation. The only linkage in Figure 1.1 which implies certainty is that a cross-gender role preference seems necessary for a cross-gender identity. This necessity arises out of the likely absence of persons in columns 5 and 6 of that figure. In column 5 are males with a masculine role-preference and a heterosexual orientation who thereby seem to lack any basis for making an inference that they are, in fact, females. Those in column 6 have a masculine role-preference and a homosexual orientation and while they could possibly be masculine homosexuals, it seems that virtually all adult homosexuals, including those who are masculine, deny any interest in being females. Hence, homosexual interests per se seem to be insufficient to induce a male to lay claim to the label of woman.

The necessity of a cross-gender role preference, rather than a homosexual orientation, for the establishment of a cross-gender identity seems to point to the importance of gender role rather than sexual orientation for the internalization of societal gender labels.

A major thesis of the present work is that, while gender-role preference is neither necessary nor sufficient for the determination of sexual orientation, it strongly influences the latter. In their recent study Bell, Weinberg, and Hammersmith (1981a, pp. 75-77) found that childhood cross-gender role preferences were the most important predictor of adult orientation. Among males the total path analytic effect of a childhood cross-gender role preference was 0.61 while among females it was 0.53. This variable dominated all others in their data and was linked to most of their adult variables. Saghir and Robins (1973, p. 18) found that 67 percent of their male homosexuals exhibited a "sissy" syndrome of behaviors and interests versus 3 percent of their heterosexual respondents. Similarly, Whitam (1977) found that 94 percent of his gay male respondents versus 26 percent of his heterosexual respondents exhibited at least one of six cross-gender characteristics during childhood. His cross-gender items included having wanted to be a girl, preferring to play with girls, being considered a sissy. Whitam (1980) has subsequently replicated his gay/nongay differences in Brazil and Guatamala. Freund (1974) has also found that gay men score considerably higher on his Feminine Gender-Identity Scale than do heterosexuals but also score considerably lower than male transexuals. Freund's scale consists of items asking about cross-gender characteristics during childhood, adolescence, and adulthood combined. It should be noted that Freund's homosexual respondents showed much greater variability on his scale than either the heterosexuals or the transexuals and had considerable overlap with the heterosexuals and only a little with the transexuals who had no overlap with the heterosexuals.

While these data show a sizable association between sexual orientation and a childhood cross-gender role preference, it appears that they have always been percentaged by the various researchers in the wrong direction. All of the researchers exploring the association of sexual orientation and a cross-gender role preference have assumed that the latter is the causative variable influencing sexual orientation. While it is conceivable that a propensity to homosexuality or heterosexuality induces an individual to adopt a role preference concordant with his sexual propensities, there are several reasons for discounting this possibility. First, studies of effeminate boys (Green 1976; Zuger 1966; Stoller 1968) have shown that their cross-gender role preferences appear to be largely established between the ages of two and six. These years seem to precede the years of crystallization of an erotic preference which typically occurs around puberty or thereafter. While Kinsey et al. (1948, pp. 164-165) have shown that prepubescent boys are often sexually excitable, their excitability seems unfocused on a particular sex, often being aroused by an immense variety of objects and activities including urinating, big fires, seeing females, and the national anthem. Their sexual excitability does not seem to have yet become differentiated from general excitability.

Second, if one were to assume that a sexual orientation preceded the establishment of a gender-role preference during very early childhood, one would be quite lacking in evidence for a gender-focused form of sexuality distinct from general excitability. Third, it is possible that there are biologically induced predispositions of temperament which dispose an individual toward a feminine or masculine gender role. However, it would be a gratuitous assumption that those things which predispose one toward a gender role also predispose one toward a concordant sexual orientation. While it has been conclusively shown (Meyer-Bahlburg 1977) that levels of prenatal sex hormones can influence the sexual behaviors of nonhuman mammals, there is as yet no evidence that such effects also occur in humans without also producing a number of physical abnormalities which are rarely found among gender deviants.

Since the extant evidence seems contrary to the hypothesis that sexual orientation influences the early development of a gender-role preference during childhood, we proceed with the reverse hypothesis. If gender-role preference is to be considered the principal independent variable it seems that all researchers on this topic have mispercentaged their data. However, the reasons for this mispercentaging seems understandable given the difficulties or impossibilities of obtaining representative samples of gender deviants. We have reworked the American data of Saghir and Robins and of Whitam using a cross-gender role preference as the independent variable and taken from Kinsey et al. (1948, p. 151) his estimate that 10 percent of the adult male population is homosexual (Kinsey 5s and 6s). So refigured, we find from the Saghir and Robins data that 71 percent of those with a "polysymptomatic effeminacy" during childhood are adult gays versus 4 percent of those without such effeminacy. A similar reworking of Whitam's data proceeds as follows. We first divide Whitam's gay and non-gay groups into those who possess more than two of six cross-gender characteristics and those who possess two or less. This cutting point seems to correspond to Saghir and Robins' criterion of "sissiness" that the respondent should have possessed several such characteristics (Saghir and Robins do not state the exact number of items they used). This cutting point results in 62 percent of whitam's gays and 8 percent of his heterosexuals being cross-gendered during childhood, results which are quite comparable to Saghir and Robins 67 versus 3 percent. Using the Kinsey et al. weights and reversing the direction of percentaging, we find that 63 percent of those with a childhood cross-gender role-preference are adult gays versus 4 percent of the others. These results are quite similar to those of Saghir and Robins and show huge differences between the childhood cross-gendered and non-cross-gendered in adult sexual orientation. While a childhood cross-gender role-preference is not determinative of sexual orientation, it makes it more likely than not that the person will be gay.

It is worth noting that the above reworked data may somewhat understate the relationship between childhood gender-role preference and adult sexual propensities since only gays and heterosexuals have been included in the data. Not included were transexuals and transvestites. Zuger (1966) and Lebovitz (1972) have restudied during adolescence and early adulthood effeminate boys who had been interviewed during childhood. Transexualism and transvestism were alternative developments to homosexuality for some of these boys, although homosexuality was the most common denouement of the three. It should be noted that Lebovitz (1972) found that less than half of his childhood-effeminate boys were nonheterosexual. However, there is reason to believe that the percentage of nonheterosexuals would have been a fair amount larger if he had re-interviewed them when they were somewhat older. Since gay men do not come to a full realization of their homosexuality until approximately 19 or 20 (Dank 1971; Harry and DeVall 1978, p. 65), more might have been found to be gay if interviewed a few years later. Also, since eight of Lebovitz's original 36 effeminate boys, while willing to be interviewed, had moved too far away to be interviewed, and since there is every reason to expect gay men to be much more geographically mobile than heterosexual men, it seems likely that there was differential mortality in Lebovitz's study by sexual orientation. The probable greater geographic mobility of gay men, principally to large cities, seems likely to create problems for future longitudinal studies of gays.

It is useful to observe that one gets somewhat different results in reworking the Whitam data if one uses the weaker criterion of possessing any of his sex indicators versus none. Applying the Kinsey et al. weights, we find that only 53 percent of the childhood cross-gendered are adult gays as compared with 63 percent using the higher cutting point. This means that heterosexuals constitute almost half of the childhood cross-gendered and that, using the weaker criterion for cross-gendering, cross-gendering might appear a not very good predictor of sexual preference. However, we interpret this difference in results as meaning that minimal amounts of cross-gendering such as that manifested in the possession of one or two cross-gender characteristics may have little significance for sexual orientation. Until such characteristics are sufficiently clustered or crystallized into an entity that may be called a gender role, they have little subjective gender significance. Rather, they may be simply gender-atypical behaviors arising out of situational influences or be gender-atypical interests such as those earlier described as correlating with gender but not defining it or derivative of it.

Although there is a strong association between a childhood cross-gender role preference and adult male homosexuality, adult transexualism is also a possible denouement. While adult gay men and transexuals are behaviorally both homosexuals, the principal difference between the two is that transexuals have acquired a cross-gender identity while gay men have not. There are possible alternative explanations as to why a childhood cross-gender role preference in some results in a cross-gender identity but not in others. Transexuals may be those who were most extreme in their cross-gender role preference while gay men may have been less extreme. Lebovitz (1972) found that transexuals seemed to manifest a cross-gender role-preference somewhat earlier in childhood than did homosexuals, although the numbers of his subjects were small. If extremeness of childhood cross-gendering is the operative variable, then it seems that at the extreme of desire to be a woman, transexuals transform the criterion of gender from physical sex to that of desire. Desire thus becomes identity and the transexual then escapes the conventional construction of gender status. While this inferential leap seems to be a rather creative reworking of gender roles and an escape from the mystification of gender, transexuals seem to have recreated the gender identity trap by insisting that there is such a thing as a "real" woman and that desire defines it. While transexuals have repudiated a particular gender status, they have not repudiated the concept of gender status.

A second interpretation accounting for why a cross-gender role preference sometimes eventuates in male homosexuality and sometimes results in transexualism involves the timing of the acquisition of the cross-gender role preference. As noted above, Lebovitz (1972) found that transexuals seemed to manifest a cross-gender role preference earlier in childhood than did homosexuals. If the acquisition of that preference occurs during the second and third years of life at the same time that gender identity appears to be formed, the two may become fused as in the case of transexualism. However, if a cross-gender role preference appears somewhat after the establishment of a male gender identity, the denouement of male homosexuality may be more likely. Answers to these questions seem possible only with longitudinal studies.

A possible hypothesis explaining homosexuality in non-cross-gendered males arises out of their possible views of and experiences with sex and sexuality during early adolescence. Kinsey et al. (1948, pp. 320-321) found that males who come to puberty earlier engage in more homosexual behaviors during adolescence. Coming to puberty and becoming sexually active at an early age may be conducive to homosexual behaviors since social groups during early adolescence are still very largely sex-segregated. Homosexual experiences during this period, supplemented by various cultural sex-role stereotypes, can lead to the identification of sexuality with the male sex such that only or principally males are viewed as sexual beings. A piece of evidence consistent with this hypothesis was found by Saghir and Robins (1973, p. 41) who reported that more of their homosexual childhood "sissies" reported heterosexual fantasies during childhood than did their homosexual nonsissies. In erotic desires those homosexual men not cross-gendered during childhood may thus be even more purely homosexual than the cross-gendered. Since our principal interests in the chapters to follow lie in the pursuit of the adult effects and correlates of gender role rather than in explaining sexual orientation, we do not follow up on this hypothesis.

GENDER CULTURE

The pervasive influence of gender in allocating persons, somewhat independently of sex, to differing erotic scripts, occupational interests, leisure recreations, and toy preferences suggests the possibility that one may legitimately speak of differing gender-cultures (Lee and Gropper 1974). Do males and females have differing cultures? If by gender-culture we mean do males and females value different activities for themselves, the answer is a massive "yes." Various researchers (Green 1976; Kohlberg and Zigler 1967; Looft 1971; Nemerowicz 1979, p. 130) have shown that from early childhood boys and girls exhibit great differences in their toy preferences and occupational aspirations. However, there is also a great consensus between the sexes that, although each sex prefers different activities for themselves, they also view the other sex's self-preferences as gender-appropriate. For example, Duncan and Duncan (1979, p. 331) found among adults "fantastically close agreement between the sexes just how sex typed" 11 household tasks for children were, although women were less sex-typing than men. Because of this great consensus, one may not legitimately speak of differing gender-cultures if one is talking about views of gender-appropriate behaviors and interests.

Language and shared meaning are at the core of a definition of culture. If males and females share a common culture, one would assume that common words have the same meanings for them. However, Diamond (1977) has shown that men and women quite systematically differ in their interpretations of a number of very basic words. He conducted many games of charades in which men and women were asked to give physical depictions of words such as "love" or "child". For the word "love", women gave facial interpretations expressing emotions while men typically provided more pelvic ones. For the word "child", women gave baby-in-arms interpretations while men depicted older children. Since there appear to be quite systematic sex differences in the meanings men and women give to words they supposedly share, one may wonder whether it is legitimate to speak of their sharing a common culture.

Bernard (1981), in her fine recent work The Female World, has documented the large number of ways in which men and women across history have organized their values and interpersonal relations. She argues that their interests have differed systematically such that men have been the on-stage actors of the Gesellschaft while women have been the keepers of the Gemeinschaft and its respective functions. However, men have often been unaware of the activities and interests of women and, if aware of them, have ignored them. This raises the question of the extent to which men and women are aware of each other's roles and cultures. Daley (1981) has provided some evidence on this question in a recent analysis of the ways in which twentieth century male and female novelists have depicted male and female personalities in their novels. She reported that male authors depict male and female characters as very similar. However, while female authors depict males as similar to the males depicted by male authors, their female characters are quite different. This suggests an asymmetry such that while female authors can understand the world of males, male authors are less able to understand and share the female world. There thus seems to be a moderate amount of evidence justifying a distinction between the cultures of men and women.

The definition of gender culture we find useful is in terms of the culture valued for itself by a particular gender independently of the degree of intergender consensus. Such gender cultures sometimes give rise to complementary gender-roles such as discussed by Parsons and Shils (1951, pp. 190-191), e.g., husband-wife, boss-secretary. However, before adolescence the gender cultures seem to give rise not to complementary roles, but to sets of parallel activities in which boys and girls engage in a largely physically and sex-segregated basis. Until the advent of sexuality and dating after puberty, boys and girls have little to do with each other and little interest in the activities of the other. This seems to be particularly true of boys. As Kohlberg and Zigler found (1967, p. 144), "girls . . . found boys more attractive than boys found girls." During childhood, girls seem at most to be cast into the passive role of audience for the activities of boys.

The degree to which gender-roles are reciprocal appears to have been exaggerated, especially for pre-adults. If boys and girls have little to do with each other and associate little with each other there seems to be only a meager basis for arguing reciprocality. There is, however, some basis for arguing reciprocality since boys and girls serve as negative reference groups for each other (Merton 1957, pp. 354-355). They define for each other what a boy or girl is not supposed to be like. However, this negative form of reciprocality only serves to physically and interactionally segregate them from each other and perpetuate the existence of parallel nonreciprocal gender roles and gender cultures. The positive contents of these roles and cultures are not defined reciprocally but are learned in largely unisexual contexts. It thus seems that one may not legitimately speak of reciprocal sex roles, but only of reciprocal heterosexual roles, the latter being acquired during adolescence or, in some highly gender-differentiating cultures, e.g., Islamic, during adulthood.

It appears to be during the period of late childhood that contrasting definitions of gender role reach their extremes of elaboration. Boys typically view gender role activities as non-overlapping and see engaging in cross-gender behavior as deeply shameful. As a second and a fourth grade boy said of their father's reactions to their own hypothetical assuming their mothers' work and housework roles, "He'd think I'm a sissy" and "He'd think I'm a faggot" (Nemerowicz 1979, p. 153). It seems clear that not only notions of appropriate gender-culture are established during childhood, but also ones of gender deviance, especially among boys. The label given to failure in the performance of gender-appropriate behaviors by boys is "sissy." Later, toward puberty, the label of sissy is given a sexual meaning in the form of "faggot." The term "homosexual" seems to enter the vocabularies of boys during late childhood.

The gender-typing of a variety of areas of achievement by children and adolescents has been found by Stein and Smithells (1969) to be very strong. These authors asked second, fourth, and twelfth grade boys and girls to rate as masculine or feminine the activities of athletics, art, reading, arithmetic, social skills, and spatial/mechanical ones. These were ordered, by the children, from masculine to feminine as follows: athletics, spatial/mechanical, arithmetic, reading, art, and social skills. The differences were quite large. There was also general consistency in the ratings between twelfth and second grade students, showing that such gender typing is established quite early. A case of inconsistency was that the twelfth graders tended to rate art as less feminine, but still feminine, than did second graders. This age-related change apparently reflected the increasing realization by the twelfth graders that the world of art is a largely male-dominated one. The reasons why young children should misperceive art as a feminine activity are somewhat unclear.

The extreme dichotomization of gender-cultures appears to abate somewhat beginning with adolescence. Impelled by age-specific gender scripts, it becomes first permissible and later mandatory for persons of differing sexes to associate with each other. Such associations result in the introduction of complementary roles into gender culture, e.g., dating. In western cultures permitting considerable cross-gender contacts prior to marriage there also seems to arise not simply complementary roles, but actual sharing of activities and interests. Such sharing involves a muting of the earlier starkly defined non-overlapping gender cultures. The learning of differing interests from each other appears to often occur in the areas of the romantic and erotic. Simon (1973) has suggested that in the course of adolescent dating males come to acquire more romanticized conceptions of the erotic while females come to acquire more eroticized conceptions of the romantic. Through a series of negotiations of their respective goals and interests, males and females are, at last, able to come together in an area of common interest.

The above sketched social and cultural structure of the worlds of children and adolescents impact with special significance and intensity on boys with a cross-gender role preference. As one adult homosexual respondent described his childhood, "It was like living in a world where the furniture was all constructed for persons with three buttocks." The troubles of homosexual males with heterosexual males appear to start early. Green (1974, p. 240) and Freund (1974) have observed that effeminate boys often have troubled relationships with their same-sex peers. They are often teased, rejected, called names, and beaten by their peers for their sissiness. As Whitam (1977; 1980) has found, far higher percentages of homosexuals than heterosexuals reported having been considered sissies during childhood. Such rejection by peers can eventuate in effeminate boys being either loners during childhood or being obliged to play with girls because boys will not play with them. In her observational study of three and four year old children, Fagot (1977) found that feminine boys play alone three times as much as other boys. In comparing adult heterosexual and homosexual males, Stephan (1973) found that the latter were more often loners as children.

While it is clear that effeminate boys are rejected by other boys, it is not as clear whether their more common playing with girls is due to that rejection. In an elsewhere stated childhood version of labeling theory (Harry and DeVall 1978, pp. 12-13), effeminate boys would be labelled sissies, excluded from the company of other boys, and thereby come to play with the outcast group--girls. However, it also seems likely that effeminate boys may prefer to play with girls, as reported by Whitam (1977). In his data, adult gay men were 28 times more likely to have preferred playing with girls than were heterosexual men. Bell et al. (1981a, pp. 84-85) also found that gay men were more likely to have had girls as friends than non-gay men during childhood and adolescence. Freund (1974) has reported a similar relationship. Hence, girls may have served as a reference group for effeminate boys for at least a considerable part of childhood.

To the extent that effeminate boys employ girls as a reference group for cultural activities, it seems they may elaborate a commitment to the opposite gender culture. One such cultural interest distinguishing the sexes during childhood is art, as noted earlier. Green (1974, p. 148) found that of his conventional boys "33 percent showed no interest in (play-acting), 50 percent showed only slight interest, and only 17 percent display a considerable interest. Of the feminine boys evaluated, however, more than 75 percent were described by their parents as showing a considerable interest in play-acting and none was said to be altogether devoid of this interest." Although the effeminate boys described by Green display a variety of artistic interests such as painting, flowers, and hair arrangement, it appears that an interest in acting is their most beloved artistic recreation. During such acting, these boys often, but not inevitably, assume a female role. In their factor analytic study of five to twelve year old effeminate boys, Bates et al. (1973) found that childhood play-acting--"play-acts, puts on little dramas"--was part of the feminine behavior factor they extracted. They also found that feminine boys were lower on an extroversion factor, suggesting that the practice of being a loner may occur early in life. Green and Money (1966) reported that "Nine of 20 effeminate boys displayed an exceptional interest in stage-acting, dramatic role taking in childhood play, or female impersonation from an early age onward. The mean age of onset of this "symptom" was four." Somewhat later during childhood, Green and Money observe, these boys tended to develop substitute interests for their acting and female impersonation as they learned that such impersonations went unrewarded or were negatively sanctioned. Their substitute interests included dressing up girls (as opposed to themselves), creating verse, expressive speech, intellectual pursuits, and interior decoration.

The extant data strongly suggest that the artistic interests developed by effeminate boys during childhood persist into adult life among male homosexuals. Saghir and Robins (1973, p. 173) found that 50 percent of their homosexual respondents had interests which were "artistic--theater, music, painting, decoration"--as compared with 18 percent among their heterosexual respondents. Stringer and Grygier (1976) found that their English male homosexuals scored significantly higher than heterosexual counterparts on a measure of "creative and artistic" interests". Goertzel et al. (1979), in studying the biographies of eminent (biographed) persons, found that homosexuals significantly more often attained their eminence in the humanities. Also, Whitam and Dizon (1979) have presented data on artist interest among American and Brazilian homosexuals and heterosexuals. They asked their respondents "If you could choose any occupation, regardless of your present occupation, education, or qualifications what would you want it to be?" Forty-two percent of the American homosexual males chose occupations in the arts and entertainment as opposed to five percent of the heterosexuals. In the Brazilian samples, the corresponding percentages were 44 and 7. They also found a positive association between childhood cross-gender behaviors among the homosexuals and choosing entertainment and the arts. These data suggest that early learned gender culture, while subject to later modification, shows strong persistence into the world of adult gender culture. However, we should note that the case of artistic interests may be a special one due to the fact that, although artistic interests are considered "sissy" by gender-conventional boys, with maturity they are recognized as legitimate interests for males, even though somewhat suspicious.

Hence, increasing social support for artistic interests by boys might help to perpetuate a formerly gender-deviant activity.

As an additional exploration of the persistance of gender-typed interests beyond childhood, we take up the case of sports. Sports is particularly important in the culture of boys and adolescent males (Coleman 1961, p. 20; Nemerowicz 1979, pp. 49-61). Also important are activities requiring much physical exertion, strength or skill. Among young boys, the emphasis on the ability to perform such activities as a uniquely male trait is so great that some second to sixth grade boys employ those abilities as gender-defining criteria (Nemerowicz 1979, p. 50). Differences in interests in sports between effeminate and gender-conventional boys which parallel those between boys and girls have been widely reported in the literature. Green (1976) has reported large differences between effeminate and conventional boys in their interest in sports. A similar difference between gay and nongay males in describing their adolescence has been reported by Stephan (1973). These differences also seem to persist into adulthood since Saghir and Robins (1973, p. 176) found that "While close to two-thirds of the heterosexual men were interested in team sports, only ten percent of their homosexual counterparts reported a similar interest ($X^2=34.64$, p. $< .001$)".

In addition to art and sports, there appears to be massive gender-cultural typing of occupational interests. The large differences between men and women in the types of occupations they hold during adulthood are anticipated by children in the types of occupations they say they would like to have when they grow up (Sewell et al. 1980). The extremity of the differences in the occupational aspirations between boys and girls have been documented by several studies (Nemerowicz 1979; Looft 1971; Siegel 1973). Boys typically mention manual, scientific and male professional occupations while girls mention nurturant ones such as teacher and nurse plus a variety of domestic-related and clerical ones. Also, the number of occupations mentioned by boys is typically twice as many as those mentioned by girls. Siegel (1973) found that the two occupations of teacher and nurse accounted for two-thirds of the choices by second grade girls whereas boys almost never mention these two occupations. The one boy in Siegel's study who did mention teacher "had been previously referred to Guidance with the complaint that he was 'too feminine'" (p. 17). The narrow range of choices that girls give anticipates the fairly narrow range of occupations in which adult women are found. It thus appears that early gender-cultural socialization defines many jobs and types of activities as either masculine or feminine and that these definitions persist across the decades. Of course, experience with a wider set of occupations during adulthood undoubtedly somewhat reduces the extremity with which children sex type occupations and activities.

We anticipate that, to the extent that gender culture shows persistence from childhood to adulthood, those gay men who were cross-gendered as children should show parallel cross-gender interests as adults. To the extent that their effeminacy persisted into adulthood, we would expect them to be more interested in the arts, less interested in sports, and to hold or aspire to occupations conventionally viewed as feminine. However, if a substantial degree of defeminization occurs among gay men with childhood histories of cross-gendering, we would anticipate that their adult cross-gender interests would be correspondingly reduced, although perhaps not eliminated. Our intent in the analyses undertaken below is to show the strong and enduring effects of childhood gender cultures independently of the sex of the body in which they are located.

DEFEMINIZATION: THE DISENGAGEMENT OF GENDER ROLE AND GENDER CULTURE

While both girls and effeminate boys internalize a feminine gender-role preference, whether that preference is located in a person of the appropriate sex is very consequential. As noted earlier, effeminate boys receive considerable negative feedback from their peers for their cross-gender role preference. Some pressure to discontinue cross-gender behaviors also comes from parents and particularly fathers. Green and Money (1966) have observed that effeminate boys often learn that their fathers disapprove of behaviors such as cross-dressing and, in response, they may discontinue such blatant forms of cross-gendering. However, it seems that, for a time, some continue to cross-dress in private when their parents are not around.

Whitam (1977) and Saghir and Robins (1973, p. 30) have described a defeminization process whereby boys who are effeminate during childhood gradually defeminize in the years between childhood and adulthood. In response to the widespread pressures toward gender conventionality they receive, effeminate boys discontinue the more blatant manifestations of a cross-gender role preference. While this defeminization process may occur to varying degrees in different boys, a measure of defeminization seems to occur in the majority of cross-gendered boys. Gender-deviance thus seems to be subject to substantial modification in the world of boys whose behaviors are closely supervised by adults and inspected by peers.

Such a defeminization process seems partly inconsistent with the earlier noted strong tendency for such gender-typed interests as art and sports to persist from childhood into adulthood. This inconsistency suggests a selectivity in persistence whereby the more blatant cross-gender behaviors are discontinued while the more subtle or gender-ambiguous ones persist. To the extent this occurs, the collection of behaviors known as gender role may gradually lose their organizing coherence and diffuse into a less visible set of gender-typed interests. In such a process, the components of gender role seem to become unglued. Gender role decrystallizes while some cross-gender culture may remain.

Whether the effeminate boy acquires, concomitant with the defeminization process, a masculine gender-role preference, and to what degree, is problematic. He certainly is pressured in that direction. He also probably has a moderate amount of experience with and knowledge of the activities gender-typed as masculine, e.g., sports, cars, fighting. Probably some defeminizing boys engage in such activities out of pressure. Yet, whether such activities are internalized as an aspect of the gender self or simply endured is unknown. While, theoretically, pressures to adopt a masculine gender-role preference might result in an eventual masculinization of the effeminate boy, the arrival during early adolescence of a focused homosexual sexuality may impede the defeminization process. Saghir and Robins (1973, p. 33) have reported that homosexual interests in the forms of fantasies and masturbation seem to have an age of onset during late childhood and early adolescence. Tripp (1975, p. 77), reporting unpublished Kinsey data, has found that homosexual males "tend to arrive at puberty" earlier than do heterosexual males and to masturbate earlier. While we have no explanation for such early sexuality, it seems that the sexualization of one's gender-role preferences may provide a new reward-value for those preferences and make subsequent change in them more difficult.

The extent to which the sexualization of one's gender-role affects the denouement of the defeminization process may involve a matter of timing. If the defeminization process is largely complete by the advent of puberty, the arriving sexuality may not become linked to a cross-gender role preference. Conceivably, in the early defeminized boy, it could become linked to a more recently acquired masculine gender-role preference and eventuate in heterosexuality. However, such a linkage would largely assume that defeminization is accompanied by a new liking for the masculine gender role. This may or may not occur. If it does not, the person would likely become culturally androgynous without any marked preference for either gender-role.

Several authors (Bates and Bentler 1973; Brown 1957; Vener and Snyder 1966) have reported a somewhat parallel defeminization process which occurs among conventional boys during early and middle childhood, and thus considerably earlier than among effeminate boys. This defeminization process is manifested in the evolution of toy preferences, the It Scale, and the Draw A Person test. Vener and Snyder (1966) found among two to five year old boys a strong age trend for boys to increasingly prefer household artifacts sex-typed for males. However, 54 percent of the youngest boys preferred feminine-typed artifacts. If such changes in conventional boys do, in fact, indicate a shift from a feminine to a masculine gender-role preference they occur considerably before the sexualization of gender-roles. Hence, the later years of childhood are spent in the elaboration of a masculine gender-role which subsequently serves as a vehicle for the focussing of sexuality into a heterosexual script.

The caution should be noted in interpreting these early changes in toy and artifact preferences that they may not be indicative of change in a gender-role preference. Rather, they may simply indicate the differentiation of the masculine gender role out of a non-gender-differentiated status of baby. One of the major conclusions of Maccoby and Jacklin's (1974) monumental review of sex differences is that during the first four years of life, boys and girls are treated very similarly by parents other than being taught the appropriate gender labels. While young boys may be very close to their mothers during these early years, it is hazardous to infer gender identities or gender-role preferences. All boys love their mothers and such "identifications" need not imply or result in identities. Heilbrun (1973) has cogently criticized the hypothesis of successive gender-role identification by boys first with the mother and later with the father as based on a confusion between "the formation of an attachment to the primary caretaker" and the formation of a self-identity one component of which is gender.

Whether the defeminization process observed by various authors in effeminate boys implies both cultural and psychological defeminization is unclear. The defeminization process has typically been assessed through observations or measurements of gender-typed preferences for such things as dolls, sports, toys, and playmates. Such preferences seem to be indicators of culturally feminine interests. They may or may not also measure psychological femininity. Researchers in this area appear to have assumed that the effeminate boys whom they were testing were also psychologically feminine. Green and Money (1974, pp. 292-304) administered to these boys such tests as the Family Doll Preference Test and the Draw A Person Test. Freund (1977) employed the Mf Scale of the MMPI to validate his Feminine Gender Identity Scale to distinguish heterosexuals, gay males, and transexuals. Other researchers on transexualism (Money and Brennan 1968) or on male homosexuals (Siegelman 1972) have used traditional measures of masculinity such as the MMPI Mf Scale or the Guilford-Zimmerman masculinity-femininity scale. Similarly, Stringer and Grygier (1976) compared heterosexual and homosexual males matched on age and education and found the latter more feminine than the former. However, all of these measures are measures of gender-typed cultural interests and activities and do not directly tap the psychological components of masculinity and femininity.

The use of these gender-typed interest or activity scales has been extensively criticized by Bem (1974) and Spence and Helmreich (1976) for not validly measuring psychological as opposed to cultural masculinity and femininity. The major criticisms have been two. First, some scales assume that masculinity and femininity constitute a bipolar dimension such that one cannot be both high or low on both masculinity and femininity. Second, all of the traditional scales measure gender-typed interests or activities rather than psychological aspects such as aggressiveness or affiliative warmth. Given that sex-typed interests have been subject to recent cultural change in the West, it is not at all evident that the presumably underlying traits of psychological masculinity and femininity have undergone a parallel evolution. In short, traditional tests measure role rather than personality.

Proceeding from these criticisms of traditional tests, Bem (1974) and Spence and Helmreich (1978) developed psychological measures of masculinity and femininity in the form of self-rating adjective checklists. They define masculinity as "instrumental aggressiveness" and femininity as "affiliative warmth." Spence and Helmreich (1978, p. 50) found these measures to be positively correlated (r=0.22). Bem found a similar association. In our Chicago sample of gay men, we found a positive correlation of 0.20. From these data we infer that, while cultural interests seem to be highly gender-typed, psychological masculinity and femininity are hardly the polar opposites which gender-attribution processes might lead one to believe.

Given that psychological and cultural femininity seem far from colinear, we may not assume that the effeminate boy is also psychologically feminine or that his manifest cultural defeminization is paralleled by a psychological defeminization. Indeed, one might speculate that those boys who are most psychologically feminine would thereby be more influencable to defeminize from social pressures. This would imply that those who did not defeminize would be the most masculine or aggressive. Differently put, persistent gender deviance takes guts. Hopefully, observers of gender-unconventional children will include in their future procedures the newer measures of psychological masculinity and femininity to see if the psychological parallels the cultural and if they are learned in different phases of preadulthood.

ADOLESCENCE: THE UGLY DUCKLING AND THE BEAUTIFUL GAY SWAN

The significance of a gender-role preference to others and to the self depends in part on the sex of the person manifesting that preference. This significance is revealed in the considerable negative feedback received by effeminate boys for behaviors which, if manifested by girls, would be considered gender-conventional (Saghir and Robins 1973, pp. 19-20). Because the sex of the person manifesting a role preference specifies the significance of that preference, sex, and thereby sexual orientation, becomes a highly consequential variable meriting the status of an independent variable or at least a control or specifying variable. While largely intrinsically meaningless, sex and sexual orientation in interaction with gender-role preference create fateful consequences and differential contingencies for effeminate and non-effeminate boys. Major consequences already noted are the tendencies for effeminate boys to be teased and rejected, to play with girls, and to be loners.

Extant data do not permit one to assess the extent to which the observed propensities of effeminate boys to play with girls and be loners is due to rejection versus a feminine gender-role preference. Both may be operative. Frequent peer rejection has been documented both in studies of effeminate boys and recall studies of adult gay men (Fagot 1977; Saghir and Robins 1973, pp. 19-20). However, a cross-gender role preference also seems operative since the presence of that preference has been commonly observed to exist during early childhood preceding the formation of childhood play groups. Based on mothers' reports of their effeminate sons' behaviors, Green (1976) found that three-quarters of these boys had begun cross-dressing before their fourth birthdays. A preference for playing with girls and, more arguably, to play alone rather than participate in the male gender culture of peers seems a logical extension of a feminine gender-role preference.

Several major consequences of peer rejection seem possible. First, there may occur a drift toward gender conformity. This seems to be the more common case as noted in the earlier cited studies dealing with defeminization. An alternative scenario seems to be one of further alienation from peers and their gender culture. Through becoming a loner the effeminate boy may not learn the culture of other males. Particularly important in the culture of boys and adolescents is appreciation of and participation in sports. Interviewing college athletes and nonathletes about their histories of participation in sports, Stein and Hoffman (1978) found that the athlete/nonathlete distinction was important during adolescence and served to structure reputations and social relationships. Being a nonathlete was a matter of some pain to the nonathletes. "The inability of the non-athlete to perform at even the minimal level of competence severely limited his membership in male peer groups. This inability to perform in sports led to feelings of inadequacy and inferiority" (pp. 148-149).

There is considerable evidence--cited earlier--that effeminate boys and adult gay men were immensely indifferent or averse to the sports element of male gender culture. Such great differences in the cultural interests of effeminate and noneffeminate youths seem to play an alienating role during the preadulthood of effeminate boys and relegate them to the social and cultural periphery of the worlds of conventional boys. Bell et al. (1981a, pp. 87-88) have documented that gay men are much more likely than non-gay men to have felt different, and particularly gender-different, during childhood and adolescence. Through being outcasts, effeminate boys may not learn the competitiveness and dominating behaviors so characteristic of the interaction of young males who have not yet attained adulthood and a security in their adulthood and masculinity (Matza 1964, pp. 53-59).

The advent of heterosexuality into the social relations of early adolescence may also serve as a further source of alienation for the effeminate boy. As Coleman (1961) has found, heterosexual relations and sports activities appear to be the two principal foci around which adolescent behaviors are organized. While academic interests are very important in some adolescent circles, such circles seem to be minority groups in an adolescent culture which accords the highest status to those who achieve in the area of sports and appear to be achieving in the area of sex and heterosexual dating.

An adolescent culture so organized around heterosexual relations and sports seems almost maximally ill-suited for the boy who is either cross-gendered, or experiencing homosexual desires, or both. Saghir and Robins (1973, p. 38) reported that it is during early adolescence, and sometimes late childhood, that homosexual males began feeling focused erotic attraction to other males. These inner promptings are troubling for many homosexuals. Harry and DeVall (1978, p. 68) found that 51 percent of their gay men agreed that "Before I came out, the idea that I might be gay troubled me a lot." (They came out at a median age of 19.2 years.) Dank (1971) has also described the adolescence of gay men as often a troubled period during which they search for a label around which to organize their erotic promptings while also being fearful of adopting the stigmatized label of "gay" or "faggot."

During the period of adolescence, there appears to be considerable sexual exploration on the part of gay as well as by heterosexual men (Saghir and Robins 1973, pp. 88-89). It appears that the majority of gay men did heterosexual dating, and sometimes intercourse, during adolescence. Some of their heterosexual activity seems to have been motivated at least as much by peer-normative expectations as by erotic promptings. However, it seems such heterosexual activities engaged in by homosexual men did not prove particularly rewarding. Comparing gay and non-gay adults, Saghir and Robins (1973, p. 92) found that none of the gays versus all of the nongays said they found their heterosexual experiences, including intercourse, sexually rewarding or exciting. Bell et al. (1981a, p. 92) found that many gay men dated during adolescence simply because it was "the thing to do." It thus seems that, although many gay men engage in normative heterosexual relations during adolescence, they remain largely indifferent to those relations or simply endure them since that is what is expected of males.

Given a substantial degree of alienation from peer culture for either effeminate or homosexual adolescents, several solutions to their problems, of varying degrees of benignity, are possible. One is a continuing state of social isolation and drift (Matza 1964, pp. 27-30). In this scenario, the adolescent is unattached to peers and their culture while not being committed to other goals. He remains an isolate until graduation from high school frees him from continued immersion in a distasteful culture. This scenario is probably accompanied by a notable measure of damage to the individual's self-esteem. A second alternative involves continuing efforts to defeminize, if he is effeminate, and to conform to the norms of gender conventionality. He dates, may participate in sports, and perhaps continues to resist proclivities toward homosexuality. This road through adolescence seems a more likely alternative for those adolescents who, while experiencing homosexual attractions, are not cross-gendered.

A third and more benign solution to alienation from adolescent culture is to develop an intense and continuing interest in the alternative conventional academic culture. This culture consists of such things as the pursuit of grades, intellectual or artistic interests, reading, and hobbies. The possibility of this option seems enhanced if the boy is denied rewards from participating in the activities of the adolescent culture. Alternatively, it is also enhanced if he does not perceive the rewards of the adolescent culture, e.g., dating and sports, as rewards. Whether self-imposed or other-imposed, the denial of the option of obtaining rewards in the adolescent culture assists him in searching for alternative rewards and may help funnel him into commitments to an academic culture and achievement in that culture.

If the option of commitment to conventional academic adult-approved culture is chosen, the boy's chances of upward mobility may be enhanced. Through reading and studying more than non-alienated students, he is likely to enter the adult world or college better prepared. Through commitment to intellectual or artistic interests, he seems more likely to go on to college. Through model deportment in high school and diligence in schoolwork, he is likely to obtain better recommendations from teachers. Through being denied success in the adolescent culture and opting for rewards in the academic culture he is denied the opportunity for academic and, indirectly, occupational failure. Hence, in a curious twist of labeling theory, rejection of gender deviants may force them into academic and occupational success or, at least direct them away from failure. In discussing the homosexual adolescent, Gagnon (1979, p. 237) has observed that "Poorly adjusted children may find many opportunities as well as problems... In school he may find opportunities to be upwardly mobile, go to college, and become successful, while his classmates are still hanging around the corner tavern."

It should be noted that our argument from peer-alienation to academic and occupational success does not apply only to effeminate or cross-gendered adolescents. It seems likely to be also operative among heterosexual youths who for whatever reasons find adolescent peer culture unappealing. However, there are reasons for believing that a benign academic solution to such alienation would be more appealing to the cross-gendered youth than to the typically not cross-gendered heterosexual adolescent. Stein and Smithells (1969) have reported that second, sixth, and twelfth grade boys and girls rate artistic activities and reading as quite feminine activities. To the extent that the cross-

gendered youth has a feminine role preference, these activities
would be more consistent with those preferences. Also, if his
feminine role preference is, in fact, accompanied by psychological
femininity we might expect him to be more conforming and obediant
in school and more dutiful about scholastic activities. It is
worth noting that academic or artistic achievement may be a
"gender-natural" solution for cross-gendered boys. It was noted
earlier that the job of teacher is much often stated as an
occupational aspiration by young girls than by boys (Nemerowicz
1979, p. 30). However, that occupation requires higher education.
Hence, both directly due to a feminine gender-role preference and
indirectly due to alienation problems, the jobs of teaching and
higher education may be outcomes of an early feminine gender-role
preference.

As a qualification to the hypothesis that peer-alienation
breeds academic interests among cross-gendered youths, it may be
that defeminization makes this less likely since, presumably,
defeminization would reduce alienation and hence academic
interests. Whether this latter alternative is true would depend
on several empirical questions. Does defeminization result in
masculinization or simple defeminization? If the latter, peer
culture would still remain unappealing to the defeminized boy.
Does defeminization involve complete defeminization or only the
eschewal of the more visible and obvious forms of a cross-gender
role preference? If the latter, the defeminized boy still retains
interests in feminine gender-culture and hence would be peer-
culture alienated, although he does not express that feminine
gender culture in the crystallized form of a gender role. Does a
cross-gender role preference both directly and indirectly through
peer alienation establish an early commitment to academic/artistic
achievement which then, because it has important reward value in
an otherwise reward-barren environment, acquires an autonomy of
its own despite further defeminization? Does gender-role
nonconformity establish an early alienation among defeminizing
youth which is subsequently replaced by an alienation more based
on homosexual desires? If the answer is "yes" to any of these
four possibilities, then academic achievement can survive the
defeminization process.

There are several reasons for believing that the cross-
gendered youth may be less delinquent than gender-conventional
youths. Gender has been found to be the major predictor of
criminality in apparently all societies (Simon 1975; Harris 1977).
This relationship is particularly strong in the area of assaultive
offenses and serious crimes in which there is a direct
confrontation with the victim. To the extent that a cross-
gendered male is committed to the feminine gender role, we might
thereby expect him to be less seriously delinquent during
adolescence. However, it is unclear which aspect of masculinity
and femininity is more important in bringing about the observed
sex-differences in criminality. Is it cultural (role) or
psychological masculinity and femininity which are the important

variables? It may be that psychological masculinity, defined as aggressiveness, leads to serious delinquency. Cullen et al. (1979) have found delinquency, and particularly serious delinquency to be associated with psychological masculinity. Gold and Mann (1972) have reported that high masculinity was associated with delinquency, although it is unclear what form of masculinity their measure taps. Grosser (1951, pp. 78-118) has offered the idea that delinquency is role-expressive for males but, with the exception of sexual activities, is only role-supportive for females. Under this interpretation, serious forms of delinquency are demonstrations to peers of one's masculine qualities. Lacking the desire to demonstrate one's commitment to the masculine role, the effeminate youth has little reason to become involved in serious delinquency, although he may engage in petty or non-gender-significant forms of delinquency. We explore the associations between gender-role preference and self-reported delinquency below.

A further reason for expecting the cross-gendered youth to be less delinquent is his isolation from peers. A very large percentage of delinquent acts are committed by groups of adolescent rather than by lone individuals. The situation of company appears to provide for boys motivations to commit crimes about which they would have been reluctant if alone (Matza 1964; Erickson 1971). Polk and Halferty (1972) have reported that time spent in association with peers is positively associated with deliqneuency among males. Hence, while delinquency has not typically been found to be characterologically (personality) significant, it does seem to be gender-significant. To the extent that the cross-gendered youth is a loner, he is denied the opportunity to be significantly delinquent. A further reason we might expect the cross-gendered youth to be less delinquent is that, contingent upon his adopting the benign academic solution to his alienation problems, such a commitment to school achievement has been repeatedly found to be strongly negatively associated with delinquency (Hirschi 1969, pp. 120-130; Bochman 1970).

The two reasons of a feminine gender-role preference and being a loner offered to suggest lower delinquency rates among cross-gendered or peer-alienated youths also suggest that a delinquent solution to his adolescent problems is less likely than among gender-conventional youths. As suggested by Cohen (1955), some youths adopt a delinquent solution to their status problems in high schools. This solution for the effeminate boy alienated from peers seems relatively foreclosed for several reasons. First, delinquent peers would probably be the most likely to reject him. Second, he tends to be a loner already. Third, significant and gender-significant delinquency is incompatible with a feminine gender-role preference. Hence, it seems that once more he may be funneled into an academic solution due to both peer-rejection and denial of an opportunity to even be seriously delinquent. Through processes such as the ones sketched above, the effeminate youth who is rejected and teased by peers may, with luck, survive the holocaust of preadulthood and be the ugly duckling who is transformed into the beautiful adult gay swan.

The empirical chapters to follow constitute an exploration of the adult gender-cultural manifestations of a childhood cross-gender role preference. While such gender-cultural studies could be performed by comparing males and females, there would often arise questions of effects possibly due to biological influences. Our use of gay men as our principal, but not sole, set of respondents sidesteps the question of biological differences by controlling sex while varying culture. Indeed, gay men appear to be the only large population in which there is much gender-cultural heterogeneity which has become sufficiently crystallized that one may speak of gender roles rather than simply gender-typed interests. While heterosexual males do show some variability in a variety of sex-typed activities and interests, e.g., interest in art, these interests do not seem to correlate or cluster sufficiently that one may speak of distinct roles or cultures which vary among heterosexual males.

It might be felt that biological interpretations can not be side-stepped through examining only gay men because the latter could be biologically different from heterosexual men and more similar to women. While this has been hypothesized, there does not yet exist any convincing direct data to support such biological interpretations among humans (Meyer-Bahlburg 1977). Also, it is clear that not all gays were cross-gendered during childhood. Hence, any biological interpretation of the childhood cross-gendering of gay men could only readily apply to some of them. For these reasons, we proceed under the assumption that the effects we are looking at are those of culture rather than biology.

2

RESEARCH METHODS
AND MEASURES

RESEARCH ON DEVIANT POPULATIONS

Gaining research access to any type of population defined as deviant presents the social scientist with considerable difficulties. To the extent that the form of deviance being examined is popularly considered serious or abhorrent the deviant will be hesitant to reveal her or himself to the researcher either out of personal embarrassment or out of fear of ensuing legal/economic or social sanctions. For example, research on unprosecuted murderers or child molesters would probably founder for lack of available subjects while students of marijuana users or alcoholics can typically glory in a surplus of subjects eager to tell their stories. The classically employed solution to the problem of subject reluctance has been to study those deviants immune to further social sanction by virtue of their already having been discredited as deviant, either voluntarily or involuntarily. Psychiatric patients and other deviants who have willingly entered various forms of therapy have been the principal subjects studied in the case of the voluntarily discredited. Prisoners have been the historical subjects for studies of the involuntarily discredited. An example of the latter type of studies is Lemert's (1967) famous study of convicted check forgers. While students of homosexuality in earlier decades were willing to study incarcerated homosexuals or homosexual psychiatric patients (Bieber et al. 1962; Bergler 1956; Doidge and Holtzman 1960), it is now recognized that such samples of homosexuals seem so grossly unrepresentative of the non-clinical, non-institutionalized broader population of homosexuals that no competent contemporary researcher would employ such samples unless he/she were particularly interested in such specialized populations. Hence, the researcher of homosexuality may now no longer adopt the convenient strategy of ready availability in

33

order to acquire a set of homosexual subjects. He must gather a sample consisting of homosexuals who are "out there" in the community at large.

As the methodological sophistication of students of deviance has increased in recent years, it has become increasingly recognized that deviants who have come to public attention by virtue of having been arrested, treated, or incarcerated are a highly and non-randomly selected subset of all deviants. Hence, researchers have increasingly abandoned the prison, the court, and the psychiatric office to avail themselves of broader and presumably more representative segments of the deviant populations. This advance from the official institutions for the discredited has occurred both in studies of homosexuals and of other forms of deviance. Examples of community-based researchers on homosexuals have been those of Bell and Weinberg (1978), Saghir and Robins (1973), and Warren (1974). Examples of similar community-based studies of other forms of deviance have been Short and Strodbeck's (1965) Delinquent Gangs, Albini's (1971) Organized Criminals, and Klockars' (1974) Professional Fences.

Once it has been accepted that the researcher must gather deviant respondents from the community rather than from institutions, most researchers have either gone to those physical locations where deviant populations are commonly located or have contacted organizations the members of which consist of the deviants of interest. Whether these approaches are feasible depends importantly on whether the deviant population of interest tends to congregate in particular locales or has reason to form organizations. If the deviant population of interest has little propensity for gathering together such approaches are not feasible. Examples of deviants who show little propensity for gathering together in numbers are rapists, bestialists, and child beaters. However, even if a particular deviant population does tend to collect itself together in sizable numbers, the researcher must still face the question of whether those who gather together are representative of the broader population who indulge in a particular disapproved behavior but may or may not gather together with their peers. Are the gathered representative of the ungathered and, if not, how unrepresentative are they and what are the relative sizes of the two types?

In order to directly deal with these problems of the unrepresentativeness of samples of gathered community-based deviant samples, researchers of the last decade have increasingly resorted to two different types of probability surveys of the general population. In the first type of survey a sample of the general population has been asked whether, how often, and by whom they may have been personally victimized by a particular form of deviant behavior such as armed robbery or burglary (Hindelang 1976). Through these victimology surveys it has been possible to gain much better estimates of the extent and social distribution of a number of important forms of deviant behaviors. However, such surveys will remain forever closed to students of homosexuality or of other forms of victimless deviance. Since persons engaging in homosexual behaviors do not consider themselves victimized in the overwhelming majority of non-prison instances, such encounters leave no-one willing to claim the status of victim. If such a survey of "homosexual victims" were attempted it would be equivalent to the second form of survey of the general population described below.

The second form of survey has been to ask a probability sample of the general population about various types of deviant or criminal behaviors in which they may have engaged. This approach has only recently been employed with adult populations (O'Donnell et al. 1976; Tittle and Villemez 1977). It represents an extension of the practice of asking representative samples of high school students about their delinquent behaviors (Short and Nye 1958; Elliott and Voss 1974). At present the technique of asking adults about their deviant behaviors has been limited to criminal behaviors rather than including other forms of deviance. In those instances where adults have been asked about such behaviors the particular questions asked have, for the most part, referred to the less serious forms of crime, e.g., marijuana use. Of course, the reasons for limiting questions to the less serious crimes has been to assure honesty in the responses of subjects. Although the omission of questions about the very serious infractions is regrettable, the technique of asking a representative sample of the general population about their deviant behaviors promises to be a major advance in the study of deviance. While such a data-gathering approach would have been unthinkable two decades ago, it appears that social scientists have gained sufficient trust in the eyes of the general public that the latter are evidently willing to be open in their responses to questions about their own deviant behaviors.

The study of homosexuality has not yet progressed to the stage at which it is possible to ask a general sample of the population about sexual orientation and non-heterosexual sexual behaviors. It can only be hoped that the inclusion of a question on the respondent's sexual orientation can be included in general social surveys in the near future. While some respondents could be expected to not answer such a question honestly, even approximate honesty would be a first major step in gaining realistic estimates of the general characteristics of the homosexual population. At present it is simply not known whether and by how much homosexuals may differ from heterosexuals on many of the most "obvious" variables of education, age, residence, and mobility patterns. Such information can only be acquired through probability samples of the general populations.

The present study of adult male homosexuals in the Chicago area sought out subjects from the gay community of that city and is thus within the tradition of gathering community-based, but not general survey, respondents. The student of homosexuality is fortunate in that his subjects have strong propensities for gathering themselves together in particular locales and within organizations. He is thereby able to avail himself of such places and organizations for research subjects. However, it should be recognized that the gathering propensities of homosexuals have been historically variable. Prior to the development of large concentrations of homosexuals in most of the major North American cities, principally in the "gay ghettos" (Harry and DeVall 1978: Ch. 8), homosexuals were considerably more covert in their lifestyles and tended to be isolated from each other or to consort together in small friendship cliques. They also occasionally gathered at the few gay bars which could be found only in the very large cities of North America. As a result of their earlier propensity for remaining covert and isolated, earlier researchers on homosexuality were presented with greater difficulties than are contemporary ones.

During the decades of the 1960s and 1970s there developed openly gay communities of homosexuals in most large American cities. Within these communities there arose a variety of institutions serving the gay community, e.g., bars, restaurants, newspapers, theaters, counseling centers, and a variety of organizations. The efflorescence of such visible institutions has created more openings for social scientists interested in studying homosexuality. Also, that considerable numbers of gay persons have become more open and less fearful about their lifestyles has probably increased the representativeness of recent studies of homosexuals, although to an unknown degree. Such changes in the openness of homosexuals and their institutions have changed the nature of research on homosexuality. They have made that research more accurate and probably more representative. They have made it possible to inquire into aspects of the lives of homosexuals about which they were formerly reluctant to respond. For example, homosexuals have frequently been reluctant to answer questions about their occupations or to give information which would identify them as individuals. They still seem reluctant to respond to such questions. Such reluctance clearly limits the types of studies which may be done on gays. For example, longitudinal studies of gays are impossible without the ability to identify individual respondents. Similarly, studies requiring access to institutional record such as grades, majors, or ability test scores presuppose the ability to identify the individual. It is hoped that, as gay persons become less fearful and more open, such studies may be done. The improvement and advance of research on gay studies depends considerably on the liberation of gay persons. As that liberation proceeds, gay studies may proceed.

DATA-GATHERING METHODS

Our sample design was created so as to permit both comparisons between gay and heterosexual males and analyses within each of these groups, particularly within the gay samples. While the problems of obtaining samples of gay respondents have been discussed above, it must be noted that the tasks of obtaining a sample of comparable heterosexuals also presents considerable difficulties. For example, if a sample of gay men is collected it will typically be found to consist of persons the majority of which are unmarried either heterosexually or homosexually while a representative sample of adult males will consist of persons the large majority of which are married. Hence, comparisons between two such samples will very largely be comparisons of married heterosexuals with unmarried homosexuals. In order to deal with this problem Saghir and Robins (1973) selected heterosexual respondents who were single for their comparison group. This, of course, precludes the possibility of comparing gay and heterosexual couples.

Another problem which arises in choosing an appropriate heterosexual comparison group is that there are likely to be different degrees of self-selection or volunteering for the two groups. While all social scientific samples not based on either torture or captivity are self-selected, what is relevant is the degree of effort or motivation required on the respondent's part in order to participate in the study. Most studies of non-clinical homosexuals have required a moderate to high amount of motivation on the respondent's part. In both the Saghir and Robins (1973, pp. 4-5) study and that by Bell and Weinberg (1978, pp. 42-44), individuals were first solicited to volunteer for the study and then later were asked to arrange for an interview. Such two-stage selection procedures require a non-trivial measure of motivation on the respondent's part and introduce the probability that the ultimate samples will differ in their motivations from those who chose not to volunteer. In comparison, the typical sampling procedures employed in area probability samples of the general population do not require such special motivation and can include all but the most recalcitrant or reluctant of respondents. For this reason a representative sample of the general population may not often be an appropriate comparison group to a sample of homosexuals. In their current study of gay and heterosexual couples, Schwartz and Blumstein (1979) first obtained samples of volunteer homosexual couples and then opted for samples of volunteer heterosexual couples, rather than random samples of heterosexual couples, in order to have groups derived from the same sampling methods and with similar biases.

In order to be able to make comparisons both within and between gay and heterosexual groups of males four different samples were obtained.
1. A sample of 204 male students systematically sampled from the list of students at the author's university in DeKalb, Illinois was obtained. This university has approximately 25,000 students the very large majority of which are from Chicago and the suburbs. Questionnaires were mailed to 398 students. Of the 398 students, 18 proved to be bad addresses. Of 213 returned, nine were excluded because the respondent indicated a sexual orientation other than "exclusively heterosexual" or "predominantly

heterosexual - only incidentally homosexual" (Kinsey 0 S or 1 S) or did not respond on the sexual orientation item. The resultant response rate was 55 percent (204/371).

2. A group of 32 gay male respondents who were also students at the author's university were also questionnaired. These respondents were obtained through the Gay Student Organization at the university and through having questionnaires distributed at several social events of local gays. The student organization is much more a social than a political one. These respondents were paid $5.00 to participate.

3. A group of 90 gay students from the Chicago area was obtained. These respondents were obtained through the same mechanisms as were employed to obtain the fourth group.

4. A group of 1,466 gay non-students was obtained from the Chicago area. The two Chicago area groups were obtained through two mechanisms. First, because it was anticipated, as in all studies of gay men, that the obtained respondents would under-represent the older, research cooperation was obtained from a Chicago area homophile organization for gay men over forty years of age. Questionnaires were mailed out by the secretary of this organization to the 275 members and 62 were returned. The median age of these respondents was 50.3 years compared with a median of 30.0 for the other Chicago respondents. There is reason to believe that the actual response rate from these organization members is considerably higher than the 62 returns out of 275 would indicate. This organization appears to retain on its mailing list many persons who have long since ceased attending meetings or paying dues. Hence, some considerable percentage of the 275 claimed membership may be members in name only.

Secondly, the very large bulk of our Chicago area respondents were acquired through the cooperation of Gay Life, the major weekly Chicago area gay newspaper. The editor and publisher of this paper were approached and their assistance obtained. Gay Life is not principally a subscription publication although a handful of individuals and institutions such as libraries subscribe. The overwhelming bulk of its 18,000 copy issues are distributed free as a throwaway or shopper to nearly all of the gay establishments in the Chicago area plus a number of heterosexual or mixed establishments in gay neighborhoods in Chicago, e.g., supermarkets, restaurants, liquor stores. Stacks of the paper are placed each week in 104 establishments catering to gays in the Chicago area. This number fluctuates slightly from month to month. Of the 104 places, 54 percent were gay bars with the others being gay organizations (5), steam baths (7), gay hotels (2), adult bookstores and arcades (17), restaurants (17), a moviehouse (1), and a medical clinic (1). Within these establishments there is typically a corner, shelf, or table containing recent gay publications, announcements, and advertisements which customers or clientele pick up while passing through.

The above list of establishments constitutes our sample of settings through which respondents were obtained. It should be noted that all major studies of gay men to date have involved samplings of settings such as gay bars or of social structures such as gay organizations or of friendship networks for the gays contained therein. The better samplings appear to be those which attempted to widely sample settings or structures. For example, Bell and Weinberg (1978, pp. 30-33) obtained volunteers from gay bars, baths, organizations, parks, and restrooms. Our setting-sampling method provided a mechanism for distributing questionnaires in a variety of settings nearly as wide as those settings sampled by Bell and Weinberg. However, in our case we took as given the settings to which _Gay Life_ distributed their newspaper.

While it has been originally intended to insert a questionnaire in each copy of a single issue of the paper it was later decided that such a procedure would very largely restrict the obtained respondents to the readership of _Gay Life_. The alternative was adopted to have the questionnaires distributed along with the newspaper. Stacks of the questionnaires, totalling 17,600, were placed alongside those of the newspaper in the recipient establishments. Each copy of the questionnaire was stamped on the cover in bright colors with the title "Lifestyle Study of Gay Men." This was designed to increase their visibility. The cover letter soliciting cooperation was printed on the front cover of the booklet-format questionnaire. It should be noted that the procedure adopted, that of not inserting the questionnaires in copies of the paper, renders the obtained set of respondents not simply a subset of the readership of the newspaper. The questionnaires could as well have been distributed by the breadman or beerman. Hence, the obtained set of respondents constitute a subset of the gay customers and clients of the recipient establishments. However, _Gay Life_ published an announcement of the research in the issue with which the questionnaires were distributed during early November, 1978.

While our sampling of settings within which respondents were obtained was similar to that employed by Bell and Weinberg, and considerably broader than the sampling of bars and organizations in the Weinberg and Williams (1974) study, the acquisition of respondents within settings occurred much differently. We basically relied on the respondents noticing our questionnaires and being sufficiently interested to fill one out and return it in the accompanying pre-paid envelope. While this gave us no control over which individuals within settings became respondents, it also imposed only minimal requirements on them in terms of effort and motivation. In contrast, the two and three stage procedures for obtaining homosexual respondents described earlier impose considerably greater effort and motivation requirements on respondents than did our procedures. Also, our procedures provided complete anonymity to respondents whereas two-stage procedures and most interview procedures do not provide this, although they provide assurances of confidentiality.

We believe that procedures which provide complete anonymity to gay respondents, rather than those which provide only assurances of confidentiality, permit a broader sampling of gay respondents. In particular, they make it possible for gay men who feel uneasy about providing identifying information about themselves to respond. Interview and two-stage procedures may not. This uneasiness about responding seems to appear in the differential completeness with which our gay respondents answered certain items. Of the 1,556 Chicago respondents only three did not provide their ages and 10 did not give their years of education. In contrast, 110 did not give their zip codes and 53 did not give their occupations. We estimate that when asked to participate in an interview situation where identification is usually unavoidable considerable numbers of potential respondents will be screened out. Our procedures avoid this problem. In short, we believe that our sampling of settings was about as broad as that accomplished in the Bell and Weinberg study and our sampling of persons within settings was at least as broad, if not more.

One thousand, seven hundred, and seventy questionnaires were returned by Chicago area respondents, including the 90 students and the members of the organization for older gay men. A total of 214 were excluded because they did not meet one or more predetermined criteria. These exclusions were:
1. 116 were excluded because they did not live within our operationalized "social commuting area." This area was defined as the city of Chicago, Gary - Indiana, plus the Chicago suburbs. It excluded such independent or satellite cities as Aurora, Joliet, Elgin, Rockford, DeKalb, and Valparaiso, Indiana.
2. 21 were excluded because they did not answer items with sufficient completeness.
3. 14 were excluded because they were from exclusive heterosexuals (Kinsey 0 S or from Kinsey 1 S) or were probable heterosexuals.
4. 15 were excluded because they did not respond on the screening item of sexual orientation even though from other indicators they were very likely to be homosexuals.
5. 48 were excluded because they were received after our cutoff date for returns of February 1, 1979. The remaining questionnaires were 1,556 in number of which 61 were from the organization for older gay men.

While ten percent of the distributed Chicago questionnaires were returned, it is not possible to calculate a traditional response rate because of the mode of distribution. It is unknown how many questionnaires even got into the hands of potential respondents. Many may have been thrown away by owners or managers of the recipient establishments who may not have wanted them present. Some stacks of questionnaires may have sat for a few days and been thrown away. A number may have been destroyed by gays opposed to surveys. For example, seven can be accounted for by one person having returned to the researcher, not questionnaires, but miscellaneous advertisements in the pre-paid return envelopes. For these reasons one may only conclude that the actual response rate is higher than ten percent by an unknown amount.

The process by which we make comparisons between our gay and heterosexual respondents involves comparisons between all four groups--gay Chicago non-students, gay Chicago students, DeKalb gay students, DeKalb non-gay students. The gay DeKalb students and the heterosexual DeKalb students are the most comparable. The former small group of gay students serves principally as a "shuttle" between the DeKalb heterosexuals and the two Chicago homosexual groups. The logic of our comparisons is to first show that there are no significant differences between the three gay groups. Then, since the DeKalb gays are most comparable to the DeKalb heterosexuals, we may compare Chicago gays with DeKalb heterosexuals. In almost all of the comparisons below there appear to be no effects of area; such effects would appear as differences between Chicago and DeKalb gay students. In a few instances there appear to be differences which are due to age. In these cases, the Chicago non-students are found to differ from the student groups. In these cases, we control for age by comparing the four groups while including only those of college age--those under 25 years of age. In other instances, we make comparisons only between the student heterosexuals and the two gay student groups combined.

In those parts of the analysis where we are interested in examining relationships only within the gays, e.g., victimization due to homosexuality, we employ the two Chicago groups combined. These two groups combined constitute our best approximation of a representative sample of gays from the Chicago area. Little internal analysis of relationships within the DeKalb gay student group is attempted due to the limited size of that group.

Table 2.1 presents the demographic characteristics of our four sample groups. As expected, there is a very large age difference between the three student groups and the non-student group. Our Chicago non-student group appears, despite our efforts, to somewhat under-represent older respondents. This is a problem found in all of the studies of male homosexuals (cf. Weinberg 1970; Bell and Weinberg 1978, pp. 274-276; Harry and DeVall 1978, p. 25). We also anticipated, as found, that the heterosexual students might be younger than the gay students. Comparing the three student groups on age, we find that 28 percent of the Chicago gay students are under 21, 19 percent of the DeKalb gay students are under 21, and 50 percent of the DeKalb heterosexual students are under 21 (X^2=19.20, df=2, p. < .001). The age difference between gay and heterosexual students appears to arise because gays do not come out or define themselves as gay until the very late teens or early twenties. Two studies have

TABLE 2.1

DEMOGRAPHIC CHARACTERISTICS BY SAMPLE GROUP (PERCENT)

Characteristic	Chicago gay non-students	Chicago gay students	DeKalb gay students	DeKalb non-gay students
Age				
16-24	17	66	78	90
25-29	27	26	12	7
30-34	21	8	9	3
35-39	13	1	0	0
40-44	8	0	0	0
45-49	5	0	0	0
50-59	6	0	0	0
60-80	2	0	0	0
N(100%)	1466	90	32	204
Race				
White	92	79	91	95
N(100%)	1461	90	32	204
Marital Status				
Never-Married	84	96	88	92
Married	2	0	6	6
Sep./Divorced	13	4	6	1
Widowed	1	0	0	0
N(100%)	1446	90	32	204
Occupational Level				
Upper-White-Collar	21			
Lower-White-Collar	53			
Blue-Collar	6			
Service Workers	17			
Unemployed	2			
Retired	1			
N(100%)	1413			

TABLE 2.1 (continued)

DEMOGRAPHIC CHARACTERISTICS BY SAMPLE GROUP (PERCENT)

Characteristic	Chicago gay non-students	Chicago gay students	DeKalb gay students	DeKalb non-gay students
Income				
Under $5,000	4	45		
$5,000 - $9,999	13	40		
$10,000 - $14,999	27	14		
$15,000 - $19,999	25	0		
$20,000 - $24,999	15	1		
$25,000 - $29,999	7	0		
Over $30,000	9	0		
N(100%)	1443	87		
Years of Education				
0-8	1			
9-11	3			
12	12			
13-15	30			
16	23			
Over 16	31			
N(100%)	1457			
Area of Residence				
Newtown	21	12		
Non-Newtown Chicago	58	66		
Indiana	3	5		
Suburban Illinois	18	17		
N(100%)	1358	88		
Class Status				
Freshman			22	20
Sophomore			12	20
Junior			25	29
Senior			9	24
Grad. Student/Other			31	7
N(100%)			32	204

Source: Compiled by the author.

found the median age of coming out to be 19 or 20 (Dank 1971; Harry and DeVall 1978, p. 64). This means that gays come out approximately half-way through their college careers and before that are not usually available to researchers. Hence, a representative sample of heterosexual male students can be expected to be somewhat younger than a sample of gay students.

Since the fact that our heterosexual students are somewhat younger than our gay students can confound comparisons by sexual orientation we examined the relationship among the student groups of age to all of our principal independent and dependent measures used in the subsequent analyses. These relationships with age are presented in Table 2.2. Age, dichotomized at over and under 21, was found to be significantly related only to psychological dominance, disinterest in the arts, and having had a high school interest in sports. These associations do not seem to create any particular problems for subsequent analyses. Since the difference between the gay and heterosexual student groups on interest in the arts and high school interest in sports are considerably larger than those associated with age, it is unlikely that they could be explained by the latter. For example, the differences by age in artistic interest and sports interest are both 12 percent. The respective percentage differences by sexual orientation groups among the students are 27 and 58. In the case of dominance, we find no significant differences among the student groups (X^2=2.03, df=4, p=NS).

The age differences among the student groups are reflected in a difference in class status between the DeKalb gay and heterosexual students. (Class status was not asked of the Chicago students at the time of gathering the Chicago data since it had not yet been decided to gather the DeKalb samples.) This difference is particularly evident in the percentage who are graduate students. However, if there exist real differences in the educational attainments of gays and heterosexuals, as suggested earlier, this difference between the DeKalb samples may not simply be an artifact of sampling but a real one. A larger percentage of gay students may, in fact, decide to go to graduate school.

Table 2.1 shows that our respondents are overwhelmingly Caucasian in all groups, although there is a significant difference between the Chicago student group and all other groups combined (X^2=17.68, df=1, p < .001). Much of the difference between the Chicago student group and the other groups is due to the fact that a number of apparently Chicano students opted for the response category "Other", rather than designating themselves as "White." As expected, the percentage ever-married among the Chicago non-students differs significantly from all other groups combined (X^2=16.55, df=1, p < .001). However, since very few of the non-students are currently married, this difference is apparently due to the fact that they are considerably older than the student groups. The 16 percent ever-married among the Chicago non-students is comparable to the 19 percent reported by Bell and

TABLE 2.2

DIFFERENCES ON BASIC MEASURES AMONG GAY GROUPS AND
BY AGE AMONG STUDENT GROUPS

| Measure | X^2 | Age Differences | | | X^2 | Group Differences | | |
		df	p	gamma		df	p	v
Childhood Cross-gendering	1.57	2	ns	-.13	5.32	4	ns	.04
Adolescent Cross-gendering	3.04	2	ns	-.15	5.96	4	ns	.04
Adult Cross-gendering	1.08	2	ns	.03	2.78	4	ns	.03
Persistent Acting Interest	0.73	2	ns	-.07	5.61	4	ns	.04
Persistent Loner	3.79	2	ns	.19	7.29	4	ns	.05
Self-Esteem	1.22	2	ns	.03	3.55	4	ns	.03
Masculinity	1.38	2	ns	.11	7.61	4	ns	.05
Femininity	1.17	2	ns	.08	0.72	4	ns	.02
Dominance	11.51	2	.01	.31	7.10	4	ns	.05
Competitiveness	1.22	2	ns	.01	0.65	4	ns	.01
Disinterest in Art	4.43	1	.04	-.26	1.09	2	ns	.03
High School Interest in Sports	4.21	1	.04	-.25	2.35	2	ns	.04
Overall Crime	0.98	2	ns	.05	8.23	4	ns	.05
Violent Crime	2.52	1	ns	-.09	0.15	2	ns	.01
Property Crime	3.89	2	ns	-.11	6.48	4	ns	.05

Source: Compiled by author

Weinberg (1978, p. 374) and the 17 percent reported by Weinberg and Williams (1974, p. 213).

As can be seen from Table 2.1, our Chicago non-students are a highly educated group with 84 percent having at least some college education. This over-sampling of the educated has occurred in all studies of gay men. Weinberg and Williams (1974, p. 95) reported that 82 percent of their respondents had at least some college education. Gagnon and Simon (1973, p. 141), reporting Kinsey's data gathered during the 1940s, found that 70 percent of their homosexual respondents and 77 percent of their exclusively homosexual respondents had at least some college education. Harry and Devall (1978, p. 26) reported a similar statistic of 69 percent while Bell and Weinberg (1978, p. 274) found 76 percent among their recruitment pool of volunteers. The percentage of the national white male population possessing at least some college education in 1977 was 34.8 (U.S. Bureau of the Census 1978, pp. 155-157). While the over-representation of the educated in the studies of gay men is likely to be in part due to sampling bias, we have suggested above and below attempt to show that there is, in fact, a real and large difference in the educational attainments of gay and heterosexual men.

As a final comment on the demographic data of Table 2.1, we observe that the Chicago students appear to be less likely to live in the Newtown "gay ghetto" area. This is probably due to the fact that some of them still live at home with their parents, to the fact that they may not be able to afford the rents of that area, and that they may prefer to live near their respective universities, only one of which is located near Newtown.

The deficiencies in our final Chicago sample are: (1) that non-whites are severely under-represented, (2) that, despite our efforts, truly older gay men are somewhat under-represented if one assumes that the age distribution of gay men should approximate that of the general male population, (3) that the educated are somewhat over-represented, (4) that residents of the "gay ghetto" are probably somewhat over-represented, and (5) that blue-collar employees are probably somewhat under-represented. The over-representation of "ghetto" residents is most likely due to the fact that many of the sampled settings at which questionnaires were distributed are located in the Newtown area. The under-representation of blue-collar respondents has been found in all studies of gay men and parallels the over-representation of the educated. In our chapter on the occupational choices of gay men, we attempt to show that gays, in fact, avoid blue-collar jobs and hence only part of the under-representation of blue-collar gays is the result of sampling. Our arguments that the under-representation of blue-collar gays and of the less educated in our data reflect real differences between gay and heterosexual men rather than sampling artifacts places the reader in a somewhat unusual position. Normally, the reader of a research report evaluates the adequacy of the results in the light of the methods employed to obtain those results. In the present case, we are asking the reader to evaluate the adequacy of the methods in the light of the results. In short, in the present work our results partly serve to validate our methods.

MEASURING INSTRUMENTS

Below we briefly describe the multi-item scales employed in our analysis. We have developed several scales measuring cross-gendering patterned after the measuring instruments of Freund et al. (1974) and Whitam (1977). However, since the interpretations of the meanings of these scales are of considerable substantive importance, consideration of these scales is deferred to the following chapter. Consideration of our scales measuring self-reported criminal behaviors are also deferred until the chapter on crimes. The standardized alpha reliabilities of the scales here described are presented in Table 2.3 for the Chicago samples, the DeKalb gay students, and the DeKalb heterosexual students.

1. Psychological femininity. We adopted the measures of psychological masculinity and femininity developed by Spence and Helmreich (1978, pp. 31-38). Our femininity scale is adjective self-rating in format and contains eight items.

2. Psychological masculinity. This scale is also adjective self-rating in format and contains eight items. Its substantive interpretation may be considered as rational or goal-oriented aggressiveness while that of the femininity scale may be considered affiliative expressiveness or emotional warmth.

3. Self-esteem. The three items of this scale are "On the whole I am quite a happy person," "I take a very positive attitude toward myself," and "On the whole I am satisfied with myself." This scale should be more interpreted as self-acceptance rather than as esteem in the sense of superiority over others. While some researchers use self-esteem scales of the latter type, e.g., Spence and Helmreich (1978, pp. 234-236), it was felt that these scales tend to excessively define self-esteem in terms of dominance and superiority, thus inflating the correlation between self-esteem and masculinity, introducing thereby a sex bias and, perhaps, a value judgement.

4. Interpersonal dominance. The four items of this scale are "When I am in disagreement with other people my opinion usually prevails," "When in a group of people I usually do what the others want rather than make suggestions," and self-ratings on "Not at all aggressive - Very aggressive," and "Very dominant - Very submissive." We note the rather modest reliability of this scale.

5. Competitiveness. The four items of this scale are "It is important to me to perform better than others on a task," "I feel that winning is very important in both work and games," "I really enjoy working in situations involving skill and competition," and "When a group plans an activity I would rather organize it myself than have someone else organize it and just help out."

TABLE 2.3

STANDARDIZED ITEM ALPHA RELIABILITIES OF SCALES
BY SAMPLE GROUPS

	Sample Group		
Scale	Chicago Groups	DeKalb Gay Students	DeKalb Non-Gay Students
Masculinity	.76	.82	.70
Femininity	.77	.77	.73
Self-Esteem	.81	.90	.81
Dominance	.53	.22	.49
Competitiveness	.65	.76	.61
Overall Crime	.67	.70	.68

Source: Compiled by the author.

3

CHILDHOOD
EFFEMINACY AND
ITS EVOLUTION

In the present chapter we empirically explore the extent of cross-gender characteristics among our several groups of respondents and see whether they collectively form a scale indicative of feminine cross-gendering as suggested in the earlier discussed researches. We also take up the question of the extent to which these characteristics persist into later phases of life and the significance of that persistence. To these ends, all of our respondent groups were asked about six cross-gender characteristics they may have manifested during each of the following three time periods of their lives: "Childhood (before age 13)", "Adolescence (ages 13 through 17)", and "Since Adolescence (18 years and over)." Taken from the various earlier described researches on childhood effeminacy among boys, the questions were: "Were you regarded as a sissy?"; "Were you usually a loner?"; "Did you ever wish you had been a girl rather than a boy?"; "Did you prefer playing or associating with girls rather than boys?"; "Did you ever dress up in female clothes (drag)?" The response categories provided for each of these 18 items were "Yes," "Don't Know," and "No." In the cross-gendering scales to be developed below we--after Freund, et al. (1974)-- scored these respective response categories 2, 1, and 0. These items are very similar to Part A of Freund et al.'s (1974) feminine gender identity scale. We opted not to use Part B of his scale because we wanted to explore cross-gendering for different phases of our respondent's lives. Also, we did not use Part C because it was felt these items might offend our respondents.

It may be questioned whether individuals are capable of accurately responding to questions about behaviors during their childhoods which may have been a decade to a half-century ago. However, we are encouraged on the accuracy of such data by the results of earlier researches in which large percentages of gay men recall cross-gender characteristics during their childhoods (Whitam 1977, 1980; Freund et al., 1974; Saghir and Robins 1973, pp. 18-21). Although there is a general tendency for events to be forgotten across time, it seems likely that cross-gender characteristics are sufficiently perceptually outstanding that they remain emblazoned in memory for years. As Saghir and Robins (1973, p. 19) reported, all of their adult gay male respondents who were effeminate during childhood "were called sissy and teased about it by their schoolmates. It was an unhappy experience that most of them recalled very vividly."

Sudman and Bradburn (1974, pp. 84-85) have found that the problem of forgetting can be exaggerated since the degree to which forgetting of prior events occurs depends on the frequency and significance of those events. They found that while individuals are likely to forget purchases they have made which are minor, recall of large purchases is nearly perfect. Hence, significant events such as being considered a sissy by peers seems likely to be more recallable than less significant ones such as the type of candy preferred during childhood. Kinsey et al. (1948, p. 152) found greater accuracy of response when they asked whether persons had ever done something than when asking how often they had done it. For this reason, we framed our cross-gendering questions in terms of ever occurring during a bounded time period.

Another source of error in obtaining accurate reports of earlier cross-gendering, and one we consider at least as important as simple forgetting, is that some respondents may be unwilling, rather than unable, to report such phenomena. The rhetoric of the gay movement of recent years has been to depict gay men as not being visibly effeminate and as being largely indistinguishable from heterosexual males. This rhetoric has been principally directed to the end of debunking the grossly distorted stereotypes which many heterosexual persons hold about gay men. To ask questions about past or present cross-gender characteristics implies the possibility that there might be, or might have been, some truth in those stereotypes. Hence, gay men sincerely committed to movement rhetoric might decline to respond accurately to such questions. We did receive a handful of questionnaires with written comments suggesting that the questions on cross-gendering were prejudicial. It thus appears that the socially desirable response among gay men is to depict the self as non-cross-gendered. Since our questions on cross-gendering and numerous other ones have socially desirable responses and may be threatening, this is likely to lead to some under-reporting. However, as Sudman and Bradburn (1974, p. 66) found, "If the topic is threatening more complete reporting may be obtained from self-administered rather than personal interviews. Self-administered forms may also be used for highly threatening questions dealing with possibly illegal behavior where anonymity is required. Where a socially desirable answer is possible on attitudinal questions, there is a greater tendency to conform on personal interviews than on self-administered questionnaires." It thus appears that for the types of questioning included in our study, our self-administered questionnaire may be superior to interview procedures where the respondent must admit to various forms of socially disapproved behaviors when face to face with an interviewer. Because some of our respondents might be unable to respond accurately and some might be unwilling to respond accurately, we consider the extent of cross-gendering reported below to be minimum estimates of cross-gender behaviors among our respondents both homosexual and heterosexual. The effect of any such under-reporting histories of cross-gendering would be that those individuals classified as cross-gendered would be or have been actually cross-gendered while those classified as not cross-gendered would include both the actually non-cross-gendered plus some of the actually cross-gendered. The effect of this measurement bias would be to reduce the magnitudes of the associations between the cross-gendering measures and other variables. Hence, the associations shown in the other measures are likely to somewhat understate the strength of the true associations. On the other hand, this also implies that when we find no significant association there could, in fact, be one although it would probably not be a very strong one.

DEFEMINIZATION

Table 3.1 presents each of our cross-gendering items for each of the three time periods by our four sample groups. The data of this table reflect two different patterns of association. One pattern involves the four items of sissy, be girl, play with girls, and cross-dressing. These four become our overall cross-gendering scales. The other two items of wanting to be an actor/performer and being a loner exhibit different patterns and have been subsequently made into separate scales. These two items reflect cross-gendering less directly than the other four. Examining the four items for childhood, we note consistent and significant differences between our sample groups with the major differences being between the heterosexual group and the other three groups. If we compare the heterosexual group with the other three groups combined, we find quite large and significant differences. In the order of the items presented in Table 3.1 for childhood, the respective gammas for the four gay/heterosexual comparisons (df=1) are 0.72, 0.70, 0.72, and 0.83. These differences confirm the findings of the earlier cited researchers on sample groups much larger than heretofore studied. If we compare only the three gay groups on these four items, we find no significant differences. Hence, there appear to be quite large differences in childhood cross-gendering between gay and heterosexual males which are reliable across groups and studies.

TABLE 3.1

CROSS-GENDERING ITEMS FOR CHILDHOOD, ADOLESCENCE, AND ADULTHOOD BY SAMPLE GROUP (Percent)

	Sample Group									
	Chicago Gay Non-Students		Chicago Gay Students		DeKalb Gay Students		DeKalb Non-Gay Students		x^2	p.
Childhood Items	%	N(100%)	%	N(100%)	%	N(100%)	%	N(100%)		
Sissy	42	1460	47	89	47	32	11	204	77.44	.001
Actor	40	1463	47	89	41	32	34	204	4.54	ns
Loner	47	1457	62	90	47	32	27	203	39.72	.001
Be Girl	22	1466	23	90	34	32	5	204	36.82	.001
Play Girls c	46	1463	58	90	50	32	12	203	91.41	.001
Cross-Dress	36	1465	39	90	44	32	5	204	80.75	.001
Adolescent Items										
Sissy	33	1454	38	87	44	32	3	203	79.23	.001
Actor	48	1458	53	90	50	32	40	203	5.71	ns
Loner	50	1449	60	90	59	32	31	202	33.90	.001
Be Girl	15	1458	12	90	9	32	5	203	15.57	.010
Play Girls c	27	1456	37	90	47	32	25	201	10.10	.020
Cross-Dress	17	1458	14	90	16	32	3	203	25.14	.001

Adulthood
Items

Items									
Sissy	8	1452	9	86	13	31	2	203	12.45	.010
Actor	36	1456	40	88	45	31	37	203	1.27	ns
Loner	39	1446	36	88	39	31	28	203	9.85	.020
Be Girl	5	1454	6	88	6	31	2	202	3.11	ns
Play c Girls	9	1454	16	88	23	31	41	201	158.92	.001
Cross-Dress	17	1456	14	88	6	31	2	203	32.06	.001

Source: Compiled by the author.

53

Turning to the items for adolescence, we also find significant differences across groups on the four direct cross-gendering items. However, the differences are not as large as for childhood. This is due to the gay groups having decreased the extent of their cross-gendering for the items sissy, be girl, play with girls, and cross-dressing and also due to the heterosexuals having increased their preference for associating with girls. Comparisons of the heterosexual respondents with the three gay groups combined reveal significant differences for the items of sissy, be girl, and cross-dressing: the respective gammas are 0.87, 0.53, and 0.70. For the item of preferring to associate with girls, there is no significant difference between the gays and the heterosexuals (gamma = 0.07). Comparing the three gay groups on these four items there is a significant difference only for the item of preferring to associate with girls with the student groups being somewhat higher on this measure. This may arise out of the students still going to school in essentially heterosexual environments and hence reflect more opportunity than motivation. Consistent with this interpretation, we observe that the DeKalb gays who attend a residential school are higher on this measure than the Chicago students who attend a largely commuter, and therefore less mixed-sex, school.

Turning to the measures for adulthood, we find significant differences across groups for sissy, cross-dressing, and preferring to associate with girls, but not for wanting to be a girl. We note that the differences are now considerably smaller than in earlier time periods for sissy and cross-dressing and they have vanished for wanting to be a girl. Comparing the combined gay groups with the heterosexuals, we find significant differences for sissy (gamma = 0.70), for cross-dressing (gamma = 0.78) but not for wanting to be a girl (gamma = 0.37). There is also a significant difference between the heterosexuals and the combined gay groups on associating with girls but it is reversed in direction from childhood (gamma = 0.73). This shows that a preference for associating with the opposite gender increases toward adulthood among heterosexual males but declines among homosexual men. Comparing the three gay groups on these four items we find, as before, a significant difference on the item of preferring to associate with females (gamma = 0.36), with the two student groups being higher on this measure.

We briefly note that there are no significant differences on the three actor/entertainer measures across all groups or among the gay groups. There is a small significant difference between the gays and the heterosexuals (gamma = 0.16, df=1, p=.03) on this measure for adolescence only. This partly conflicts with Whitam's (1979) finding of a difference between gays and heterosexuals on such an interest. On the measure of being a loner, there are significant differences across all groups for all time periods and between gays and heterosexuals for all time periods. This agrees with earlier studies (Bell et al. 1981a, p. 84). Comparing the three gay groups on the loner measures, there is a significant difference only for childhood with the Chicago students having been more often loners. The actor and loner measures do not exhibit the pattern of declining frequencies from childhood to adulthood. Rather, they show persistence across time among both homosexuals and heterosexuals. Whatever the causal status of these correlates of childhood cross-gendering, it appears that such propensities are established early in life, and are enduring characteristics of the individual.

Turning to the hypothesis of defeminization of gay men between childhood and adulthood, the relevant comparisons in Table 3.1 are the vertical differences across time periods within columns. Again, we separately analyze the four cross-gendering items and the two of actor/entertainer and loner. It is clear that for all four of these items for all three gay groups, there is a strong trend toward the elimination of cross-gender characteristics. Among the heterosexuals there is either no trend or only a very slight one. However, we should note that Bates and Bentler (1973) reported a defeminization process for conventional boys which occurred between the ages of four and ten. Their measure of defeminization was choices of different games and toys. Vener and Snyder (1966) have also found increasing defeminization with age among conventional pre-school boys in terms of choice of masculine or feminine artifacts. It may be that there is a defeminization process which occurs much earlier in heterosexual males than in homosexual ones and to a lesser degree. Of course, such an early defeminization process is substantially beyond the reach of our recall methods.

In order to further explore the relative persistence into adulthood of cross-gendering, Table 3.2 presents each childhood item against the same item for adulthood among our Chicago respondents. This cross-tabulation is necessary in order to explore persistence since those in Table 3.1 responding affirmatively to an item during adulthood need not have responded affirmatively to that item during childhood. It may be seen from Table 3.2 that for all six items the greatest stability across time is in the "No" responses. Of those without a given trait during childhood, the lowest percentage also without that trait during adulthood is 77 percent for the loner item. Since the "No" responses are the most socially acceptable ones for all time periods, we would expect the greatest stability among them across time. In contrast, the "Yes" responses for childhood reveal quite variable persistence into adulthood and may be divided into the two groups of actor plus loner versus the four others. Among the latter four, the highest percentage of respondents possessing a given trait during both childhood and adulthood is 25 percent for the cross-dressing item. These low percentages of persistence directly reveal the defeminization process, i.e., non-persistence is the majority case.

Additional information about the defeminization process may be learned if we examine the column percentages (in parentheses) of the sub-tables of Table 3.2. For all six items, a majority of

TABLE 3.2

CHILDHOOD CROSS-GENDERING ITEMS BY ADULT CROSS-GENDERING ITEMS
AMONG CHICAGO RESPONDENTS (Percent)[a]

Childhood Items		Adult Items			
Considered Sissy	Yes	Yes 12 (68)	No 88 (40)	N(100%) 649	X^2=34.27,p<.001
	No	4 (32)	96 (60)	887	d_c=0.28,d_a=0.08[b]
Be Actor	Yes	60 (66)	40 (25)	620	X^2=241.58,p<.001
	No	21 (34)	79 (75)	921	d_c=0.40,d_a=0.39
Was Loner	Yes	55 (69)	45 (35)	736	X^2=164.31,p<.001
	No	23 (31)	77 (65)	796	d_c=0.34,d_a=0.32
Be Girl	Yes	14 (59)	86 (20)	336	X^2=68.13,p<.001
	No	3 (41)	97 (80)	1206	d_c=0.40,d_a=0.12
Play c Girls	Yes	16 (81)	84 (43)	714	X^2=76.21,p<.001
	No	3 (19)	97 (57)	826	d_c=0.38,d_a=0.13
Cross-Dress	Yes	25 (52)	75 (32)	549	X^2=36.57,p<.001
	No	13 (48)	87 (68)	994	d_c=0.20,d_a=0.12

[a]The column-based percentages are within parentheses; the row-based are without. For each subtable a childhood measure is cross-tabulated against the same measure for adulthood.
[b]d_c is Somer's asymmetric d predicting the childhood measure.
d_a is Somer's asymmetric d predicting the adult measure.
Source: Compiled by the author.

those possessing a given trait during adulthood also possessed that trait during childhood. This implies that the acquisition of cross-gendering during adulthood is less likely and that by far the most common pattern is for early acquisition of that trait whether or not it persists into adulthood. Hence, among these data it is considerably easier to predict from adult cross-gendering to childhood cross-gendering than in the reverse direction. Whereas a person possessing one of the non-actor/non-loner items during childhood is unlikely to possess that trait during adulthood due to defeminization, if he possesses it during adulthood, he is quite likely to have also possessed it during childhood. This asymmetry of predictability is shown in the different values of the asymmetric Somer's ds (see Table 3.2) for each of the four direct cross-gendering measures. In contrast, the greater persistence (non-defeminization) for the actor and loner items results in asymmetric Somer's ds for these items of equivalent magnitudes, e.g., 0.40 and 0.39 for the actor item.

Briefly examining persistence in the cross-gendering items among our heterosexual respondents we find no significant associations between childhood and adulthood for the items of sissy, be girl, and cross-dressing. Indeed, of the five respondents who cross-dressed during adulthood, none are among the ten who cross-dressed during childhood. These data suggest that the possession of cross-gender characteristics among heterosexuals is of minimal significance as indicators of enduring aspects of their personalities and largely arises out of transient situational influences. We did find a significant association between childhood and adulthood for the "prefer to associate with girls" item. However, as the data on trends in this item suggest, such a preference is probably indicative of heterosexual interests among heterosexuals while being indicative of cross-gender interests among homosexuals. Among the heterosexuals the two items of actor and loner are strongly and significantly associated between childhood and adulthood as they are among the homosexuals. That the actor and loner items show considerable persistence among both heterosexuals and homosexuals is consistent with the notion that such behaviors are more socially acceptable than the other four cross-gendering items and not subject to intense pressures for gender conformity.

Having shown how our individual cross-gendering items reveal defeminization across time among the homosexuals only, we now turn to a further examination of the defeminization process by exploring how these items aggregate or not into more global measures of cross-gendering during each of the three time periods. In particular, we ask whether these items constitute a scale or syndrome of items for each time period and does this occur among both heterosexuals and homosexuals? Also, does such a complex persist across the defeminization process, or is there selective defeminization? Table 3.3 presents the Pearsonian inter-item correlations within each time period for each of the three time periods for the Chicago homosexuals.

58

TABLE 3.3

PEARSONIAN CORRELATIONS AMONG CROSS-GENDERING ITEMS WITHIN
CHILDHOOD, ADOLESCENCE, AND ADULTHOOD (Chicago respondents)[a]

Items	Items					
	Considered Sissy	Be Actor	Was Loner	Be Girl	Play c Girls	Cross-Dress
Considered Sissy	X	.19**	.18**	.31**	.37**	.25**
N	X	1546	1541	1549	1547	1548
Be Actor	.12**	X	.03	.22**	.16**	.20**
N	1538	X	1544	1552	1550	1551
Was Loner	.14**	-.04	X	.09**	.11**	.04
N	1529	1538	X	1547	1545	1546
Be Girl	.21**	.17**	.07*	X	.35**	.36**
N	1538	1547	1538	X	1553	1555
Play c Girls	.27**	.14**	.08*	.27**	X	.27**
N	1536	1545	1536	1545	X	1552
Cross-Dress	.21**	.17**	-.01	.32**	.19**	X
N	1538	1547	1538	1547	1545	X
Considered Sissy	X	.15**	.05	.18**	.20**	.21**
N	X	1535	1525	1534	1533	1536
Be Actor		X	-.01	.09**	.12**	.21**
N		X	1532	1540	1540	1542
Was Loner			X	.09**	.08*	-.02
N			X	1530	1530	1532
Be Girl				X	.22**	.22**
N				X	1538	1541
Play c Girls					X	.13**
					X	1540

[a]The childhood correlations are above the diagonal of the upper
panel; those for adolescence are below. The adulthood
correlations are in the lower panel.
**Indicates .001 two-tailed significance
*Indicates .01 two-tailed significance

Source: Compiled by the author.

From the pattern of correlations in Table 3.3 for childhood among the four items of sissy, be girl, play with girls, and cross-dressing, it is apparent that these constitute the core of a potential cross-gendering cluster. The actor item is somewhat less strongly related to this cluster while the loner item is still more peripheral. Only the four direct cross-gendering items form an adequate scale with a standardized item alpha-reliability of 0.65. These four items constitute our scale of childhood cross-gendering used in subsequent analyses. Inspection of the patterns of correlations for adolescence and adulthood among the Chicago homosexuals reveals a general decline in the magnitudes of the coefficients as we move from childhood to adulthood. These declines are reflected in the declining values of the alpha coefficients of the three four-item cross-gendering scales for the three time periods. The respective standardized alpha coefficients for childhood, adolescence, and adulthood are 0.65, 0.57, and 0.49. The decline in the magnitudes of these coefficients has the substantive meaning that a fairly coherent childhood complex of cross-gendering disintegrates across time. This disintegration effect should be distinguished from the earlier observed defeminization process. While the latter may be expressed as a decline in the mean level of cross-gendering, the former is a result of the declining magnitudes of the correlations among the items constituting a given scale. Hence, while a boy possessing any of these cross-gendering traits is also likely to possess some of the others during childhood, a gay adult who possesses one is not as likely to also possess the others.

Validity for the childhood and adulthood cross-gendering scales is conferred by their sizeable associations with each other and with responses to the self-assessed item, "Do you think of your appearance as: Very Masculine, Masculine, A Little Feminine, or Quite Feminine?" Table 3.4 shows that, despite defeminization and disintegration across time, childhood and adulthood cross-gendering are notably associated with each other and with self-assessed adult appearance. Of course, the stronger association of self-assessed femininity with adult cross-gendering than with childhood cross-gendering is due to defeminization. Many of the self-assessed masculine gay men were once cross-gendered as children. In the cross-tabular analyses below employing our childhood and adult cross-gendering scales we employ the same cutting points for both scales. While this results in very unequal marginal frequencies for the adulthood scale, it permits more meaningful comparisons, particularly in distinguishing between those with any versus no cross-gendering as adults. Table 3.5 presents the Pearsonian correlations among the six cross-gendering items for each of the three time periods found among our heterosexual respondents. It is evident that for the childhood period there is little tendency for the formation of a cross-gendering cluster comparable to that found among our Chicago homosexuals. The meaning of these differing patterns of

TABLE 3.4

CHILDHOOD AND ADULT CROSS-GENDERING BY EACH OTHER
AND BY SELF-ASSESSED MASCULINE-FEMININE APPEARANCE (Percent)

Childhood Cross-Gendering	Appearance		
	Very Masculine	Masculine	Feminine or Quite Feminine
None	40	30	11
Some	46	49	41
High	15	22	48
N(100%)	147	1188	193

$x^2 = 81.99$ df = 4   p < .001   gamma = 0.39

Adult Cross-Gendering			
None	84	74	40
Some	16	25	48
High	1	1	12
N(100%)	147	1178	187

$x^2 = 149.93$ df = 4   p < .001   gamma = 0.54

Adult Cross-Gendering	Childhood Cross-Gendering[a]		
	None	Some	High
None	88(35)	69(46)	53(18)
Some	11(12)	28(51)	41(37)
High	1(8)	2(38)	6(55)
N(100%)	433	723	370

$x_2 = 124.03$ df = 4   p < .001   gamma = 0.49

a.   Row percentages in parentheses; column percentages outside parentheses.

Source: Compiled by the author.

TABLE 3.5

PEARSONIAN CORRELATIONS AMONG CROSS-GENDERING ITEMS WITHIN CHILDHOOD, ADOLESCENCE, AND ADULTHOOD (non-gay respondents)[a]

Items						
	Considered Sissy	Be Actor	Was Loner	Be Girl	Play c Girls	Cross-Dress
Considered Sissy	X	.11	.19*	.09	.06	.16^x
N	X	204	203	204	203	204
Be Actor	-.02	X	-.09	.05	.06	-.11
N	203	X	203	204	203	204
Was Loner	.31**	.11	X	.17^x	.06	.10
N	202	202	X	203	202	203
Be Girl	.16^x	.02	.14	X	.15^x	.02
N	203	203	202	X	203	204
Play c Girls	.04	.02	.02	.05	X	-.04
N	201	201	200	201	X	203
Cross-Dress	.10	.03	.07	.34**	.09	X
N	203	203	202	203	201	X
Considered Sissy	X	-.03	.24**	.36**	.01	.03
N	X	203	203	202	201	203
Be Actor		X	.16^x	.09	.13	.01
N		X	203	202	201	203
Was Loner			X	.26**	.10	.13
			X	202	201	203
Be Girl				X	.03	.38**
N				X	200	202
Play c Girls						.08
N						201

[a]The childhood correlations are above the diagonal of the upper panel; those for adolescence are below. The adulthood correlations are in the lower panel.
**Indicates .001 two-tailed significance
*Indicates .01 two-tailed significance
^{x}Indicates .05 two-tailed significance
Source: Compiled by the author.

correlations between our homosexual and heterosexual respondents is that, while occasional cross-gender behaviors or feelings are not rare among the heterosexuals, they are apparently ephemeral, not part of a cross-gendering complex, and not expressions of enduring gender-role preference. Rather, they appear to be probably situationally induced behaviors lacking substantial significance as indicators of gender-role preference.

The correlations for adolescence and adulthood in Table 3.5 show a tendency for the formation of a cross-gendering cluster. However, no significance can be attached to these correlations since they arise due to, variously, three to five individuals out of more than 200. The virtual lack of variation of these items beyond childhood among our heterosexual respondents makes any use of them for analytic purposes--other than the actor or loner items--unreliable. Hence, in subsequent analysis we make no use of measures of adolescent or adult cross-gendering among the heterosexuals. We employ for the heterosexuals the aggregate measure of childhood cross-gendering while noting that its significance is different for the heterosexuals than for the gays. Among the former, such a measure only indicates the number of ways in which they may have at various times acted cross-gendered while among the homosexuals it measures the number of ways in which they may have expressed cross-gendering or been cross-gendered.

In the analyses below, we have created a scale measuring persistent interest in being an actor/entertainer and another for being a persistent loner. Each of these measures combines the three items from the different time periods. For the actor measure, the respective standardized alpha reliabilities among the Chicago gays and the heterosexuals are 0.79 and 0.69; for the loner measure, the respective reliabilities are 0.72 and 0.73. While the other cross-gendering items show considerable fluctuation across time, interest in being an actor or being a loner both appear to be established during childhood and to show great persistence.

Table 3.6 presents our overall measures of childhood cross-gendering, of persistent acting interest, and being a persistent loner by the four sample groups. A large difference in childhood cross-gendering is apparent between the heterosexual and homosexual respondents. There are no significant differences between the three gay groups ($X^2 = 5.32$, df=4, p=ns) while there is a large and significant difference between the heterosexuals and the three gay groups combined ($X^2 = 154.25$, df=2, p. < .001). These findings replicate on considerably larger samples the findings of Whitam (1977; 1979) and Saghir and Robins (1973, p. 18). Also replicating earlier findings is the relationship between sample group and being a persistent loner. The differences here are also due to the gay/non-gay comparison ($X^2 = 42.93$, df=2, p. < .001) rather than to any differences among the three gay groups ($X^2 = 7.29$, df=4, p=ns). The reasons for the gay/non-gay difference in being a loner are not completely clear. While there is ample reason to believe that to some degree cross-gendered children are

TABLE 3.6

CHILDHOOD CROSS-GENDERING, PERSISTENT ACTOR, AND PERSISTENT LONER
BY SAMPLE GROUPS (PERCENT)

Childhood Cross-Gendering	Chicago-Gay Non-students	Chicago-Gay Students	DeKalb Gay Students	DeKalb Non-Gay Students
None	29	20	16	70
Some	47	53	56	30
High	24	27	28	1
N(100%)	1457	89	32	203

x^2=159.11 df=6 p < .001

Persistent Actor

None	40	34	29	38
Some	37	38	52	44
High	23	28	19	18
N(100%)	1453	87	31	203

x^2= 8.86 df=6 p=ns

Persistent Loner

None	33	22	26	55
Some	39	50	52	30
High	28	28	23	15
N(100%)	1444	88	31	202

x^2= 50.06 df=6 p < .001

Source: Compiled by the author.

excluded from the company of other boys, it is possible that their having been loners was a voluntary or quasi-voluntary choice. Rather than having been loners due to labeling as a sissy and rejection by other boys, Green (1974, p. 146) has reported that many are loners voluntarily. Such a "voluntary" choice may arise out of an intense disinterest in the conventional play activities of other boys. As we show below, being a persistent loner is related to an adolescent disinterest in sports. In our present data, we are unable to directly deal with the separate effects of rejection versus "voluntary" self-exclusion.

Table 3.6 does not replicate the findings of Green (1974, p. 148) and of Bates and Bentler (1973) that feminine boys have a notably greater interest in acting than conventional boys. However, this appears to be due to our different data-gathering methods. His non-conventional experimental group (and those of other researchers on childhood effeminacy) consisted of boys who had been referred to clinical attention due to effeminacy whereas a sizeable minority of our gay respondents were not effeminate during childhood. However, among our Chicago respondents we find a sizeable association between childhood cross-gendering and a persistent acting interest ($x^2 = 96.56$, df=4, p. < .001, gamma=0.34). Among those with no childhood cross-gendering, 54 percent had no acting interests as compared with 24 percent among those highly cross-gendered during childhood. Hence, it would appear that the inclusion in our gay samples of persons who were not cross-gendered during childhood reduces or eliminates the gay-heterosexual differences. This is borne out by the fact that, if we exclude from the analysis those gay respondents who were not cross-gendered during childhood and hence would not have been referred to clinical attention for effeminacy, a significant difference between the heterosexuals and the three gay groups combined appears ($x^2 = 7.40$, df=2, p. < .03). There are no significant differences on this measure among the three gay groups ($x^2 = 4.46$, df=4, p=ns).

Table 3.4 presents the relationship between our overall measure of childhood cross-gendering and that for cross-gendering during adulthood. This table reveals a strong, although asymmetrical, relationship between cross-gendering in childhood and adulthood. While those cross-gendered during childhood may or may not be also cross-gendered during adulthood, those highly cross-gendered during adulthood were virtually certain to have been cross-gendered during childhood. Only eight percent of those highly cross-gendered during adulthood displayed no cross-gendering during childhood. Of course, the reason for the asymmetry of this relationship is that large numbers of those cross-gendered during childhood defeminized by adulthood.

DEFEMINIZATION AND PSYCHOLOGICAL WELL-BEING

Having replicated the findings of other pertinent researches and established the existence of a large-scale defeminization process among gay men, we now turn to an analysis of the relationships of childhood and adult cross-gendering with measures of psychological well-being. For this analysis, we employ only the gay Chicago respondents since, as earlier shown, adult cross-gendering and defeminization do not seem to exist among heterosexual males to any significant extent. In the analyses below, we retain our cross-tabular mode of presentation but utilize log-linear likelihood ratio tests of statistical significance. The advantages of these procedures are that they retain for the reader the simplicity of cross-tabular forms of presentation while also permitting one to test for the presence of interaction effects as in the analysis of variance. In the presentation below, we use analysis of variance terminology to refer to the order of interaction effects rather than the less well known terminology of log-linear analysis. Thus, an interaction between two independent variables we refer to as a first-order interaction rather than a three-way interaction. The log-linear approach also permits a more economical analysis of zero-order, partial, and interaction relationships than separate presentation of all such relationships.

Table 3.7 presents the relationships of adult self-esteem with childhood and adult cross-gendering. In our likelihood ratio tables exemplary abbreviations for our variables are childhood cross-gendering (C), adult cross-gendering (A), and self-esteem (S). Thus, the association between childhood and adult cross-gendering is symbolized as "AC" while the term symbolizing any interaction is "SCA." The chi-sqaureds associated with each of these associations are printed in the upper half of the table with the percentages in the lower half. A readable introduction to log-linear analysis may be found in Reynolds (1977). The computer program used to produce the log linear analyses was that contained in BMDP (Brown 1977). Table 3.7 reveals that there are significant zero-order and first-order partial relationships among all three variables. It is also apparent from these data that those individuals who were cross-gendered during childhood but who defeminized have higher self-esteem than those who are persistently effeminate. A direct comparison of the defeminized with the always-effeminate reveals a significant difference (X^2=15.52, df=2, p. < .001), although the defeminized are still somewhat and significantly lower than the never-effeminate (X^2=9.37, df=2, p. < .01). We should note that, lacking measures of self-esteem prior to the occurrence of defeminization, we cannot determine whether those with higher self-esteem subsequently defeminized or defeminization resulted in the acquisition of higher self-esteem.

TABLE 3.7

LIKELIHOOD RATIO ANALYSIS OF SELF-ESTEEM BY
CHILDHOOD AND ADULT CROSS-GENDERING

Partial (1st Order) Associations				Marginal (0-Order) Associations	
Effect	df	LR Chi-squared	P	LR Chi-squared	P
SC	2	9.61	.008	18.02	.000
SA	2	20.13	.000	28.53	.000
CA	1	84.41	.000	92.81	.000
SCA	2	1.60	.448		

Adult Cross-Gendering(A)	Childhood Cross-Gendering(C)	Self-Esteem (S) (Percentages)			
		Low	Med	High	N(100%)
Some	Some	39	42	19	391
	None	31	52	17	52
None	Some	28	46	26	697
	None	21	46	33	377

Source: Compiled by the author.

Psychological masculinity has been found by various researchers to be the major predictor of self-esteem among men, women, and male homosexuals (Spence and Helmreich 1978, p. 67; Bem 1974; Kelly and Worell 1977). Among our Chicago respondents the respective Pearsonian correlations of self-esteem with masculinity, femininity, dominance, and competitiveness are 0.56, 0.17, 0.30, and 0.19; among our heterosexual respondents the comparable correlations are 0.51, 0.18, 0.37, and 0.16. Since these characteristics appear to be the major predictors of self-esteem, we proceed to an analysis of how defeminization relates to them. Table 3.8 presents the likelihood ratio analysis of masculinity by childhood and adult cross-gendering. Masculinity is significantly negatively related to both childhood and adult cross-gendering at both zero-order and partial levels. The defeminized are significantly more masculine than the always-effeminate (X^2=6.83, df=2, p. < .04) while still significantly less masculine than the never-effeminate (X^2=13.89, df=2, p. < .001). It seems that these differences may account for some

TABLE 3.8

LIKELIHOOD RATIO ANALYSIS OF MASCULINITY BY CHILDHOOD
AND ADULT CROSS-GENDERING

Partial (1st Order) Associations				Marginal (0-Order) Associations	
Effect	df	LR Chi-squared	P	LR Chi-squared	P
MC	2	9.85	.007	15.12	.000
MA	2	13.68	.001	18.95	.000
CA	1	82.92	.000	88.19	.000
MCA	2	4.81	.090		

Adult Cross-Gendering(A)	Childhood Cross-Gendering(C)	Masculinity (M) (Percentages)			
		Low	Med	High	N(100%)
Some	Some	35	42	23	382
	None	40	42	17	52
None	Some	28	44	28	691
	None	24	37	39	372

Source: Compiled by the author.

of the self-esteem differences in the preceding table.   We
earlier hypothesized that psychological femininity might be
associated with cross-gendering.   Table 3.9 tests the
relationships of femininity with childhood and adulthood cross-
gendering.   There are significant, although modest, zero-order
and first-order partial relationships of femininity with
childhood cross-gendering but none with adult cross-gendering.
The modestness of the strength of these associations shows that
apparent role femininity need not be expressive of psychological
femininity and that theorizing assuming a close relationship
between the two seems hazardous.

TABLE 3.9

LIKELIHOOD RATIO ANALYSIS OF FEMININITY BY
CHILDHOOD AND ADULT CROSS-GENDERING

Partial (1st Order) Associations				Marginal (0-Order) Associations	
Effect	df	LR Chi-squared	p	LR Chi-squared	p
FC	2	11.32	.004	15.20	.000
FA	2	3.92	.141	7.81	.020
CA	1	91.11	.000	95.00	.000
FCA	2	1.86	.394		

Adult Cross-Gendering(A)	Childhood Cross-Gendering(C)	Femininity(F) (Percentages)			N(100%)
		Low	Med	High	
Some	Some	32	32	36	388
	None	32	42	26	50
None	Some	33	36	30	693
	None	42	36	22	375

Source: Compiled by the author.

Competitiveness and dominance are the major predictors of masculinity among both our Chicago and heterosexual respondents. Among the former, the respective correlations are 0.39 and 0.59; among the latter, they are 0.53 and 0.46. All these coefficients are statistically significant. Tables 3.10 and 3.11 explore whether defeminization status--childhood cross-gendering cross-

cut by adult cross-gendering--is also related to these other
"masculine virtues." In Table 3.10, we see that those effeminate

TABLE 3.10

LIKELIHOOD RATIO ANALYSIS OF DOMINANCE BY
CHILDHOOD AND ADULT CROSS-GENDERING

Partial (1st Order) Associations				Marginal (0-Order) Associations	
Effect	df	LR Chi-squared	p	LR Chi-squared	p
DC	2	0.75	.688	2.51	.284
DA	2	10.17	.006	11.94	.003
CA	1	88.97	.000	90.74	.000
DCA	2	1.10	.577		

Adult Cross-Gendering(A)	Childhood Cross-Gendering(C)	Dominance (D) (Percentages)			N(100%)
		Low	Med	High	
Some	Some	36	35	29	385
	None	40	33	27	52
None	Some	29	36	35	695
	None	26	38	36	377

Source: Compiled by the author.

as adults are less dominant while childhood cross-gendering does
not appear to be directly related to dominance. The defeminized
do not differ significantly from the never-effeminate (X^2=1.52,
df=2, p=ns), although they do differ from the always-effeminate
(X^2=6.60, df=2, p. < .04). Turning to the examination of

competitiveness (Table 3.11), the relationship of that variable
to adult cross-gendering is borderline and weak. While they are
significantly related at the zero-order level, this relationship
vanished in the partials. Childhood cross-gendering per se has
no notable direct inhibiting effect on adult competitiveness.

TABLE 3.11

LIKELIHOOD RATIO ANALYSIS OF COMPETITIVENESS BY
CHILDHOOD AND ADULT CROSS-GENDERING

Partial (1st Order) Associations				Marginal (0-Order) Associations	
Effect	df	LR Chi-squared	p	LR Chi-squared	p
PC	2	1.34	.512	2.90	.235
PA	2	4.42	.109	5.98	.050
CA	1	92.86	.000	94.42	.000
PCA	2	0.54	.765		

Adult Cross-Gendering(A)	Childhood Cross-Gendering(C)	Competitiveness(P) (Percentages)			
		Low	Med	High	N(100%)
Some	Some	41	32	26	389
	None	42	29	29	52
None	Some	36	33	31	687
	None	32	35	33	378

Source: Compiled by the author.

The above data have shown that cross-gendering is
significantly and negatively related to self-esteem and the
masculine virtues. However, defeminizing appears to be nearly as
important a predictor of psychological well-being as cross-
gendering. Those who defeminize between childhood and adulthood
approach the never-effeminate in self-esteem and masculinity. In
the cases of dominance and competitiveness, the defeminized equal
the never-effeminate since childhood cross-gendering had no
significant inhibiting effect on these two measures. In the above
data, the persistently effeminate were clearly the lowest in
psychological well-being. Similar to them are the small group of

those who became effeminate between childhood and adulthood. We give brief attention to this small group in the next chapter. Contrary to our expectations, we found only a weak relationship of psychological femininity with childhood cross-gendering and none with adult cross-gendering. From this, we infer that psychological femininity may have little explanatory value in interpreting the behaviors of effeminate gay men.

GAYS VERSUS NON-GAYS ON PSYCHOLOGICAL WELL-BEING

We now turn to comparisons among our four sample groups on measures of psychological well-being. There is no overall significant difference on self-esteem among these four groups. There are no significant differences among the three gay groups (X^2=3.55, df=4, p=ns). There is no significant difference between the heterosexuals and the three gay groups combined (X^2=1.00, df=2, p=ns). These findings are consistent with earlier studies which find either no differences between gay and heterosexual males or very small ones in favor of the latter (Hart et al. 1978). Turning to masculinity we observe an overall significant difference. There are no significant differences among the three gay groups on masculinity (X^2=7.61, df=4, p=ns). There is a significant difference between the three gay groups combined and the heterosexuals (X^2=20.08, df=2, p. < .001). However, it is difficult to interpret this difference as having a direction. either the heterosexuals are lower on masculinity than the gays or they are simply more homogeneous. The tendency for the heterosexuals to be somewhat less masculine than the gays does not appear to be due to their somewhat younger age since, among the heterosexuals age seems slightly negatively related to masculinity (r=0.13, p=.06) and is unrelated to masculinity among the Chicago respondents.

On femininity the gays seem definitely higher. There are no significant differences on this measure among the gay groups (X^2=0.72, df=4, p=ns), but there is a significant difference between the heterosexuals and the homosexual groups combined (X^2=27.69, df=2, p. < .001). We infer that at least part of this difference is associated with the already exhibited difference between gays and heterosexuals in childhood cross-gendering. The modest differences and non-differences on masculinity and femininity between our gay and non-gay respondents seem similar to the non-significant trends reported by Heilbrun and Thompson (1979) in comparing their gay and non-gay men on psychological masculinity and femininity. On dominance, there are no differences among all groups, among the three gay groups (X^2=7.10, df=4, p=ns), or between the gays and heterosexuals (X^2=1.44, df=2, p=ns). On competitiveness, there is no overall significant chi-squared, nor are there significant differences among the three gay groups (X^2=0.65, df=4, p=ns), although there is a difference between the combined gays and the heterosexuals (X^2=11.73, df=2,

TABLE 3.12

PSYCHOLOGICAL MEASURES BY SAMPLE GROUPS (percent)

Self-Esteem	Sample Groups			
	Chicago Gay Non-Students	Chicago Gay Students	DeKalb Gay Students	DeKalb Non-Gay Students
Low	29	25	22	30
Med	45	43	44	48
High	25	32	34	22
N(100%)	1459	88	32	204

X^2 = 4.58   df = 6   p = ns

Masculinity

Low	29	19	34	25
Med	41	55	38	58
High	29	26	28	17
N(100%)	1437	89	32	201

X^2 = 27.60   df = 6   p < .001

Femininity

Low	35	34	34	49
Med	35	32	38	38
High	30	33	28	13
N(100%)	1445	87	32	201

X^2 = 28.44   df = 6   p < .001

Dominance

Low	31	20	23	26
Med	36	44	48	39
High	33	36	29	34
N(100%)	1450	89	31	201

X^2 = 8.57   df = 6   p = ns

Competitiveness

Low	37	38	41	30
Med	33	31	28	28
High	30	32	31	42
N(100%)	1447	88	32	204

X^2 = 12.39   df = 6   p = ns

Source: Compiled by the author.

p. < .01). Presumably, this difference arises due to the lesser competitiveness of those gays who are cross-gendered as adults. Since there are age differences among our sample groups, we also compared those groups on the psychological variables including only those under 25 years of age. The pattern of differences and non-differences remained as reported above.

We note that the relative lack of disadvantage of the gay groups compared with the heterosexuals on most of these psychological measures seems a little surprising, given the low psychological well-being of the sizeable minority of gay men who are cross-gendered as adults. This lack of sizeable differences between gay and non-gays appears to be due to the relatively high levels on these measures of the never-effeminate and the defeminized. For example, comparing our heterosexual respondents with the never-effeminate homosexuals, the latter are significantly higher on self-esteem than the former (x^2=9.81, df=2, p. < .01). Also, the heterosexuals do not differ on self-esteem from either the defeminized (x^2=1.02, df=2, p=ns) or even the persistently effeminate (x^2=5.08, df=2, p=ns). Similarly, on masculinity the heterosexuals are significantly lower than the never-effeminate homosexuals (x^2=33.39, df=2, p. < .001), do not differ from the defeminized (x^2=3.82, df=2, p=ns), but are higher than the always-effeminate (x^2=12.79, df=2, p. < .01). Only on competitiveness are the heterosexuals generally higher than most of the homosexual groups. It would thus seem that sexual orientation per se has little or no negative effect on self-esteem and masculinity, that childhood cross-gendering may reduce levels on these measures relative to other homosexuals but not relative to heterosexuals, and that only the persistently effeminate have notably lower levels of the masculine psychological virtues.

4

THE PSYCHOLOGIES
OF EFFEMINACY

In the preceding chapter, it was shown how there occurs a defeminization process in a large minority of gay men. There remains to be examined the problem of why many gay men do not defeminize despite the tremendous pressures to do so that they must have encountered in the course of growing up. While it is conceivable that a few pre-gay children may have lived in such protected environments that they were able to avoid major masculinizing pressures, such a possibility seems remote in American culture for a very large majority of effeminate boys. Hence, we now examine what special meanings effeminacy may have had for some gay men who perpetuated across the decades a personal style of effeminacy despite strong negative pressures.

GENDER ROLE AS ACHIEVED ROLE

Most children have fantasies about doing something for which they will be admired. Common fantasies involve being an astronaut, president, athlete, moviestar, or more recently, a rock musician. Quite common among these childhood fantasies is an interest in being an actor, entertainer, or moviestar. Table 3.1 above showed that approximately equal percentages of our gay and heterosexual respondents had had such interests during childhood. Also, Table 3.6 showed that such interests persisted to an equal degree in both gay and non-gay respondents.

Such fantasies seem to be a rather primitive form of achievement motivation in which the individual desires a status for which he will be admired or recognized. However, an interest in being an actor or entertainer also implies a certain egoism since it suggests that the individual is to be admired or rewarded simply for being entertaining rather than for productively rendering the audience a service or product which is not uniquely dependent on the personality of the performer. The egoism involved flows from the unique dependence of the service on the personality of the performer. In its more self-aggrandizing form, actorization seems a manifestation of attention getting while in its socialized forms it may be more focused on occupations involving attentive audiences and publicity. The egoism involved in actorization is shown in Table 4.1 which presents responses to

TABLE 4.1

"BE IN LIMELIGHT" AND "IDEAL OCCUPATION IS GLAMOROUS"
BY PERSISTENT ACTORIZATION AMONG NON-GAYS

	Persistent Actorization		
	None	Some	High
"Like to be in Limelight" Percent Yes	37	57	61
N(100%)	78	88	36
	$X^2 = 8.54$	df = 2	p < .02
"Ideal Occupation Would be Glamorous" Percent Yes	38	63	69
N(100%)	78	89	36
	$X^2 = 13.89$	df = 2	p < .001

Source: Compiled by the author.

the item, "When I do things with people I like to be in the limelight or spotlight," by persistent actorization among the heterosexual respondents. (The two items of this table were asked only of DeKalb respondents.) The second item of this table, "My ideal occupation would be one which was in some way glamorous," also has a rather strong relationship to actorization among the heterosexuals and shows how occupational ideals may be informed with values established in childhood. Although the numbers involved in our DeKalb gay group are quite small, we also there find a strong trend for an association between actorization and the occupational glamor item (Fisher's exact two-tailed p=0.07). Among the never-actorized, 35 percent like occupational glamor

(N=17) versus 71 percent among the ever-actorized (N=14). Among the DeKalb gay respondents, there is also a significant relationship of the occupational glamor item with childhood cross-gendering. Among the highly cross-gendered during childhood (N=17), 94 percent liked occupational glamor as compared with 60 percent (N=15) among the less cross-gendered (Fisher's exact two-tailed p=0.03). Hence, it seems that actorization and its correlate, childhood cross-gendering, are associated with some primitive achievement ideals involving glamor, publicity, and recognition.

Several researchers cited above have shown how the majority of effeminate boys have a disproportionate interest in playacting, although they usually prefer to play feminine roles during early childhood. Whitam and Dizon (1979) have shown how gay men, compared to heterosexuals, disproportionately were interested in being performing artists during their childhoods. They found this both in the United States and Brazil. The data of Table 4.2 show

TABLE 4.2

PERSISTENT ACTORIZATION BY CHILDHOOD AND
ADULT CROSS-GENDERING

Childhood Cross-Gendering	Persistent Actorization			
	None	Some	High	N(100%)
None	54	33	13	432
Some	40	38	22	726
High	24	39	37	373

$x^2 = 96.56$ df = 4   p < .001   gamma = 0.34

Adult Cross-Gendering				
None	45	37	18	1079
Some	29	38	33	405
High	25	30	45	40

$x^2 = 54.60$ df = 4   p < .001   gamma = 0.32

Source: Compiled by the author.

how a persistent interest in being an actor or entertainer among our Chicago respondents is positively related to both childhood and adult cross-gendering at the zero-order level. Apparently a strong interest in glamor or recognition is a correlate of cross-gendering in gay men during both childhood and adulthood. [We examined the relationship of childhood cross-gendering with persistent actorization among the heterosexuals and found only a non-significant trend (X^2=3.45, df=2, p=.18).] In order to see whether cross-gendering persisting into adulthood is also associated with persistent actorization, we present Table 4.3

TABLE 4.3

LIKELIHOOD RATIO ANALYSIS OF PERSISTENT ACTING INTEREST
BY CHILDHOOD AND ADULT CROSS-GENDERING

Partial (1st Order) Associations				Marginal (0-Order) Associations	
Effect	df	LR Chi-squared	p	LR Chi-squared	p
PC	2	35.81	.000	54.72	.000
PA	2	31.65	.000	50.57	.000
CA	1	74.97	.000	93.88	.000
PCA	2	2.97	.227		

Adult Cross-Gendering(A)	Childhood Cross-Gendering(C)	Persistent Acting(P) (Percentages)			N(100%)
		Low	Med	High	
Some	Some	27	37	36	392
	None	46	40	13	52
None	Some	39	39	21	698
	None	54	32	13	379

Source: Compiled by the author.

which shows persistent actorization by both childhood and adult cross-gendering. We see that persistent actorization has sizeable zero-order and partial relationships with both childhood and adult cross-gendering. We find that the persistently effeminate are highest on actorization and differ significantly from the defeminized (X^2=33.56, df=2, p. < .001) who, in turn, differ from the never-effeminate (X^2=24.61, df=2, p. < .001). Apparently, the

persistently effeminate are persistently actorized while the
defeminized may have undergone a measure of de-actorization
between childhood and adulthood. That persistent actorization is
associated with persistent effeminacy implies that, among those
who defeminized, early rather than late defeminization may be
associated with lower levels of actorization. It is possible for
us to explore this implication in our data by comparing among the
defeminized those who defeminized by adolescence with those who
defeminized later (cf. Table 4.4). We find that lower levels of

TABLE 4.4

EARLY VERSUS LATE DEFEMINIZATION BY PERSISTENT ACTOR (Percent)[a]

Defeminization	Persistent Actor		
	None	Medium	High
Early	50	42	36
Late	50	58	64
N(100%)	273	275	149
	$X^2 = 7.62$	df = 2	p < .05

[a]Only the defeminized are included.
Source: Compiled by the author.

actorization are associated with earlier defeminization. These
data thus appear to replicate the association of persistent
actorization and persistent effeminacy.

Since persistent actorization is associated with persistent
effeminacy, we now ask what it is about actorization which,
combined with childhood cross-gendering, may give rise to the
persistence of the latter? Our attempted answer is that
actorization combined with cross-gendering constitutes an
idealization and glamorization of the feminine role and its
associated culture and artifacts. To the extent that the feminine
role is viewed as an ideal, it is a role to be achieved by the
effeminate youth. Once achieved, the performer of that role is in
a position to be admired for that achievement, just as an actor or
entertainer hopes to be admired for her/his performances.

While both gender identities and gender roles are ascribed by
societies, the individuals who are expected to internalize and
enact them do not always conform as the cases of transexuals and
effeminate pre-gay boys make evident. While ascribed identities
are most commonly internalized by the persons expected to adopt

them, there is considerably less match between the enactment of expected gender roles and the expectations. This is true in quite gender-conventional persons because of the idealization of many aspects of gender roles. There are public images of what an ideal man or ideal woman should act and look like. The advertising industry bases much of its communications on the general acceptance of gender ideals. Given the idealized nature of gender roles, most persons, gender-conventional or not, have to spend some time making themselves more like the ideals. Charm schools and body-building salons assist in such transformations. To the extent that gender roles, or some parts of them, are idealized, it is possible, even demanded, that one achieve within the ascribed role of gender. To the extent that gender roles are idealized the child who is not aware of the routinization and mundaneness of gender roles as practiced is invited to treat them as roles of achievement rather than of ascription. Ascribed roles which have been so idealized have the built-in irony that the individual has to try so hard to become what he is supposed to naturally or biologically be, and then having achieved competence in the role, to pretend to others and to self that that is what he was all along.

Effeminate boys appear to have focused their images of the ideal on the feminine gender role. They then engage in play enactments of that role in which the culture and artifacts of the role constitute the media of their preferred art form and mode of achievement. The feminine enactments of actorized pre-gay boys seem psychologically indistinguishable from those of female impersonators performing "glamor drag." As Newton (1979, p. 52) has described the world of female impersonators, the intent of glamor drag is not to be mistaken for a woman, but to be recognized as a very professional imitator of a woman. One wants, as an adult imitator, to be seen as accomplishing the image of a beautiful woman and "not look like an ordinary woman (for) ordinary women are not beautiful;" one wants, as a child imitator, to be applauded for a feminine rendition of "cute" behavior. The imitation of a woman is seen as an achievement or even an idealized art form combining the abilities of an actor with the cultural artifacts of the feminine role.

In support of these interpretations of actorization and persistent cross-gendering, we present data from responses to the question, "If you could choose any occupation, regardless of your present occupation, education, or qualifications, what would you want it to be?" [This question is identical to one asked by Whitam and Dizon (1979).] The intent here is to show how the gender typedness of occupational ideals appears to be influenced by and a manifestation of his gender-role preferences and how such ideals express gender-role specified achievement motivations. We note that the non-response rate on this item was 14.2 percent among the Chicago respondents. From several comments written on the questionnaires, it appears that a number of respondents could not think of an ideal occupation or were quite happy with their current jobs. The responses were coded into 21 categories according to the cultural content of the job, rather than according to the social organizational rank or context of the work. Thus, a respondent who wanted to be an owner of a florist shop was coded "florist" rather than "businessman." The 21 codings were subsequently grouped into the five gender-typed categories presented in Table 4.5. These groupings are as follows: The Arts includes the major traditional non-acting or entertaining arts plus a variety of minor arts such as puppetry, woodcarving, and closonne. Acting includes acting, entertaining, and opera singing. Nurturant includes both such nurturant occupations as nursing, teaching, hospital aides, social workers, various kinds of therapists such as psychiatrists (but not other physicians), and domestic-related occupations such as cooking, hair and pet grooming, clothes management, and floristry. [A spatial analysis of perceived occupational similarities revealed psychiatrists to be nearer to psychologists than to other physicians (Cole and Hansen 1973).] The intent of this category was to capture the traditional domestic and nurturant functions of the feminine gender role while acting/entertaining captures the more glamorous components of that role. The masculine category includes sports, law enforcement, the military, science and technology, the traditional professions such as law, accounting and non-psychiatric medicine, business, manual work, politics, the clergy, and farming. Other includes travel and "Other." Most of the occupations included in the "Other" category are rather nondescript lower level clerical, service, and administrative jobs such as bank teller or postal worker.

The data presented in Table 4.5 differ somewhat from most of the other log-linear tables presented in the present work. The "Effects" section of that table shows the usual Chi-squareds indicating significant zero-order and partial relationships among ideal occupation, persistent actorization, and childhood cross-gendering. However, in the present data, we are interested not only in overall relationships among these three measures, but also in the relationships of actorization and childhood cross-gendering with particular columns and cells of the nominal occupation measure. Hence, we have presented both the percentage distributions and the standardized lambdas. The standardized lambdas are the logs of the model-predicted frequencies for each cell of a given table divided by their respective standard errors where the model predicting these frequencies is the one best fitting the data. In the present case, it is the model involving associations among all three measures. Since the predicted frequencies have been divided by their standard errors, they may be interpreted as z-scores in a normal distribution with absolute values greater than 1.96 indicating a significant difference of a cell's predicted frequency from a prediction of no association based solely on the marginal distributions. The lambdas of the two subtables of Table 4.5 may be interpreted as "standardized partial lambdas" since the effects of the third variable have been controlled.

TABLE 4.5

LIKELIHOOD RATIO ANALYSIS OF IDEAL OCCUPATION BY CHILDHOOD
CROSS-GENDERING BY PERSISTENT ACTORIZATION

Effect	df	Partial (1st Order) Associations		Marginal (0-Order) Associations	
		LR Chi-Squared	p	LR Chi-Squared	p
IA	8	162.09	.000	173.27	.000
IC	4	20.20	.000	31.38	.000
AC	2	30.31	.000	41.49	.000
IAC	8	4.92	.766		

Standardized Lambdas

Ideal Occupation (I)

Actorization (A)	The Arts	Acting	Nurturant	Masculine	Other
Low	0.88	-6.66	3.99	5.98	3.31
Med	0.96	2.11	-1.70	-1.22	-0.71
High	-1.58	7.80	-1.78	-3.94	-2.22

Ideal Occupation

Childhood Cross-Gendering (C)	The Arts	Acting	Nurturant	Masculine	Other
Some	-0.48	0.75	2.39	-2.96	-0.92
None	0.48	-0.75	-2.39	2.96	0.92

Ideal Occupation (Percent)

Persistent Actorization	Childhood Cross-Gendering	The Arts	Act-ing	Nurtur-ant	Mascu-line	Other	N(100%)
Low	Some	22	2	23	41	12	315
	None	17	1	14	57	11	184
Med	Some	27	14	17	33	10	374
	None	32	10	9	39	9	120
High	Some	22	31	16	24	6	264
	None	22	25	9	31	13	55

Source: Compiled by the author.

These data show that the actorized seem averse to occupations culturally typed as masculine since the highly actorized are considerably under-represented in the masculine occupations while the non-actorized are very much over-represented in those occupations. Also, and somewhat obviously, the actorized were very much more likely to choose acting or entertaining as their ideal occupation. This appears to attest to the great persistence of their fantasy of being an entertainer. More interesting is the propensity of the non-actorized to choose nurturant and domestic occupations thus suggesting that if the gay man does not tend toward the glamorous entertaining aspect of the feminine gender-role, he is considerably more inclined toward its less glamorous home-related activities.

Turning to the sub-table of lambdas showing the associations of ideal occupations with cross-gendering, we see that the cross-gendered are averse to those occupations sex-typed for men. Rather, the cross-gendered are more inclined toward nurturant and domestic activities. It is also worth noting that, although childhood cross-gendering and actorization are positively associated, they have opposite associations with the nurturant category. Cross-gendering unaccompanied by actorization seems associated with the less glamorous aspects of the feminine role while actorization focuses on the glamor parts of that role. More broadly interpreting these data, the childhood cross-gendering/actorization complex appears to be a rather global feminine gender-role factor of cultural interests displaying two oblique sub-factors. One of those factors is actorization representing a desire for display of self as feminine. Within that subfactor, the feminine gender role is seen as an achievement and (as we shortly show in the data on psychological measures) seems to have served as a focus for the investment of achievement energies. The second sub-factor is more focused on the less dramatic aspects of the feminine gender role involving household chores and nurturant activities. However, some of these chores, such as interior design and clothes management, may also have stagey or display aspects and thereby express the interests proper to both subfactors.

Both Newton (1979, p. 57) and Tripp (1975, p. 28) have identified these two sub-factors as aspects of the feminine role well exemplified by the drag-queen and the transexual. The actorized man, like the drag-queen, aggressively puts his effeminacy on glamorous display for the admiration of audiences while the transexual wants only to be a housewife and spend his time doing housewifely chores. Of course, many effeminate gay males may possess a measure of both sets of interests and attempt to combine the two in such activities as interior decorating or hairdressing. It should be noted that we are not presently claiming that the cross-gendered who are not actorized are transexuals, but rather that their interests seem similar to those described by other observers who have noted the highly primitive, unglamorous, and culturally conservative interpretations which transexuals have of the feminine gender role (Kando 1973, pp. 22-24). Some of our non-actorized cross-gendered may be quasi-transexuals as we shortly show.

The data of Table 4.5 revealed no significant associations between artistic occupational choices and either actorization or childhood cross-gendering. This seems somewhat inconsistent with other studies showing an association between childhood cross-gendering and artistic interests (Green 1976). As an alternative exploration of the relationships of persistent actorization and childhood cross-gendering with esthetic values, Table 4.6 presents

TABLE 4.6

LIKELIHOOD RATIO ANALYSIS OF INTEREST IN THE ARTS BY
PERSISTENT ACTORIZATION AND CHILDHOOD CROSS-GENDERING

Partial (1st Order) Associations				Marginal (0-Order) Associations	
Effect	df	LR Chi-squared	p	LR Chi-squared	p
IA	2	27.16	.000	34.44	.000
IC	1	12.19	.000	19.48	.000
AC	2	48.45	.000	55.73	.000
IAC	2	2.71	.258		

Childhood Cross-Gendering (C)	Actorization (A)	Interest in the Arts (I) Yes	No	(Percent) N(100%)
Some	Low	78	22	380
	Med	88	12	421
	High	86	14	295
None	Low	67	33	231
	Med	81	19	144
	High	88	12	57

Source: Compiled by the author.

the relationships of these measures with the item, "I am not very interested in the arts." It is apparent that both actorization and childhood cross-gendering have sizeable relationships with artistic interest both at the zero-order and partial levels.

(Further analyses of the artistic interest item with childhood and adult cross-gendering showed that adult cross-gendering is unrelated to artistic interest at either zero-order or partial levels.)

Comparing the relationships of actorization and childhood cross-gendering with artistic interest in Table 4.6 with the relationships found in Table 4.5, there appear to be some inconsistencies. Artistic interest was significantly related to both measures in the second table and artistic occupational choices to neither in the first table. These differences can be fairly readily reconciled if we assume that the actorized mean principally the acting/entertaining arts by the expression, "the arts." If this is true, then the interest of the actorized in "the arts" is consistently found in both tables. The lack of consistency between the two tables in the relationship of childhood cross-gendering and artistic interest or choices seems less easily reconcilable. However, it is possible that the childhood cross-gendered may have transmuted their earlier interests in art from the vocational to the avocational.

As a final comparison of artistic interests, Table 4.7 presents the artistic interest item by our sample groups. It is

TABLE 4.7

INTEREST IN THE ARTS BY SAMPLE GROUP

	Sample Group			
	Chicago Non-Student Gays	Chicago Student Gays	DeKalb Student Gays	DeKalb Student Non-Gays
Percent Interested in the Arts	81	86	81	59
N(100%)	1463	90	32	203
	$X^2 = 56.84$	df = 3	p < .001	

Source: Compiled by the author.

apparent that the gay groups are generally more interested in the arts than are the heterosexuals. There are no significant differences among the three gay groups (X^2=1.09, df=2, p=ns), but between the three groups combined, and the heterosexuals, the difference is highly significant and large (X^2=54.49, df=1, p. < .001, gamma=0.51). This difference between the gays and the heterosexuals does not seem to be due to their differing years of education or ages since the difference between the DeKalb gay and

DeKalb heterosexual groups is also significant (X^2=5.09, df=1, p. < .03, gamma=0.51). The latter two groups also differ significantly on the related item, "I am not very interested in the fine arts (X^2=11.61, df=1, p. < .001, gamma=0.76). This item was asked only of DeKalb respondents.

The above data have shown that actorization seems to express a somewhat egoistic desire for recognition or reward for achievement as an entertainer and that it is related to adult visions of an ideal occupation. In its more primitive and childish forms it seems to express an interest in achievement as a woman. Hence, we infer that persistent actorization results in the persistent pursuit of that recognition and that persistent effeminacy is the performance for which recognition is sought. Persistent actorization differs somewhat from childhood cross-gendering in their associated adult ideals. Whereas actorization expresses an interest in the glamorous side of femininity, cross-gendering unaccompanied by actorization expresses an interest in the more domestic and nurturant aspects of femininity, while both express an aversion to activities and occupations culturally sex-typed as masculine. We now turn to an elaboration of the psychological correlates of actorization versus cross-gendering and show their relationships with transexualism.

PSYCHOLOGICAL CHARACTERISTICS OF THE EFFEMINATE

If the actorized view the feminine gender role as one to be achieved, this implies that effeminacy so motivated may have associated with it a number of instrumental characteristics, and not be simply an expressive manifestation of a role preference. If a feminine gender role is to be achieved, so motivated individuals are then achievers, but of a very special nature. If they are achievers, then they would not be expected to conform to the stereotypes of the effeminate as weak and withdrawing individuals. To explore the psychology of effeminacy and actorization, we present Tables 4.8 through 4.12, which show the relationships of adult cross-gendering and actorization with self-esteem, psychological masculinity, competitiveness, dominance, and being a persistent loner. The percentages of these tables are presented in four-fold format so that they may be compared with the succeeding block of tables which, since they include only the adult cross-gendered, must necessarily be so presented.

Table 4.8 shows that self-esteem is negatively associated with adult cross-gendering both at the zero-order and partial levels and that actorization has neither a significant zero-order or partial association with self-esteem. However, there is a significant interaction such that among the adult cross-gendered actorization is positively related to self-esteem (gamma=0.31), while among the non-cross-gendered it is either unrelated or weakly negatively related to self-esteem. This interaction

TABLE 4.8

LIKELIHOOD RATIO ANALYSIS OF SELF-ESTEEM BY PERSISTENT
ACTORIZATION AND ADULT CROSS-GENDERING

Partial (1st Order) Associations				Marginal (0-Order) Associations	
Effect	df	LR Chi-squared	p	LR Chi-squared	p
ST	1	0.48	.488	2.04	.154
SA	1	22.21	.000	23.77	.000
TA	1	34.12	.000	35.68	.000
STA	1	5.75	.016		

Adult Cross-Gendering (A)	Actorization (T)	Self-Esteem (S) Low	High	(Percent) N(100%)
Some	Some	36	64	317
	None	44	56	125
None	Some	28	72	594
	None	23	77	479

Source: Compiled by the author.

implies that actorization, when combined with cross-gendering, may
be a source of psychological strength or pride for the effeminate
gay man. Table 4.9 shows that masculinity is negatively related
to adult cross-gendering and that actorization is not, both at the
zero-order and partial levels. However, there is also a
significant interaction. The form of this interaction is
indicated by there being a .26 positive gamma between masculinity

TABLE 4.9

LIKELIHOOD RATIO ANALYSIS OF MASCULINITY BY PERSISTENT
ACTORIZATION AND ADULT CROSS-GENDERING

Partial (1st Order) Associations				Marginal (0-Order) Associations	
Effect	df	LR Chi-squared	p	LR Chi-squared	p
MT	1	0.04	.835	0.58	.446
MA	1	14.40	.001	14.94	.000
TA	1	32.52	.000	33.06	.000
MTA	1	5.10	.024		

Adult Cross-Gendering (A)	Actorization (T)	Masculinity (M) Low	High	(Percent) N(100%)
Some	Some	75	25	309
	None	84	16	124
None	Some	69	31	589
	None	66	34	473

Source: Compiled by the author.

and actorization among the cross-gendered and one of -0.08 among
the non-cross-gendered.

In Table 4.10, there is an interaction effect of the same
form as in the instances of masculinity and self-esteem. Among
the cross-gendered, actorization is positively related to
competitiveness (gamma=.32) but is unrelated among the non-cross-
gendered (gamma=-.01). In the case of dominance (Table 4.11),
there are significant negative relationships of dominance with
adult cross-gendering at the zero-order and partial levels. The
presence of an interaction is suggested, although that term is not
significant. Among the cross-gendered, there is a positive gamma
of 0.24 between actorization and dominance, while among the non-
cross-gendered the gamma is 0.03.

The above interactions collectively suggest that the
effeminate are psychologically a rather heterogeneous group among
whom actorization specifies the relationship of cross-gendering to
the "masculine virtues." Whereas those lacking in actorization
seem low on these measures of psychological well-being, the

TABLE 4.10

LIKELIHOOD RATIO ANALYSIS OF COMPETITIVENESS BY PERSISTENT
ACTORIZATION AND ADULT CROSS-GENDERING

Partial (1st Order) Associations				Marginal (0-Order) Associations	
Effect	df	LR Chi-squared	p	LR Chi-squared	p
CT	1	1.27	.260	0.73	.393
CA	1	3.59	.058	3.05	.081
TA	1	35.59	.000	35.05	.000
CTA	1	5.49	.019		

Adult Cross-Gendering (A)	Actorization (T)	Competitiveness (C) Low	High	(Percent) N(100%)
Some	Some	70	30	314
	None	82	18	126
None	Some	69	31	586
	None	68	32	478

Source: Compiled by the author.

TABLE 4.11

LIKELIHOOD RATIO ANALYSIS OF DOMINANCE BY PERSISTENT
ACTORIZATION AND ADULT CROSS-GENDERING

Effect	df	Partial (1st Order) Associations		Marginal (0-Order) Associations	
		LR Chi-squared	p	LR Chi-squared	p
DT	1	1.82	.177	0.90	.342
DA	1	7.63	.006	6.72	.010
TA	1	35.08	.000	34.17	.000
DTA	1	2.20	.138		

Adult Cross-Gendering (A)	Actorization (T)	Dominance (D) Low	High	(Percent) N(100%)
Some	Some	69	31	312
	None	78	22	124
None	Some	64	36	594
	None	65	35	477

Source: Compiled by the author.

actorized seem to be aggressive and outgoing persons. Table 4.12
shows the relationships of adult cross-gendering and persistent
actorization with being a persistent loner. The same interaction
appears as in the preceding tables. Among the cross-gendered,
persistent actorization is negatively related to lonerization
(gamma=-0.36) whereas they are unrelated among the non-cross-
gendered (gamma=0.00).

That cross-gendering, when combined with actorization, is
related to the masculine virtues suggests that those gay men who
are most effeminate in a staged, even flaunting way, are pretty
tough individuals who are able to withstand considerable negative
feedback without major damage to their psychological well-being.
It seems that, at some stage in these men's lives, a combination
of cross-gendering and actorization became a vehicle for the
expression of the masculine virtues and achievement. These data
document and partially explain the occasionally made observation
that effeminate males are not really feminine because their
presented selves are too aggressive and harsh and that, while
transexuals are often genuinely feminine, effeminate gay men are

TABLE 4.12

LIKELIHOOD RATIO ANALYSIS OF BEING PERSISTENT LONER BY
PERSISTENT ACTORIZATION AND ADULT CROSS-GENDERING

Partial (1st Order) Associations				Marginal (0-Order) Associations	
Effect	df	LR Chi-squared	p	LR Chi-squared	p
LT	1	2.80	.094	2.83	.092
LA	1	0.00	.970	0.04	.847
TA	1	31.64	.000	31.68	.000
LTA	1	8.00	.005		

Adult Cross-Gendering (A)	Actorization (T)	Persistent Loner (L) Low	High	(Percent) N(100%)
Some	Some	77	23	313
	None	62	38	128
None	Some	72	28	594
	None	72	28	476

Source: Compiled by the author.

not (Tripp 1975, pp. 26-32). The latter possess psychological
strengths in their effeminacy and are willing, even eager, to
display their cross-gendering before available audiences rather
than being persistent loners. After all, a star needs an
audience.

Table 4.13 shows the relationships of actorization and adult
cross-gendering with femininity. These data show that
actorization, but not cross-gendering, is related to femininity
both at the zero-order and first-order partial levels. There is
no interaction. It thus seems that actorization and cross-
gendering combined constitute a positive psychological androgyny
factor. The factor of stagey cross-gendering apparently serves as
a vehicle for the satisfaction of both expressive and achievement
needs. Since it serves such multiple needs its persistence, once

TABLE 4.13

LIKELIHOOD RATIO ANALYSIS OF FEMININITY BY PERSISTENT
ACTORIZATION AND ADULT CROSS-GENDERING

Partial (1st Order) Associations				Marginal (0-Order) Associations	
Effect	df	LR Chi-squared	p	LR Chi-squared	p
FT	1	13.08	.000	14.33	.000
FA	1	0.73	.392	1.98	.159
TA	1	33.30	.000	34.56	.000
FTA	1	0.27	.607		

Adult Cross-Gendering (A)	Actorization (T)	Femininity (F) (Percent)		
		Low	High	N(100%)
Some	Some	29	71	313
	None	40	60	124
None	Some	32	68	591
	None	41	59	475

Source: Compiled by the author.

formed, seems more likely. Persistent cross-gendering thus seems
like the occupational ideals of many conventional persons which
combine into one role avocational interests and achievement
motivations, e.g., the ski enthusiast who becomes a ski
instructor. Persistent cross-gendering may thereby have an
advantage in motivational strength over conventional gender-roles
which tend to separate the instrumental and expressive into
different sets of activities.
    The above data have shown that, although persistent
actorization and adult cross-gendering are positively associated
with each other, they have opposite associations with the
masculine virtues and thus serve as suppressors of each other's
effects. The persistently effeminate are thus a quite
heterogeneous group since persistent actorization specifies the
relationship between adult cross-gendering and the masculine
virtues in that it variously nullifies or reverses the negative
effects of adult cross-gendering. While the persistently
effeminate are on the average low on the masculine virtues it
seems that that category includes rather diverse subgroupings.

Thus, the reasons for a gay man's persistent effeminacy seem to be important determinants of his psychological well-being. While many, perhaps most, gay men who are persistently effeminate are so out of actorization, some may be effeminate out of transexual or quasi-transexual feelings. In order to test this idea, we test developed a quasi-transexualism scale from the three items of having wanted to be a girl. In validation of this scale, we present Table 4.14 which shows the relationships among the adult

TABLE 4.14

LIKELIHOOD RATIO ANALYSIS OF ATTRACTION TO HETEROSEXUAL MEN BY ACTORIZATION AND TRANSEXUALISM AMONG THE ADULT CROSS-GENDERED

Partial (1st Order) Associations				Marginal (0-Order) Associations	
Effect	df	LR Chi-squared	p	LR Chi-squared	p
HT	1	0.30	.587	0.03	.872
HR	1	6.07	.014	5.80	.016
TR	1	10.84	.001	10.58	.001
HTR	1	0.02	.881		

Tran-sexualism (R)	Actor-ization (T)	Attraction to Heterosexual men (H)		(Percent) N(100%)
		Low	High	
Some	Some	59	41	175
	None	55	45	49
None	Some	70	30	139
	None	68	32	78

Source: Compiled by the author.

cross-gendered of actorization and transexualism with the item, "I often find straight men more attractive than gay men." Freund (1974) has found that the very large majority of transexuals are principally attracted to heterosexual men, apparently because only such men who are interested, by definition, in women, can validate their gender identities as female. Table 4.14 shows that actorization and transexualism are positively associated at both the zero-order (gamma=0.33) and partial levels. However, only transexualism is associated with attraction to heterosexual men. The differences in such attraction in Table 4.14 are not particularly large because the transexualism variable has been dichotomized into "ever" versus "never" wanted to be a girl. Had they been dichotomized at a higher level of transexual interests, these differences would be considerably greater. However, we chose the presented cutting points in order to have sufficient numbers of transexualized-but-not-actorized subjects to analyze.

In order to explore the differing psychologies of the actorized versus the transexualized, the next block of tables presents the psychological characteristics by actorization and transexualism. Since the transexualism scale partially overlaps in item content the childhood and adult cross-gendering scales, the former scale is not introduced into the same analyses as the latter two. Also, since we are here principally interested in comparing the psychology of those who are effeminate due to actorization with that of those who are effeminate due to transexualism, the following tables include only those who are cross-gendered during adulthood.

Tables 4.15 through 4.20 present self-esteem, masculinity, dominance, competitiveness, lonerization, and femininity by actorization and transexualism among those cross-gendered as adults. In Table 4.15, we see that transexualism is negatively

TABLE 4.15

LIKELIHOOD RATIO ANALYSIS OF SELF-ESTEEM BY TRANSEXUALISM
AND ACTORIZATION AMONG THE ADULT CROSS-GENDERED

Partial (1st Order) Associations				Marginal (0-Order) Associations	
Effect	df	LR Chi-squared	p	LR Chi-squared	p
ST	1	4.37	.036	2.66	.103
SR	1	9.72	.002	8.01	.005
TR	1	11.20	.001	9.49	.002
STR	1	0.63	.427		

Tran-sexualism (R)	Actor-ization (T)	Self-Esteem (S) Low	High	(Percent) N(100%)
Some	Some	41	59	176
	None	57	43	49
None	Some	29	71	141
	None	36	64	76

Source: Compiled by the author.

related to self-esteem at both the zero-order and first order partial levels and is positively related to actorization. However, actorization has no significant zero-order relationship with self-esteem but is positively related to self-esteem when transexualism is controlled. Evidently, transexualism suppresses the positive association of actorization with self-esteem. The same pattern of suppressor effects appears in Table 4.16 in the

TABLE 4.16

LIKELIHOOD RATIO ANALYSIS OF MASCULINITY BY TRANSEXUALISM AND ACTORIZATION AMONG THE ADULT CROSS-GENDERED

Partial (1st Order) Associations				Marginal (0-Order) Associations	
Effect	df	LR Chi-squared	p	LR Chi-squared	p
MT	1	5.07	.024	3.52	.060
MR	1	7.20	.007	5.65	.017
TR	1	10.90	.001	9.35	.002
MTR	1	0.02	.900		

Tran-sexualism (R)	Actor-ization (T)	Masculinity (M) Low	High	(Percent) N(100%)
Some	Some	81	19	170
	None	90	10	48
None	Some	69	31	139
	None	80	20	76

Source: Compiled by the author.

case of masculinity. In the case of dominance, a positive and
significant association of actorization with dominance appears
after transexualism is controlled; a negative relationship of

TABLE 4.17

LIKELIHOOD RATIO ANALYSIS OF DOMINANCE BY TRANSEXUALISM AND
ACTORIZATION AMONG THE ADULT CROSS-GENDERED

Partial (1st Order) Associations				Marginal (0-Order) Associations	
Effect	df	LR Chi-squared	p	LR Chi-squared	p
DT	1	4.73	.030	3.67	.055
DR	1	3.62	.057	2.55	.110
TR	1	10.57	.001	9.50	.002
DTR	1	0.12	.734		

Tran-sexualism (R)	Actor-ization (T)	Dominance (D) Low	High	(Percent) N(100%)
Some	Some	73	27	172
	None	81	19	48
None	Some	64	36	140
	None	76	24	76

Source: Compiled by the author.

transexualism and dominance barely misses significance. Turning to competitiveness, we only find a positive relationship of that variable with actorization. In the case of persistent

TABLE 4.18

LIKELIHOOD RATIO ANALYSIS OF COMPETITIVENESS BY TRANSEXUALISM
AND ACTORIZATION AMONG THE ADULT CROSS-GENDERED

Partial (1st Order) Associations				Marginal (0-Order) Associations	
Effect	df	LR Chi-squared	p	LR Chi-squared	p
CT	1	7.52	.006	6.55	.010
CR	1	1.91	.167	0.94	.332
TR	1	11.70	.001	10.73	.001
CTR	1	1.64	.200		

Tran-sexualism (R)	Actor-ization (T)	Competitiveness (C) (Percent)		
		Low	High	N(100%)
Some	Some	71	29	174
	None	90	10	48
None	Some	68	32	140
	None	77	23	78

Source: Compiled by the author.

lonerization, actorization is negatively related to being a persistent loner while transexualism is positively related.

TABLE 4.19

LIKELIHOOD RATIO ANALYSIS OF PERSISTENT LONER BY TRANSEXUALISM AND ACTORIZATION AMONG THE ADULT CROSS-GENDERED

Partial (1st Order) Associations				Marginal (0-Order) Associations	
Effect	df	LR Chi-squared	p	LR Chi-squared	p
LT	1	14.23	.002	10.86	.001
LR	1	9.96	.002	6.59	.010
TR	1	13.24	.000	9.86	.002
LTR	1	0.11	.736		

Tran- sexualism (R)	Actor- ization (T)	Persistent Loner (L) Low	High	(Percent) N(100%)
Some	Some	72	28	174
	None	50	50	50
None	Some	83	17	139
	None	69	31	78

Source: Compiled by the author.

Finally, in the case of femininity (Table 4.20), only actorization is related to femininity while transexualism has no relationship at all to that measure.

TABLE 4.20

LIKELIHOOD RATIO ANALYSIS OF FEMININITY BY TRANSEXUALISM
AND ACTORIZATION AMONG THE ADULT CROSS-GENDERED

Partial (1st Order) Associations				Marginal (0-Order) Associations	
Effect	df	LR Chi-squared	p	LR Chi-squared	p
FT	1	5.51	.019	5.11	.024
FR	1	0.57	.451	0.17	.682
TR	1	9.71	.002	9.31	.002
FTR	1	0.04	.836		

Tran- sexualism (R)	Actor- ization (T)	Femininity (F) Low	(Percent) High	N(100%)
Some	Some	31	69	172
	None	42	58	48
None	Some	27	73	141
	None	40	60	76

Source: Compiled by the author.

The above data show that whether a gay man is motivated toward cross-gendering out of actorization versus transexual feelings makes a sizeable difference in his psychological well-being. Among the cross-gendered, those with no transexual interests who are also actorized are the best off while the "pure" transexuals (those who are transexually motivated but not actorized) are the worst off. That the effeminate are a psychologically very heterogeneous group is further explicated by comparisons of the various subcategories of the effeminate with the non-effeminates of Tables 4.8 through 4.12. (The cutting points in these two sets of tables are the same such that "high self-esteem" means the same level of self-esteem in both sets of tables.) For example, the cross-gendered and actorized but non-transexual respondents of Table 4.15 do not differ on self-esteem from the non-cross-gendered of Table 4.8 (X^2=0.72, df=0, p=ns). A similar comparison of the cross-gendered and actorized but non-transexual respondents of Table 4.16 with the non-cross-gendered of Table 4.9 reveals no significant difference (X^2=0.11, df=1, p=ns) in masculinity. A further comparison of the cross-gendered and actorized non-transexual respondents of Table 4.19 with the non-cross-gendered of Table 4.12 on lonerization shows that the former are significantly less likely to be persistent loners than the latter (X^2=5.27, df=1, p < .03). In the light of these data, it seems clear that future research on homosexuals must take into consideration the differing psychologies among effeminate persons.

The above data show that gay men who are effeminate due to actorization and those who are effeminate due to transexual feelings resemble each other only superficially. Table 4.16 shows that both actorization and transexualism are independently related to persistent cross-dressing. However, given the differing

TABLE 4.21

LIKELIHOOD RATIO ANALYSIS OF CROSS-DRESSING BY ACTORIZATION
AND TRANSEXUALISM AMONG THE ADULT CROSS-GENDERED

Partial (1st Order) Associations				Marginal (0-Order) Associations	
Effect	df	LR Chi-squared	p	LR Chi-squared	p
CT	1	10.68	.001	14.15	.000
CR	1	10.24	.001	13.72	.000
TR	1	6.97	.008	10.45	.001
CTR	1	0.00	.974		

Tran- sexualism (R)	Actor- ization (T)	Ever Cross-Dressed (C) Low	(Percent) High	N(100%)
Some	Some	12	88	176
	None	24	76	50
None	Some	24	76	140
	None	41	59	79

Source: Compiled by the author.

psychologies of the actorized and the transexualized, it would appear that all they have in common are their dresses. Other observers have pointed out related differences between transexuals and those gays with female impersonating interests. Tripp (1975, p. 27) has observed that "the transexual characteristically (has) more interest in the housedress than in the flowing gown, and virtually no interest in the showy cosmetic femininity with which the female impersonator in his high heels, frills, and jewelry reaches an image of high style." These external deportments of cross-gendering are consistent with the interpretation that, while transexuals want to be a woman on a full-time basis, those with acting or impersonating interests are only interested in temporary imitations for effect and do not take such deportments seriously except, as forms of art or achievement.

Esther Newton (1979, pp. 49-51) has made similar observations in her anthropological study of female impersonators. She reports that there is a distinction in the world of female impersonators between "glamour" drag and "transy" drag and that the latter is disvalued as deviant since it is both unglamorous and expresses deviant motivations. "Transy drag violates the implicit aesthetic in the glamour standard, for transy drag makes one look like an ordinary woman and ordinary women are not beautiful (p. 51)." Transy drag also implies deviant motivations because it implies the desire to be a woman rather than be a good impersonator. For example, the wearing of female undergarments during an impersonation act is considered inappropriate because such garments are unnecessary for the performance and imply motivations other than those of being an entertainer.

The preceding data have shown that persistent actorization and an interest in the arts are intimately and intricately linked to childhood and adult cross-gendering in gay men. The combination of cross-gendering and persistent actorization appear to provide the effeminate gay or pre-gay youth with psychological strengths useful in resisting the negative sanctions he undoubtedly encounters both in the course of growing up and later in life. These strengths of toughness seem to be singularly lacking in the transexual form of cross-gendering. That among the cross-gendered, persistent actorization seems to predict psychological characteristics opposite to those predicted by transexualism, provides another reason for doubting the utility of feminine gender-identity as a concept for explaining male homosexuality. The psychology of cross-gendered gay men simply seems to be very different from the psychology of transexuals despite their occasional similarities in cross-gender deportment. To underscore the differences between the actorized cross-gendered and the transexualized cross-gendered, we present Table 4.22 which

TABLE 4.22

LIKELIHOOD RATIO ANALYSIS OF DOMESTIC/NURTURANT OCCUPATIONAL
IDEALS BY PERSISTENT ACTORIZATION BY TRANSEXUALISM AMONG
THE ADULT CROSS-GENDERED

Partial (1st Order) Associations				Marginal (0-Order) Associations	
Effect	df	LR Chi-squared	p	LR Chi-squared	p
NT	1	1.27	.259	0.59	.443
NR	1	5.60	.018	4.92	.027
TR	1	9.69	.002	9.00	.003
NTR	1	0.03	.871		

Transexualism (R)	Actorization (T)	Domestic/Nuturan[Ideals (N) Low	High	(Percent) N(100%)
Some	Some	76	24	155
	None	69	31	39
None	Some	85	15	128
	None	82	18	65

Source: Compiled by the author.

shows domestic/nurturant occupational ideal choices by
actorization and transexualism among the adult cross-gendered.
Only transexualism is positively related to such ideal choices.
The positive association between transexualism and actorization
seems to partly suppress the association between transexualism and
domestic/nurturant choices. These data provide support for
Tripp's above-cited observations on the differences between drag
queens and transexuals. While the former are principally
interested in a glamorized appearance of femininity, the latter
seem more interested in a feminine gender identity and its prosaic
domestic accoutrement[.

These data show that the actorized cross-gendered seem to
possess instrumental qualities one might not expect among
effeminate gay men while the cross-gendered but not actorized
possess these qualities in considerably lesser degree. It would
seem that the latter are principally expressing a feminine gender-
identity while the former are expressing a role ideal to be

strived for. That striving is manifested in their possession of the masculine virtues, in their preference for ideal occupations which bring them direct acclaim, and in their disinterest in the more nurturant and domestic aspects of the feminine role. Such strivings result in persistent effeminacy.

If persistent actorization is an expression of psychological strengths for cross-gendered gay men, one may ask whether it is also a source of strength for heterosexuals. A persistent interest in being an actor or entertainer, or a persistent interest in being many things, may be interpreted as a form of ambition or desire for recognition and hence a strength. We explored this possibility among our heterosexual respondents by examining the relationships of persistent actorization with self-esteem, masculinity, femininity, dominance, and competitiveness. There were no significant relationships with these measures, although there was a weak (X^2=10.27, df=4, p < .04, gamma=0.04) and irregular relationship with dominance. Persistent actorization was also found to be significantly related to interest in the arts (X^2=3.84, df=1, p=.05, gamma=0.59). Among those highly persistently actorized, 75 percent were interested in the arts versus 55 percent of those with some or no actorization.

One may wonder whether actorization or actorization and transexualism in varying combinations of strength are sufficient to explain the persistence of effeminacy from childhood to adulthood despite the fairly general opposition which such individuals must have encountered in the course of growing up. For example, 17 percent (N=147) of those Chicago respondents describing themselves as "very masculine" responded positively to the question, "Have you ever been beat up or assaulted by straights because you were gay?" as compared with 22 percent (N=1191) of those describing themselves as "masculine" and 39 percent (N=194) of those describing themselves as "a little" or "quite feminine" (X^2=29.15, df=2, p < .001). Given this negative feedback, one might wonder what rewards he has received for persistent effeminacy and whether early internalized visions of glamorous femininity are sufficient to explain persistent effeminacy independently of contingencies encountered in growing up. To what audiences other than himself does he play so as to receive at least occasional reward for his self-representations?

One important way in which the effeminate youth may receive rewards for cross-gendered behaviors is through the pursuit of activities which, while not necessarily publicly expressing cross-gender interests, are often or ambiguously defined by the culture as more appropriate for women than for men. Art is one area about which Americans feel ambivalent as to its gender-appropriateness. Heterosexual boys define artistic interest as principally appropriate for girls. Adults, however, tend to recognize artistic interests as within the legitimate domain of male interests, even though some adult males may still question the masculinity of males with major artistic commitments. Given the cultural ambivalence surrounding male artistic interests, gay youths are in a position to exploit the pursuit of such interests and be rewarded for them. However, to the extent that the gay youth himself defines such interests as feminine in nature, he is able to be rewarded for cross-gendering, and that cross-gendering will tend to persist. To the extent that he brings to art intra-psychic scripts (Gagnon and Simon 1973, p. 19ff) which define, consistent with the conventional but primitive and gender-role dichotomizing culture of childhood, art as "sissy stuff," the practice of art becomes the practice of cross-gendered behaviors in more subtle and acceptable ways.

Whether or not the interpersonal scripts of those rewarding the pursuit of artistic interests define art as feminine, if the gay youth so defines it, the rewards he receives are rewards for cross-gendering and not only for art. In the pursuit of art the gay youth is pursuing legitimate interests (art) out of illegitimate motives (cross-gendering). Similarly, a gay youth may be rewarded for helping with the household chores when his private but not necessarily unconscious motives are those of acting like a housewife. The lack of a perfect fit between public and private motives for doing the same thing makes it possible for conventional persons to reward deviant motives without being aware of it. For example, many a gay high school student has attended sporting events as much motivated by the opportunity to admire attractive male bodies as by interest in the game being played. For these reasons, the feedback to cross-gendered behaviors seems mixed and those gay youths strongly motivated toward cross-gendered interests may be able to receive rewards sufficient to inhibit the defeminization process.

Remembering that our actorized and cross-gendered respondents seemed a rather aggressive lot, it seems likely that in their youthful years they may have sought out settings in which their cross-gender interests could be rewarded. Rather than being passive individuals allowing others to form their own destinies and selves, they may have sought settings in which an expression of culturally feminine interests could be rewarded even though they were denied the opportunities of occupying socially feminine statuses. In essence, they may have separated feminine culture from the feminine role. As an exploration of the validity of the notion that effeminate youths seek out culturally feminine activities, a group of young gay college students were interviewed about their interests and activities during high school. A number of them reported that they were principally interested in theater and band. They also reported that many of the other students who participated in these high school activities were also gay or "sissies." Another reported that as a youth, he used to raise flowers and win awards for his displays in garden shows. Such activities provide rewards consistent with the role-preferences of cross-gendered gay youths.

DEFEMINIZATION AND AGE

Having shown the existence of a large-scale defeminization process from childhood to adulthood, we turn to a further analysis of this process as it relates to age among our adult respondents. Table 4.23 presents childhood and adult cross-gendering by age

TABLE 4.23

CHILDHOOD AND ADULT CROSS-GENDERING BY AGE (Percent)

Childhood Cross-gendering	Age							
	-24	25-29	30-34	35-39	40-44	45-49	50-59	60-
None	21	28	28	38	29	33	30	28
Some	51	48	49	39	43	51	50	36
High	28	24	23	23	28	15	20	26
N(100%)	306	417	317	196	111	78	93	25
	$x^2=26.52$		df=14		$p < .05$		gamma=0.09	
Adult Cross-gendering								
None	64	66	71	78	76	79	82	87
Some	33	30	27	21	22	20	16	13
High	3	3	2	2	3	1	2	0
N(100%)	297	414	316	196	110	77	93	23
	$x^2=28.06$		df=14		$p < .05$		gamma=0.19	

Source: Compiled by the author.

among the Chicago respondents. Both are significantly related to age, although the association of childhood cross-gendering with age is quite weak. The association with adult cross-gendering suggests that defeminization continues throughout adulthood and that effeminacy is chiefly a characteristic of younger gay men.

The association of age with childhood cross-gendering is not so directly interpretable unless older gay respondents tend to have forgotten their childhood cross-gendering or were, in fact, less cross-gendered than younger ones. Another interpretation of the relationship of age with childhood cross-gendering is that it is due to adult cross-gendering. Since the very large majority of those cross-gendered as adults were also cross-gendered as children, it seems likely that there would be a relationship of age with childhood cross-gendering due to the intervening effect of adult cross-gendering.

Table 4.24 presents the relationship of childhood cross-gendering with age while controlling for adult cross-gendering. As shown before, childhood cross-gendering and adult cross-

TABLE 4.24

LIKELIHOOD RATIO ANALYSIS OF AGE BY CHILDHOOD AND ADULT
CROSS-GENDERING

Partial (1st Order) Associations				Marginal (0-Order) Associations	
Effect	df	LR Chi-squared	p	LR Chi-squared	p
AC	2	5.93	.052	9.59	.008
AN	2	14.81	.001	18.47	.000
CN	1	91.06	.000	94.73	.000
ACN	2	1.25	.535		

Adult Cross-Gendering (N)	Childhood Cross-Gendering (C)	Age (A) (Percentages)			N(100%)
		-24	25-44	45-	
None	None	14	71	14	380
	Some	19	66	15	698
Some	None	15	73	12	52
	Some	25	67	7	397

Source: Compiled by the author.

gendering are all significantly related to each other at the zero-order level. Looking at the partial relationships, we find that age is significantly negatively related to adult cross-gendering but not to childhood cross-gendering. It thus seems that the relationship of age with childhood cross-gendering is due to the intervening variable of adult cross-gendering and there is no direct linkage of the former two measures. Effeminacy thus seems to be a characteristic of the young gay who has either resisted defeminization or not yet completed it. We note in passing that association of adult cross-gendering with being young does not mean that the earlier shown associations of adult cross-gendering with various psychological characteristics may be due to age differences. Only self-esteem is related to age with those 40 to 45 years having lower self-esteem. We discuss this age group at length in Chapter 8.

Since our composite measure of adult cross-gendering is based on a series of questions asking whether the respondent has "ever" done a particular thing, it tends more to reflect lifetime effeminacy during adulthood rather than current effeminacy. In order to explore the relationships of effeminacy with age using a measure of more current effeminacy, we examine the relationship of age with self-reported masculinity/femininity. (Cf. Table 4.25). While this measure has the advantage of being an indicator of current effeminacy, rather than adult lifetime, it has the disadvantage that some gay men are apparently reluctant to admit to being effeminate. Hence, positive responses to a direct question of effeminacy should be taken more as sufficient, rather than necessary, indicators of effeminacy. In Table 4.25, we see a significant negative relationship of age with self-reported masculinity/femininity. The significance of this relationship seem very largely due to the disproportionate numbers of respondents under 25 years of age who admit effeminacy. These data suggest more strongly than do our adult cross-gendering measure that effeminacy occurs most often among those in their early twenties and thereafter rapidly declines until by the age of 30 there is no further decline. These data are also consistent with Gagnon and Simon's (1973, pp. 147-149) suggestion of a stage of flamboyant effeminacy which occurs in the gay man's early twenties shortly after he has come out.

In Table 4.25, we see a significant negative association between age and persistent acting interest. Most of the decline with age seems to occur in the early twenties after which the decline is minimal. This pattern of decline parallels that of effeminacy and points once more to the link between adult cross-gendering and actorization. We earlier suggested that there occurred deactorization from childhood to adulthood among the defeminized and that persistent effeminacy was associated with persistent actorization. The present relationships with age seem to reveal that the defeminization process which extends into adulthood is paralleled by a deactorization process. In order to see whether the defeminization and deactorization processes are

TABLE 4.25

PERSISTENT ACTING INTEREST AND SELF-REPORTED
MASCULINITY/FEMININITY BY AGE

Persistent Acting Interest	Age							
	-24	25-29	30-34	35-39	40-44	45-49	50-59	60-
None	31	36	45	47	44	50	40	48
Some	39	37	37	36	36	36	41	16
High	29	28	18	17	21	14	18	36
N(100%)	300	418	318	196	110	78	92	25

X^2=39.90   df=14   p < .001   gamma=-0.14

Self-Reported Masculinity/ Femininity								
"Very Masculine" or "Masculine"	78	87	91	93	93	89	88	92
"A Little" or "Quite" Feminine	22	13	9	7	7	11	12	8
N(100%)	304	410	319	195	110	79	92	25

X^2=44.63   df=7   p < .001   gamma=-0.49

Source: Compiled by the author.

directly linked during adulthood independently of age, Table 4.26 presents an analysis of self-reported masculinity/femininity by age and actorization among those who were cross-gendered during childhood. The data reveal significant zero-order and partial

TABLE 4.26

LIKELIHOOD RATIO ANALYSIS OF SELF-REPORTED MASCULINITY/FEMININITY
BY AGE BY PERSISTENT ACTING INTEREST[a]

		Partial (1st Order) Associations		Marginal (0-Order) Associations	
Effect	df	LR Chi-squared	p	LR Chi-squared	p
MA	2	19.29	.000	20.72	.000
MT	2	5.59	.061	7.03	.030
AT	1	4.64	.031	6.07	.014
MAT	2	6.75	.034		

Persistent Acting Interest (T)	Age (A)	Masculinity/ Femininity (M) Masculine	Feminine	(Percent) N(100%)
None	-24	89	11	65
	25-44	88	12	259
	45-	87	13	53
Some	-24	69	31	167
	25-44	87	13	461
	45-	87	13	78

[a]Includes only the cross-gendered during childhood.
Source: Compiled by the author.

associations among all three variables although the partial relationship of actorization and masculinity/femininity is of borderline significance. The reason for that borderline significance becomes apparent when we observe the significant interaction effect. Effeminacy declines with age only among the actorized, while it has no observable relationship with age among the never-actorized. We interpret these relationships to mean that, to the extent that effeminacy was originally due to actorization, defeminization can only readily occur among the actorized. The immense extent to which effeminacy among the young is associated with actorization is shown in Table 4.27, which percentages actorization by age by masculinity/femininity. (These are the data of Table 4.26 percentaged differently.) Among the young effeminates the percentage who have had acting interests at some time is 88. Hence, actorization seems almost a necessary condition for effeminacy among the young. Among the older, however, actorization seems unlinked to effeminacy since for our oldest age group the percentages of the masculine or effeminate who are actorized are identical.

TABLE 4.27

PERSISTENT ACTING INTEREST BY AGE BY SELF-REPORTED
MASCULINITY/FEMININITY (Percent)[a]

Masculinity/ Femininity	Persistent Acting Interest	Age		
		-24	25-44	45-
Feminine	None	12	33	41
	Some	88	67	59
	N(100%)	59	91	17
Masculine	None	34	36	40
	Some	66	64	60
	N(100%)	173	629	114

[a]Includes only those cross-gendered during childhood.
Source: Compiled by the author.

The above data have shown that defeminization, although it seems to occur principally between childhood and early adulthood, continues some years beyond the attainment of majority status. The twenties is the adult decade of continuing defeminization after which little more appears to occur. There also occurs a process of deactorization which seems to undercut some of the motivational support for effeminacy. However, during later adulthood those few gay men who remain effeminate may do so for reasons additional to actorization.

THE CURIOUS CASE OF THE NEWLY EFFEMINATE

The small number of our gay respondents (3 percent) who exhibited some cross-gendering during adulthood but who had none during childhood are inconsistent with the generally developmental explanations we have offered. The cross-gendering of the newly effeminate can conceivably be explained as a result of adult social influences in the gay world. Some may have experimented with cross-gendering as a result of influences from gay peers toward such behaviors as cross-dressing or "camping." This is strongly suggested by the fact that 25 (48 percent) of the 52 newly effeminate were cross-gendered only on the one item of having cross-dressed at some time during adulthood. In contrast, 35 percent of the always-effeminate have only cross-dressed during adulthood. As two of these respondents wrote on their questionnaires, they did it "only as a lark." Such superficial forms of cross-gendering seem analogous to the occasional prankish cross-dressing done by fraternity members and seem unlikely to reflect any enduring predispositions of the individual or to speak to his psychological characteristics.

Such an interpretation of the cross-gendering of the newly effeminate as situational and of superficial meaning, however, is contra-indicated by their low levels on self-esteem and the masculine virtues earlier shown in Tables 3.7 through 3.11. Because of these low levels of psychological well-being, they may not readily be seen as errant never-effeminate gay men who through situational influences engaged in some cross-gendering. In order to examine more closely the internal diversity among the newly effeminate they were divided into the two groups of the 25 superficially cross-gendered through having only cross-dressed, and the group of 27 others who are generally more cross-gendered. Since the numbers involved in comparing these two groups are quite small, statistical comparisons cannot readily be significant. Hence, the following comparisons may be taken as a form of descriptive deviant case analysis.

On self-esteem, 20 percent of the superficially cross-gendered are low versus 41 percent of the others. On masculinity, 32 percent of the superficially cross-gendered are low versus 48 percent of the others. On femininity, 12 percent are high versus 38 percent of the others. On dominance, 36 percent are low versus 44 percent of the others, and on competitiveness, 32 percent are low versus 52 percent of the others. Also, the superficially cross-gendered do not really appear to be effeminate since only 4 percent (1) rated themselves as feminine on self-reported masculinity-femininity versus 26 percent of the others. These differences are all in the same direction and support the notion that the newly effeminate consist of a superficially effeminate group and a truly effeminate group having extremely low levels of psychological well-being. If we compare the non-superficial newly effeminates with the other defeminization status group (cf. Tables

3.7 through 3.11) on self-esteem and the masculine virtues, it becomes apparent that they are lower than all other groups.

The superficially newly effeminate appear to have psychological profiles similar to those of the never effeminate. This similarity is apparent if we compare them with the psychological scores of the never effeminate in Tables 3.7 to 3.11. For example, while 20 percent of the superficially cross-gendered have low self-esteem, 21 percent of the never effeminate have low self-esteem. It thus appears that the superficially effeminate are basically errant never-effeminates for whom their cross-dressing has little significance. While we were tempted to reclassify them as never-effeminates, this would do violence to our overall set of measures and greatly complicate the analyses. That the superficially effeminates seem to be psychologically never-effeminates means that effeminacy during adulthood which was not preceded by childhood cross-gendering is even rarer than our operationalizations indicate. Thus, childhood cross-gendering is almost, but not quite, a necessary condition for serious adult cross-gendering.

To attempt to explain the low levels of psychological well-being of the newly effeminate who are not superficially cross-gendered, we offer an explanation for which we can only offer partial support. The source of the problems of this small group may be in the lack of continuity in their sexual identities. During their childhoods and adolescence they appear to have been rather conventional in their gender behaviors. The shift during adulthood to cross-gendering, whatever its causes, constituted a sharp break from their pasts and required considerable psychological redefinition. In contrast to their presents, they were similar to the never effeminate during adolescence in their degrees of interest in girls and sports (these data are reported in the chapter on adolescence). Hence, they seem to have acquired some effeminacy without reasons of either prior cross-gendering or social approval.

That the newly effeminate who are not superficially cross-gendered have not reached a harmonious accommodation with their homosexuality is suggested by the fact that, in response to the item, "I have utterly no interest in becoming straight," 37 percent disagreed in contrast to 20 percent of the superficially cross-gendered. Also, their social integration into the gay world appears to be less since 56 percent of the non-superficials versus 44 percent of the superficially cross-gendered report that their friends are "all" or "almost all" other gays. In general, the newly effeminate who are not superficially cross-gendered appear to have fairly severe psychological difficulties which may arise out of the discontinuity between their pasts and their presents.

5

GAY ADOLESCENCE

Basing our interpretations on the findings of other researchers who have found that during adolescence many gay youths are somewhat socially isolated and alienated from adolescent culture, it was hypothesized that such alienation might have a number of positive effects. To the extent that gay youths are uninterested in heterosexual relationships and sports, they may be disproportionately inclined to pursue as alternatives intellectual, artistic or cultural interests. Coleman (1961, pp. 30-31) has reported that in most high schools adolescent interests and interpersonal relationships tend to cluster around three foci: athletic activities, intellectual interests, and sociability. Sociability and athletic interests, however, were found to be strongly associated such that athletic participation was correlated with popularity while intellectual interests were somewhat negatively associated with athletic interests and were a sub-dominant cluster in the culture and status structure of the high school. To the extent that gay adolescents are uninterested in athletics and conventional heterosexual activities such as dating, it seems that they might drift more into the intellectual cluster of interests and associations often found in high schools. The intellectual interests of adolescents tend to be approved by adults more than the athletic, and particularly the hedonistic and sometimes criminogenic (Polk and Halferty 1972) interests to which large numbers of adolescents are devoted (Coleman 1961, p. 33). If such interests are pursued seriously they may be more likely to facilitate success as adults in terms of both educational and occupational attainments. In the present chapter, we first attempt to show that there were differences between gay and non-gay men in their respective adolescent interests. Then we attempt to relate such interests to childhood cross-gendering. We then see whether cross-gendering and the hypothesized differing interests are related to having been better students during high school.

GAY ADOLESCENTS AND ADOLESCENT CULTURE

Table 5.1 compares our four sample groups on responses to the items, "During high school I was quite interested in sports," "As a teenager were you seriously interested in girls?", "As a teenager how often did you date girls?", and on a measure of being an academically good student. The latter measure consists of the two Likert-format items, "During high school I read more than most other male students" and "During high school I was more serious about my studies than most other male students." The latter measure has a standardized alpha reliability of 0.67, 0.54, and 0.49 among our Chicago, DeKalb gay, and heterosexual respondents, respectively. This global measure of being a good student during high school was preferred to asking respondents about their grade averages because of grade inflation over the years and because of probable difficulties in recall. We see a large, but hardly surprising difference between the three gay groups and the heterosexuals in their adolescent interests in girls. (The percentages presented are those responding "Some" and "Very Much" versus the responses of "Not Much" and "Never".) Since there are no significant differences among the three gay groups on this item (X^2=1.15, df=2, p=ns), the only notable difference is that between the three gay groups combined versus the non-gays (X^2=104.96, df=1, p < .001, Gamma=0.79). While the gay/non-gay difference in interest in girls is unsurprising, its significance is that a lack of such an interest excludes gay adolescents from one of the major cultural foci around which a large part of adolescent activity centers. Non-participation in adolescent heterosexual activities leaves a major social vacuum for gay adolescents. There are similar but smaller differences between the four sample groups on the frequency of dating measure which was dichotomized as "Never" and "Infrequently" versus "Occasionally" and "Often." There are no significant differences in dating among the three gay groups (X^2=2.65, df=2, p=ns) and a moderate difference between the gays and non-gays (X^2=14.05, df=1, p < .001, Gamma=0.30). That the gay/non-gay difference in dating frequency is smaller than the difference in interest in girls suggests that some of the dating by gays may have been in part due to normative pressures to express heterosexual interests.

That the motivations for adolescent dating may differ between gays and non-gays is suggested by the data of Table 5.2 which show the relationships of interest in girls by frequency of dating for the Chicago gays and the heterosexuals. While the relationships for both groups are strong, the forms of these relationships differ by group. Among the gays the relationship between motivation and dating behavior is quite symmetrical while among

TABLE 5.1

ADOLESCENT INTEREST IN GIRLS AND SPORTS, AND
BEING A GOOD STUDENT BY SAMPLE GROUPS (Percent)

| | Sample Groups | | | |
	Chicago Gay Non-Students	Chicago Gay Students	DeKalb Gay Students	DeKalb Non-Gay Students
Interested in Girls	52	47	53	90
N(100%)	1466	90	32	204
	X^2=107.67	df=3	p < .001	
Interested in Sports	33	29	22	80
N(100%)	1434	89	32	204
	X^2=172.15	df=3	p < .001	
Was Good Student				
Low	30	32	38	41
Medium	34	33	31	38
High	36	36	31	21
N(100%)	1422	89	32	204
	X^2=21.06	df=6	p < .01	
Frequent Dates	56	48	56	70
N(100%)	1466	90	32	204
	X^2=17.29	df=3	p < .001	

Source: Compiled by the author.

the heterosexuals it is not. We also find an identical symmetrical relationship if we look only at the gay students (data not presented). Among the gays dating behavior reflects interest in girls and, to the extent there is a departure (the off-diagonal cells), there is more likely to occur dating unmotivated by an interest in girls than there occurs non-dating by persons interested in girls. Among the heterosexuals behavior also reflects interest in girls. However, the off-diagonal cell of males who are interested in girls but not dating is relatively larger than that of daters who are uninterested in girls. Relative to their respective interests in girls, the non-gays do

TABLE 5.2

ADOLESCENT INTEREST IN GIRLS BY DATING FREQUENCY
BY SAMPLE GROUP (Percent)

	Sample Group			
	Chicago Gays		Heterosexuals	
	Dating Frequency		Dating Frequency	
	Low	High	Low	High
Interested in Girls	19	78	75	96
N(100%)	684	872	61	143

X^2 = 529.26 df = 1 p < .001 X^2 = 19.20 df = 1 p < .001

Q = 0.87 d_d = 0.58[a] d_g = 0.59   Q = 0.80 d_d = 0.50 d_g = 0.21

[a]These coefficients are asymmetric Somer's ds with the subscript indicating the predicted variable.

Source: Compiled by the author.

too little dating and the gays do too much. The relationship of dating with interest in girls is quite similar to that among all Chicago gays if we look at only the gay students. Twenty-eight percent of the infrequent daters were interested in girls (N=61) versus 69 percent of the frequent daters (N=61) (X^2=18.91, df=1, p < .001). These data suggest that adolescent gays spend time dating and thereby appearing to conform to demands that they be interested in activities in which they often are not. Bell et al. (1981a, pp. 106-107) also found that adolescent dating was less likely to be motivated by interest among their gay than among their heterosexual respondents.

Table 5.1 also shows a very large difference between the four sample groups in adolescent interest in sports. Again, there are no significant differences among the three gay groups (X^2=2.35, df=2, p=ns) and the only notable difference is that between the three gay groups combined and the heterosexuals (X^2=167.96, df=1, p < .001, Gamma=0.87). Once more the significance of this difference is that a lack of interest in sports among adolescent gay youths creates a sociocultural vacuum to be either filled by apparent interest in what one finds uninteresting or by other interests. It may also create a basis for social exclusion of the adolescent boy who is disinterested in sports as Stein and Hoffman (1978) have found occurs among heterosexual adolescent males. We note that the differential interest in sports between gay and non-gay men extends to adulthood. In response to the item (asked only of DeKalb respondents) "I find sports fascinating", 50 percent of the gay students answered affirmatively (N=32) versus 85 percent of the heterosexual respondents (N=202) (X^2=18.56, df=1, p < .001, Gamma=0.69).

Since there is a sizable difference in age between the Chicago non-student gays and the other three groups, we explored the possibility that the above difference in adolescent interests might be due to age. Using respondents under 25 years of age only and comparing the heterosexual group with the three gay groups combined, there still remained large and significant differences on sports interest, interest in girls, and frequency of dating (data not presented). There were no significant differences on these three measures among the three gay groups for those under 25 years of age. Among the Chicago respondents, there were also no significant relationships of these three measures with age. Hence, age does not seem to account for these between-sample-group differences.

Table 5.1 also shows that adolescent gays seem more seriously interested in the academic side of high school life since they report having been better students. There are no significant differences in being a good student among the three gay groups (X^2=1.02, df=4, p=ns) while there is a significant difference between the non-gays and the combined gay groups (X^2=20.06, df=2, p < .001). However, unlike the preceding measures of adolescent interests, there are reasons for believing that the gay/non-gay difference in being a good student could be artifacts of sampling. Being a good high school student is related to years of education (X^2=137.44, df=4, p < .001, gamma=0.39) and our Chicago gay non-student group includes many older men who have graduated from college or graduate schools. These older persons, as we subsequently show in Chapter 7, were better high school students. Hence, comparisons of our heterosexual students with the Chicago non-student gays would involve comparisons of those who may or may not graduate from college or graduate school with many who have so graduated. For this reason, we limit our gay/non-gay comparisons

on being a good student to comparisons between the combined gay
student samples and the heterosexual students.

Comparing the non-gay respondents with the two gay student
groups combined, we find a significant difference with the gays
having been better students (X^2=7.93, df=2, p < .02). In order to
assess whether this difference may be due to the gays' non-
involvement in heterosexual adolescent culture, Tables 5.3 through
5.5 show the effects of interests in that culture on the gay/non-
gay difference in being a good student. In Table 5.3, there are
significant zero-order associations among interest in girls, being
a good student, and sample group. Those who were more interested
in girls during adolescence were poorer students. This
relationship holds among both gays and heterosexuals. When
interest in girls is controlled, the relationship between being a
good student and being a gay student vanishes. It thus seems that
the disproportionate being a better student by the gays arises
partly out of their disinterest in girls (or its correlates) and,
by inference, as a reaction or alternative to heterosexual
involvements.

In Table 5.4, we see a set of relationships identical to that
found in the preceding table. The sample-group difference in
being a good student vanishes once frequency of dating is
controlled, while at the zero-order level involvement in dating
behaviors is associated with being a poorer student. These
findings are consistent with a variety of findings by other
researchers who have found a negative association between early
adolescent expressions of sexuality and educational aspirations or

TABLE 5.3

LIKELIHOOD RATIO ANALYSIS OF BEING GOOD STUDENT BY
ADOLESCENT INTEREST IN GIRLS BY SAMPLE GROUP*

Partial (1st Order) Associations				Marginal (0-Order) Associations	
Effect	df	LR Chi-squared	p	LR Chi-squared	p
BI	2	10.53	.005	17.24	.000
BG	2	0.97	.616	7.68	.022
IG	1	60.53	.000	67.23	.000
BIG	2	1.77	.412		

Sample Group (G)	Interest in Girls (I)	Being Good Student (B) (Percent)			N(100%)
		Low	Med	High	
Gay Students	Low	27	24	28	62
	High	39	41	20	59
Non-Gay Students	Low	30	40	30	20
	High	42	38	20	184

*Student groups only

Source: Compiled by the author.

attainments among heterosexual adolescents (Miller and Simon 1974). It thus seems that the substantial psychological, and, to a lesser extent, behavioral exclusion of gay adolescents from the social world of teenage sexuality may operate with special force for gays so as to propel them toward academic interests.

TABLE 5.4

LIKELIHOOD RATIO ANALYSIS OF BEING GOOD STUDENT
BY ADOLESCENT DATING FREQUENCY BY SAMPLE GROUP*

		Partial (1st Order) Associations			Marginal (0-Order) Associations	
Effect	df	LR Chi-squared	p		LR Chi-squared	p
BD	2	9.30	.010		11.98	.002
BG	2	5.00	.082		7.68	.021
DG	1	10.70	.001		13.37	.000
BDG	2	0.69	.708			

Sample Group (G)	Dating Frequency (D)	Being Good Student (B) (Percent)			N(100%)
		Low	Med	High	
Gay Students	Low	23	33	44	61
	High	43	32	25	60
Non-Gay Students	Low	33	41	26	61
	High	44	37	18	143

*Student groups only

Source: Compiled by the author.

Table 5.5, which presents being a good student by adolescent interest in sports by sample group, reveals a picture consistent with the findings of the preceding two tables but one which is not as clear. At the zero-order level, there is a negative relationship between being a good student and sports interest and also a relationship between sample group and good student. However, both relationships vanish in the partials. That sports interest is negatively associated with good student is somewhat inconsistent with the findings of other researchers who have found

high school grades to be positively associated with participation
in high school athletics (Schafer 1972; Keating 1961). However,
since the negative association of sports interest with being a
good student in Table 5.5 seems to occur principally among the gay
students, that relationship may hold only for gays. We return to
this question below.

TABLE 5.5

LIKELIHOOD RATIO ANALYSIS OF BEING GOOD STUDENT BY ADOLESCENT
SPORTS INTEREST BY SAMPLE GROUP*

Partial (1st Order) Associations				Marginal (0-Order) Associations	
Effect	df	LR Chi-squared	p	LR Chi-squared	p
BS	2	3.47	.176	9.16	.010
BG	2	2.21	.331	7.91	.019
GS	1	81.51	.000	87.20	.000
BGS	2	1.10	.576		

Sample Group (G)	Sports Interest (S)	Being Good Student (B) (Percent)			N(100%)
		Low	Med	High	
Gay Students	Low	31	29	40	87
	High	39	39	21	33
Non-Gay Students	Low	37	39	24	41
	High	42	38	20	163

*Student groups only

Source: Compiled by the author.

CHILDHOOD MEASURES AND ADOLESCENT INTERESTS

Having documented the existence of different interests between gay and non-gay males during adolescence, we now attempt an explanation of those differences in terms of our earlier developed concepts. In particular, we address the question of the origins of those differences. While some may flow from earlier cross-gendering others may arise out of the social situation in which gay youths find themselves. While some of these differences may be adaptations to being immersed in a teenage culture in which they are uninterested, others may represent unfoldings of earlier identities.

TABLE 5.6

YOUTHFUL LONER BY CHILDHOOD CROSS-GENDERING*

Youthful Loner	Childhood Cross-Gendering		
	None	Some	High
None	49	32	31
Some	22	29	21
High	29	39	48
N(100%)	432	725	373
	$X^2 = 52.40$	df = 4	p < .001

*Chicago respondents only

Source: Compiled by the author.

One of the problems of gay youths found above (cf. Table 3.1) and reported by others (Stephan 1973) is that they often tend to be loners. Also, as found earlier, there tends to be considerable persistence of being a loner into adulthood among both gays and non-gays. Hence, there is the suggestion that being a loner is rather an enduring aspect of personality or individual interests and may not substantially be a reaction to responses of others. Table 5.6 shows that being a youthful loner is significantly related to childhood cross-gendering. (In the analyses of the present chapter and the one on crime we employ a measure here called "youthful loner", rather than the elsewhere employed "persistent loner" measure. Since adolescence is presently being considered, it seemed more appropriate to use a measure of lonerization referring more directly to that time period. The three categories of the youthful loner measure are: (1) never a loner for either childhood or adolescence; (2) a loner for one of these periods; (3) a loner for both periods.) One may ask whether the above reported disinterest in sports on the part of gay youths arises directly out of an identification with feminine culture or if it is a manifestation of a more general propensity to solitariness. Alternatively, being a loner may be a consequence of disinterest in sports since the adolescent male so disinterested thereby deprives himself of a considerable basis for peer interaction. The subsequent tables present analyses of the adolescent interests measures by childhood cross-gendering and being a youthful loner.

Table 5.7 presents the relationships between adolescent interest in sports, childhood cross-gendering, and being a youthful loner among the Chicago respondents. Both youthful loner and childhood cross-gendering have strong negative associations with sports interest at the zero-order and partial levels with cross-gendering being the stronger of the two. It thus appears that childhood cross-gendering has a direct relationship with the very common gay disinterest in sports. Youthful gays seem averse to the cultural activities embodied in the conventional masculine role. Childhood cross-gendering also has an additional indirect relationship with sports interest through youthful loner. It seems that sports has little to offer the gay who was either cross-gendered as a child or who tends to be a loner.

Table 5.8 presents the relationships among adolescent interest in girls, being a youthful loner, and childhood cross-gendering. Interest in girls is significantly related only to youthful loner while there is a borderline zero-order relationship with childhood cross-gendering. It seems that being a loner is an intervening variable between cross-gendering and interest in girls. The same pattern of significant and non-significant relationships appears when we examine the associations among childhood cross-gendering, youthful loner, and frequent dating (data not presented). Only loner is significantly related to dating. It thus seems that those gay youths who are loners opt for isolation rather than participate in the adolescent culture of sports, girls, and dating. Of course, the loner variable can not begin to explain the huge difference in adolescent interest in girls between our gay and non-gay groups. Among the non-gay students, the percentage interested in girls is 90 while the highest percentage interested in girls among the gay sub-groups of Table 5.8 is 68.

If childhood cross-gendering and youthful loner alienate and isolate the gay youth from teenage culture, are these characteristics which are so common among gay childhoods

TABLE 5.7

LIKELIHOOD RATIO ANALYSIS OF ADOLESCENT SPORTS INTEREST
BY YOUTHFUL LONER BY CHILDHOOD CROSS-GENDERING

Partial (1st Order) Associations				Marginal (0-Order) Associations	
Effect	df	LR Chi-squared	p	LR Chi-squared	p
SL	2	38.09	.000	54.45	.001
SC	1	57.80	.000	74.16	.001
LC	2	26.15	.000	42.51	.001
SLC	2	3.26	.196		

Childhood Cross-Gendering (C)	Youthful Loner (L)	Sports Interest (S) (Percent) Low	High	N(100%)
Some	Low	66	34	340
	Med	73	27	286
	High	79	21	452
None	Low	39	61	208
	Med	51	49	92
	High	68	32	120

Source: Compiled by the author.

TABLE 5.8

LIKELIHOOD RATIO ANALYSIS OF ADOLESCENT INTEREST IN GIRLS
BY YOUTHFUL LONER BY CHILDHOOD CROSS-GENDERING

Partial (1st Order) Associations				Marginal (0-Order) Associations	
Effect	df	LR Chi-squared	p	LR Chi-squared	p
GL	2	49.47	.000	52.47	.000
GC	1	0.58	.446	3.57	.059
LC	2	38.73	.000	41.72	.000
GLC	2	3.28	.194		

Childhood Cross-Gendering (C)	Youthful Loner (L)	Interest in Girls (G) (Percent) Low	High	N(100%)
Some	Low	40	60	346
	Med	48	52	290
	High	58	42	462
None	Low	32	68	212
	Med	48	52	95
	High	61	39	125

Source: Compiled by the author.

completely malign in their effects or, differently, is teenage
culture totally malign in its effects on gay youths? Table 5.9
shows that youthful loner is positively related to being a good
student while childhood cross-gendering is unrelated. It thus
seems that the isolation produced by childhood cross-gendering
appears to propel gay youths into being good students. Given that
the major cultural alternatives available in most high schools are
the hedonistic culture of adolescents and the more serious
intellectual, artistic, and vocationally oriented ones of teachers
and other adults, many gay youths appear to opt for the latter due
to an aversion for the former.

TABLE 5.9

LIKELIHOOD RATIO ANALYSIS OF BEING GOOD STUDENT BY YOUTHFUL
LONER BY CHILDHOOD CROSS-GENDERING

		Partial (1st Order) Associations			Marginal (0-Order) Associations	
Effect	df	LR Chi-squared	p		LR Chi-squared	p
GL	4	36.22	.000		37.48	.000
GC	2	0.50	.779		1.76	.415
LC	2	40.02	.000		41.28	.000
GLC	4	3.34	.503			

Childhood Cross-Gendering (A)	Youthful Loner (L)	Good Student (G) (Percent) Low	Med	High	N(100%)
Some	Low	36	35	29	337
	Med	33	35	32	283
	High	23	32	46	452
None	Low	37	33	30	203
	Med	30	35	35	94
	High	22	40	38	117

Source: Compiled by the author.

Table 5.10 presents the relationships among being a good
student, youthful loner, and sample group among our student
groups. The intent of this table is to see whether the loner
variable accounts for the difference in good student between gays
and non-gays. It is apparent that the association between loner
and good student is considerably stronger than that between sample
groups and good student. Also, the loner measure seems to explain
all of the difference in good student by sample group just as did
interest in girls. Different interpretations of these data are
possible. A labelling interpretation would assert that cross-
gendered youths are rejected, become loners, and, as an
alternative, are forced to become good students. The alternative
interpretation is that cross-gendered students prefer to be loners
rather than participate in conventional adolescent culture and
choose academic interests as an alternative. Since we have no
means of determining the extent to which the solitariness of gay

TABLE 5.10

LIKELIHOOD RATIO ANALYSIS OF BEING GOOD STUDENT
BY YOUTHFUL LONER BY SAMPLE GROUP*

Partial (1st Order) Associations				Marginal (0-Order) Associations	
Effect	df	LR Chi-squared	p	LR Chi-squared	p
BL	4	16.98	.002	23.01	.000
BG	2	1.94	.379	7.96	.019
LG	2	33.84	.000	39.87	.000
BLG	4	0.76	.944		

Sample Group (G)	Youthful Loner (L)	Good Student (B) (Percent)			N(100%)
		Low	Med	High	
Gay Students	Low	46	36	18	28
	Med	31	36	33	39
	High	28	28	44	54
Non-Gay Students	Low	48	38	14	114
	Med	38	40	21	52
	High	25	36	29	38

Source: Compiled by the author.

youths is a voluntary one we cannot choose among these alternatives. We can, however, observe that being a good student does not flow directly from being cross-gendered as a child since there were found no significant zero-order or partial relationships between childhood cross-gendering and being a good student among our Chicago respondents. Hence, it appears that the gay youth's disproportionate propensity for being a good student arises out of an interaction between the cultural preferences he brings to the high school setting and the cultural options there available to him. It is also worth noting that being a loner and thereby not participating in the adolescent culture is beneficial for academic success among both heterosexuals and homosexuals.

While the youthful loner measure explains the difference between our gay and non-gay students in being a good student, we also found that adolescent dating frequency and interest in girls also explained that difference. This arises because of the quite strong positive associations found in all sample groups among interest in sports, interest in girls, and dating. Collectively, these items measure participation in adolescent heterosexual culture while being a good student has moderate negative associations with these items. That being a youthful loner is negatively associated with these items indicates that it is also a measure of non-participation in adolescent heterosexual culture. Although these items are all rather strongly inter-correlated it would still be useful to separate out the respective contributions of being a loner and interest in girls to being a good student by sample group. However, since the sizes of our student groups preclude a four variable cross-classification we proceed indirectly by analyzing good student by youthful loner by interest in girls among our Chicago respondents (cf. Table 5.11). Since youthful loner and interest in girls are negatively related among both gay and non-gay groups, it would be desirable to separate out their respective contributions to being a good student. We see that while youthful loner is positively related to good student and interest in girls is negatively related to good student, controlling for youthful loner reduced the latter relationship to non-significance. An identical set of relationships is found when frequency of dating is related to youthful loner and good student (data not presented). It would thus seem that interest in girls and frequency of dating make no direct independent contribution to being a good student. Rather, they may be causally prior to being a loner such that, lacking an interest in girls, one is deprived of many opportunities for social participation in adolescent society. It thus seems, consistent with the findings of others, the adolescent, gay or non-gay, is offered the options of heterosexual social participation versus being a good student but that for the young gay the choice may be more determined in favor of being a good student due to his lower interest in heterosexual activity and his propensities, voluntary or involuntary, for being a loner.

Table 5.12 presents the relationships of good student, youthful loner, and interest in sports among the Chicago respondents. In these data, the results differ somewhat from those for interest in girls and dating. Interest in sports is unrelated to good student at the zero-order level but is significantly and positively related to good student once youthful loner is controlled. It thus seems that the negative association between youthful loner and this culturally masculine form of social participation suppresses the modest positive association between good student and sports interest. As noted above, the positive relationship between high school sports participation and high school grades has been found in other studies of heterosexual adolescents. We observe that the effect of sports interest seems to be stronger in reducing the percentage of respondents who are "low" on good student more than increasing the percentage who are "high." As Schafer (1972) has reported, high school athletic participation seems to improve the grades most of those least

TABLE 5.11

LIKELIHOOD RATIO ANALYSIS OF BEING GOOD STUDENT BY
YOUTHFUL LONER BY INTEREST IN GIRLS

Partial (1st Order) Associations				Marginal (0-Order) Associations	
Effect	df	LR Chi-squared	p	LR Chi-squared	p
BL	4	30.75	.000	36.59	.000
BG	2	5.70	.058	11.54	.003
LG	2	46.46	.000	52.30	.000
BLG	4	4.95	.292		

Interest in Girls (G)	Youthful Loner (L)	Good Student (B) (Percent)			N(100%)
		Low	Med	High	
Low	Low	33	37	30	202
	Med	28	39	33	182
	High	21	31	48	337
High	Low	39	32	29	341
	Med	36	32	32	197
	High	25	37	38	236

Source: Compiled by the author.

TABLE 5.12

LIKELIHOOD RATIO ANALYSIS OF BEING GOOD STUDENT BY
YOUTHFUL LONER BY ADOLESCENT SPORTS INTEREST

Partial (1st Order) Associations				Marginal (0-Order) Associations	
Effect	df	LR Chi-squared	p	LR Chi-squared	p
BL	4	38.74	.000	35.60	.000
BS	2	6.11	.047	2.97	.185
LS	2	59.10	.000	55.96	.000
BLS	4	7.81	.099		

Sports Interests (S)	Youthful Loner (L)	Good Student (B) (Percent)			N(100%)
		Low	Med	High	
Low	Low	42	33	26	298
	Med	33	31	36	250
	High	24	33	43	434
High	Low	30	35	34	237
	Med	32	42	27	123
	High	20	34	46	147

Source: Compiled by the author.

likely to do well--working-class adolescents and those with lower
IQs. It seems to motivate them to obtain acceptable, but not
high, grades so they may pursue athletics which is closer to their
hearts.

The above tables seem to fairly compellingly show that
adolescent peer culture offers little of great interest to the
young gay. Heterosexual activities and athletics are ones to
which he is largely indifferent or which he views with distaste.
Since these activities, plus more recently drugs, are the dominant
foci of high school culture his options are considerably narrower
than those of heterosexual youths. Peer culture offers him
choices of participating in activities in which he is not
particularly interested, of being an isolate, or of being a good
student. Apparently disproportionately large numbers of gay
youths choose the latter.

ADOLESCENT INTERESTS AND ADULT CHARACTERISTICS

It was above shown that childhood cross-gendering did not seem to have any direct relationship with being a good student; rather, it had only an indirect and positive one through youthful loner. Table 5.13 shows that it has another indirect but negative association with good student through adult cross-gendering. (The

TABLE 5.13

LIKELIHOOD RATIO ANALYSIS OF BEING GOOD STUDENT
BY CHILDHOOD AND ADULT CROSS-GENDERING

Partial (1st Order) Associations				Marginal (0-Order) Associations	
Effect	df	LR Chi-squared	p	LR Chi-squared	p
GC	2	3.58	.167	1.92	.383
GA	2	11.38	.003	9.72	.008
CA	1	94.86	.000	93.20	.000
GCA	2	4.77	.092		

Adult Cross-Gendering (A)	Childhood Cross-Gendering (C)	Being Good Student (G) (Percent)			N(100%)
		Low	Med	High	
Some	Some	34	31	35	384
	None	47	37	16	49
None	Some	27	35	38	683
	None	29	36	35	366

Source: Compiled by the author.

intent here is not to show that adult cross-gendering causally intervenes between childhood cross-gendering and good student. It is to show that that subset of the childhood cross-gendered who persisted in effeminacy into adulthood were poorer students than those who didn't.) Table 5.13 shows no significant relationship of childhood cross-gendering with good student but also reveals that the adult cross-gendered were more likely to have been poorer students.

In order to sort out the separate relationships of adult cross-gendering and youthful loner with good student, Table 5.14 presents an analysis of these three measures. These data show

TABLE 5.14

LIKELIHOOD RATIO ANALYSIS OF BEING GOOD STUDENT
BY YOUTHFUL LONER BY ADULT CROSS-GENDERING

Partial (1st Order) Associations				Marginal (0-Order) Associations	
Effect	df	LR Chi-squared	p	LR Chi-squared	p
BL	4	35.88	.000	36.26	.000
BA	2	8.39	.015	8.77	.012
LA	2	0.47	.790	0.85	.653
BLA	4	2.89	.576		

Adult Cross-Gendering (A)	Youthful Loner (L)	Good Student (B) (Percent)			N(100%)
		Low	Med	High	
Some	Low	44	33	22	160
	Med	36	30	34	115
	High	27	31	42	157
None	Low	33	35	32	381
	Med	30	38	32	259
	High	21	34	45	403

Source: Compiled by the author.

that both youthful loner and adult cross-gendering are independently related to good student and that loner is the stronger of the two measures. A series of comparisons was made between the defeminization status groups taken two at a time. The only new findings were that the defeminized were significantly better students than the persistently effeminate but there was no difference between the latter and the never-effeminate.

131

The difference found between the defeminized and the persistently effeminate in being a good student suggests the possibility that the former have attempted the solution to their alienation of greater conformity to adult expectations. Through both defeminization and being better students, the defeminized avoid negative feedback from peers for cross-gendered behaviors and obtain the rewards otherwise denied them in the adolescent culture. Their solution may be one of becoming general conformists. That their tendency to conformity has some generality across a wider set of areas of activity is shown in Table 5.15 which presents responses to the question "As a teenager did you ever take part in 'gang fights'"? by childhood and adult cross-gendering. This table shows that while childhood cross-

TABLE 5.15

LIKELIHOOD RATIO ANALYSIS OF ADOLESCENT GANG FIGHTS
BY CHILDHOOD AND ADULT CROSS-GENDERING

		Partial (1st Order) Associations			Marginal (0-Order) Associations	
Effect	df	LR Chi-squared	p	LR Chi-squared		p
FC	1	15.05	.000	10.32		.001
FA	1	9.34	.002	4.61		.032
CA	1	100.86	.000	96.13		.000
FCA	1	0.01	.912			

Adult Cross-Gendering (A)	Childhood Cross-Gendering (C)	Gang Fights (F) (Percent) Never	Ever	N(100%)
Some	Some	79	21	394
	None	67	33	52
None	Some	85	15	698
	None	77	23	294

Source: Compiled by the author.

gendering is negatively related to having participated in group fights adult cross-gendering is positively related to such behaviors. Thus those who were cross-gendered as children but not as adults--the defeminized--are the least likely to have engaged in group fights.

The data of Table 5.15 show that non-participation in fights does not seem to be a straightforward consequence of a cross-gender role preference. While one might expect those males with a cross-gender role preference to be disinclined to engage in violent behaviors, the fact that the persistently effeminate are higher than the defeminized on fighting behavior implies that factors other than role preference are operative. Drawing on earlier presented ideas in our discussion of the psychologies of effeminacy. we note that those who were both cross-gendered and actorized as adults displayed a psychological toughness through being high on all the masculine virtues. In order to see whether actorization may explain the pugnacious propensities of the persistently effeminate. we performed a four-variable analysis of gangfights by actorization, youthful loner, and defeminization status. Not included in this analysis are the newly effeminate who are too few in number to further break down. The notational system used for associations in this table requires some comment since it differs from those in preceding tables. In tables in the present work involving four or more variables, we employ the notational system used in partial correlation. For example, "FA.LM" refers to the association between gangfights and actorization controlling for youthful loner and defeminization status. Also in our analyses involving four or more variables, we exclude those partial effects which control for variables that are clearly only dependent ones. In the case of Table 5.16, gangfights is considered to be always a dependent variable and is thus never controlled for.

We find in Table 5.16 that actorization is significantly positively related to having ever been in gangfights. It would appear that the actorized, even though they are typically cross-gendered, are rather aggressive individuals. We also find that the youthful loners are less likely to have been in gangfights as was earlier hypothesized. The significant interaction among gangfights, youthful loner, and actorization appears to mean that at high levels of lonerization, lonerization suppresses the pugnacity associated with actorization.

The greater conformity, or gentleness, of the defeminized is also exhibited in Table 5.16 by the significant association of defeminization status with gangfights both at the zero-order and second-order partial levels. The standardized lambdas indicating that a defeminization status group is high on gangfights are -2.82 for the defeminized, 1.95 for the never effeminate, and 0.48 for the persistently effeminate. The actorization measure appears to

TABLE 5.16

LIKELIHOOD RATIO ANALYSIS OF GANGFIGHTS BY ACTORIZATION
BY YOUTHFUL LONER BY DEFEMINIZATION STATUS

		Partial Associations		Marginal (0-Order) Associations	
Effect	df	LR Chi-squared	p	LR Chi-squared	p
FA.YM	1	7.23	.007	6.41	.011
FY.AM	1	13.17	.001	17.85	.001
FM.AY	2	12.11	.002	15.02	.001
AY.M	1	2.15	.143	0.36	.551
AM.Y	2	63.80	.001	61.68	.001
YM.A	2	39.32	.001	37.46	.001
FAY.M	1	1.31	.788		
FAM.Y	2	4.53	.106		
FYM.A	2	1.44	.750		
AYM	2	4.29	.117		
FAYM	2	3.81	.149		

Defeminization Status (M)	Youthful Loner (L)	Actorization (A)	Ever in Gangfights (F) (Percent Yes)	N(100%)
Persistently Effeminate	Low	Low	16	32
		High	28	118
	High	Low	12	72
		High	21	168
Defeminized	Low	Low	14	77
		High	22	144
	High	Low	8	192
		High	15	278
Never Effeminate	Low	Low	25	109
		High	35	84
	High	Low	22	96
		High	12	88

Source: Compiled by the author.

explain the greater fighting behavior of the persistently effeminate compared to the defeminized. Despite their greater lonerization and their childhood cross-gendering--both negatively associated with fighting--the actorization of the persistently effeminate appears to raise their fighting level to that of the never-effeminate. In contrast, for the defeminized all variables seem to propel them in the direction of greater pacificity and, more broadly, conformity, e.g., their childhood cross-gendering, their high lonerization, their deactorization since childhood, and their non-cross-gendering during adulthood. The strong tendencies of the defeminized to conform to a variety of adult demands suggests a greater responsiveness to social demands for conformity. To further underscore their greater responsiveness to external demands, we present Table 5.17 which shows responses to the item "Before I came out the idea that I might be gay troubled me a lot." We assume that this item reflects former agreement with the conventional societal condemnation of homosexuality and that such guilt is a socially conformist response. This table shows significant relationships of both childhood and adult cross-gendering with pre-coming out guilt. While those cross-gendered as children were more likely to have been troubled, those cross-gendered as adults were less likely to have been troubled. The increases in magnitudes of the relevant chi-squareds as one goes from the zero-order to the partial relationships indicates that the two cross-gendering measures suppress each other's effects. Since two different studies of gay men have shown the median age of coming out to be 19 or 20 (Dank 1971; Harry and DeVall 1978, p. 64), the time period referred to by the item "Before I came out . . ." is for most respondents adolescence. Hence, during this period the defeminized seem more likely to have internalized some of the negative societal condemnation of homosexuality as part of their greater responsiveness to external demands in contrast to the more strong-willed persistently effeminate.

One may hypothesize that adolescent guilt over one's incipient homosexuality could have a number of negative or positive consequences for the pre-gay adolescent. It could impel him into social isolation. In extreme degree, it could interfere with his schoolwork. Alternatively, it could provide some of the motivational impetus for a conformist solution to his alienation such that, in order to make up for his felt deficiencies, he becomes a better student. We found that adolescent guilt was not significantly related to youthful loner at the zero-order level (X^2=4.38, df=4, p=ns). However, it was found to be significantly related to being a good student during high school (X^2=10.31, df=4, p < .04). In order to see whether guilt made any independent contribution to being a good student, we proceeded to a four-variable analysis of good student by guilt by youthful loner by defeminization status (cf. Table 5.18). Table 5.18 shows a significant interaction among guilt, youthful loner, and being a good student. The percentages of this table show that the positive effect of guilt on good student is limited to those who

TABLE 5.17

LIKELIHOOD RATIO ANALYSIS OF PRE-COMING OUT GUILT
BY CHILDHOOD AND ADULT CROSS-GENDERING

Partial (1st Order) Associations				Marginal (0-Order) Associations	
Effect	df	LR Chi-squared	p	LR Chi-squared	p
GC	1	9.02	.003	5.80	.016
GA	1	7.76	.005	4.55	.033
CA	1	98.67	.000	95.46	.000
GCA	1	0.21	.645		

Adult Cross-Gendering (A)	Childhood Cross-Gendering (C)	Pre-Coming Out Guilt (G) (Percent)		N(100%)
		Low	High	
Some	Some	56	44	392
	None	62	38	52
None	Some	47	53	695
	None	57	43	380

Source: Compiled by the author.

136

TABLE 5.18

LIKELIHOOD RATIO ANALYSIS OF BEING GOOD STUDENT BY PRE-COMING
OUT GUILT BY YOUTHFUL LONER BY DEFEMINIZATION STATUS

		Partial Associations		Marginal (0-Order) Association	
Effect	df	LR Chi-squared	p	LR Chi-squared	p
BG.LM	1	0.47	.494	1.14	.286
BL.GM	1	23.99	.001	25.92	.001
BM.GL	2	5.95	.051	7.89	.019
GL.M	1	1.39	.238	2.83	.093
GM.L	2	9.40	.009	10.84	.004
LM.G	2	33.67	.001	36.36	.001
BGL.M	1	4.62	.032		
BGM.L	2	3.58	.167		
BLM.G	2	3.39	.183		
GLM	2	1.38	.500		
BGLM	2	0.97	.615		

Defeminization Status (M)	Youthful Loner (L)	Pre-Coming Out Guilt (G)	Percent Good Students (B)	N(100%)
Persistently Effeminate	Low	Low	29	87
		High	37	60
	High	Low	51	124
		High	57	109
Defeminized	Low	Low	39	109
		High	53	108
	High	Low	60	205
		High	57	251
Never Effeminate	Low	Low	44	102
		High	46	85
	High	Low	58	99
		High	36	77

Source: Compiled by the author.

are non-loners while among the loners there is either no effect or a modest negative one. These data suggest that while both guilt and being a loner have positive effects on being a good student, the combination of lonerization and guilt may be sufficiently psychologically disabling so as to eliminate the separate positive effects of both variables. Guilty adolescent loners must carry their guilt alone without sharing it with others while also not receiving the usual therapeutic rewards which come with sociability.

In order to test this interpretation of the disabling effects of a combination of being guilty and a loner, we explored adult self-esteem by adolescent guilt by youthful loner by defeminization status (cf. Table 5.19). These data show that adolescent guilt appears to leave a residue in terms of lessened adult self-esteem at the zero-order level of association. However, there is also a significant interaction involving guilt, youthful loner, and self-esteem. The association of guilt with adult self-esteem is stronger among the loners than among the non-loners. These data support the disablement hypothesis and suggest that while guilt and loner have positive effects in terms of achievement their combination can be too much of a good thing. We briefly note that Table 5.19 shows a significant zero-order association between being a loner and low self-esteem. Across various tables, that association hovers usually below the level of statistical significance and here we treat it as either non-existent or of only minimal strength. Since the measures of both self-esteem and of pre-coming out guilt are present in our earlier study of Detroit gay men, a replication of the association between such guilt and adult self-esteem was attempted. Of the unguilty, 50 percent had high self-esteem as adults (N=109) as compared with 33 percent of the guilty (N=114) (X^2=6.72, df=1, p < .02). Since replication is a major means of validating findings based on non-probability samples, further replications using the earlier Detroit data are attempted where possible.

Returning to some of the other findings of Table 5.18, it is worth observing that the defeminized are highest on both guilt and lonerization. The respective standardized lambdas showing high guilt for the persistently effeminate, the defeminized, and the never effeminate are -1.47, 2.99, and -1.19. The corresponding lambdas for high lonerization are 0.98, 4.76, and -5.23. Both of these variables appear to be operative in impelling the defeminized to be better students since Table 5.18 also shows that defeminization status is associated with good student at the zero-order level. However, this association vanishes once guilt and lonerization are controlled. Since the defeminized are high on both guilt and lonerization, it would seem that the disablement hypothesis may be particularly operative among the defeminized. Fortunately, for our respondents as a whole, guilt and lonerization are at least not significantly associated at the zero-order level.

TABLE 5.19

LIKELIHOOD RATIO ANALYSIS OF SELF-ESTEEM BY PRE-COMING OUT
GUILT BY YOUTHFUL LONER BY DEFEMINIZATION STATUS

		Partial Associations		Marginal (0-Order) Associations	
Effect	df	LR Chi-squared	p	LR Chi-squared	p
SG.YM	1	13.35	.001	12.96	.001
SY.GM	1	2.33	.127	4.13	.042
SM.GY	2	29.63	.001	30.05	.001
GY.M	1	1.38	.240	3.06	.080
GM.Y	2	11.48	.003	11.78	.003
YM.G	2	33.89	.001	36.38	.000
SGY.M	1	4.74	.029		
SGM.Y	2	0.00	.999		
SYM.G	2	1.10	.576		
GYM	2	1.93	.382		
SGYM	2	0.56	.755		

Defeminization Status (M)	Youthful Loner (L)	Pre-Coming Out Guilt (G)	Percent with High Self-Esteem (S)	N(100%)
Persistently Effeminate	Low	Low	37	90
		High	33	60
	High	Low	39	128
		High	27	109
Defeminized	Low	Low	50	114
		High	45	108
	High	Low	52	211
		High	38	254
Never Effeminate	Low	Low	58	106
		High	58	86
	High	Low	57	105
		High	39	77

Source: Compiled by the author.

The fairly strong association between youthful loner and being defeminized suggests the possibility that lonerization may distinguish the defeminized in the same way that persistent actorization distinguishes the persistently effeminate. Under such an interpretation, one's relative levels during childhood of lonerization versus actorization may influence whether the cross-gendered child defeminizes or remains persistently effeminate. These possibilities were explored through examining both persistent lonerization and being a childhood loner by defeminization status. For childhood, 49 percent of the persistently effeminate were loners compared to 55 percent of the defeminized and 38 percent of the never effeminate. It thus seems that there is only a very modest difference between the persistently effeminate and the defeminized in the extent to which they were loners during childhood while the only notable difference in childhood lonerization is between the childhood cross-gendered and the noncross-gendered. On the measure of persistent lonerization the respective percentages who were never loners for the persistently effeminate, the defeminized, and the never effeminate were 30, 26. and 44. Again, persistent lonerization only distinguishes the childhood cross-gendered and the noncross-gendered. These data fairly compellingly show that lonerization does not seem to play a role parallel to that of actorization. An alternative formulation that the never effeminate tend to be neither childhood loners nor actors while the defeminized were loners but not actors and the persistently effeminate were both loners and actors also receives only very modest support. Fifty percent of the persistently effeminate were childhood actors as compared with 43 percent of the defeminized and 26 percent of the never effeminate. Hence, lonerization and actorization do not seem to have a cumulative effect in creating persistent effeminacy and, it will be recalled from Chapter 4 that among the persistently effeminate it was found that they were negatively associated. It thus seems that the principal factor distinguishing the defeminized from the persistently effeminate during childhood was the extent of their cross-gendering (cf. Table 3.4). Among the defeminized, 28 percent were highly, as opposed to moderately. cross-gendered during childhood as compared with 44 percent among the persistently effeminate. Childhood lonerization and actorization seem to only modestly add to degree of childhood cross-gendering in influencing adult gender-role outcome and degree of social conformity.

It was found above that the defeminized appear to have been socially conformist in a variety of ways before adulthood. They were better high school students, were involved in fewer gangfights, and were guiltier than our other gay groups. The data do not permit one to speak directly to the origins of their greater conformity. While our item measuring guilt over their incipiently perceived homosexuality seems to measure their feelings during adolescence, their guilt may have arisen during childhood. They may have felt guilty over their childhood cross-gendering and that guilt may have served as the basis of efforts to defeminize. Subsequent guilt over their perceived homosexuality may have simply been an extension of their earlier guilt and been one of their conformist manifestations of that guilt.

Since age has some modest associations with defeminization status, being a good high school student, and youthful loner (cf. Table 6.1), an examination of the associations of being a good student with youthful loner and defeminization status while controlling for age is in order. Table 5.20 shows that good student retains a sizable association with youthful loner with both age and defeminization status controlled. However, the association of good student with defeminization status vanishes when both age and youthful loner are controlled. An examination of the first-order partials (not presented) shows that the control for youthful loner has the greater effect in reducing the good student/defeminization status association, although the control for age also appears to have some effect.

Table 5.20 also reveals a significant third-order interaction. It should be noted that highest order interactions are less reliable than lower order interactions because they depend on the frequencies in each and every cell of a multi-way table, rather than resulting from averaging across cells. Hence, they are most subject to sampling errors. However, because similar interactions among these variables appear in subsequent tables, the following limited interpretation of this interaction is attempted. It seems that youthful loner is most strongly related to being a good student among the childhood cross-gendered while among the never effeminate its effects are more mixed. Since youthful loner has its largest positive effects on good student among the persistently effeminate, and since the persistently effeminate were the poorest students among the three defeminization status groups, it seems that being a youthful loner most helps those most in need of help.

The above data have shown several reasons why a large percentage of gay youths may be more motivated to be better students during high school than heterosexual youths. Gays are more likely to be loners than are heterosexual males as found in our data and in those reported by Whitam (1977). Being a loner has a sizable association with being a better student among both heterosexuals and homosexuals. Also, adolescent interest in persons of the opposite sex seems negatively related to being a good student, although this relationship may, in part, be simply another manifestation of degree of lonerization. Another factor which seems to motivate a segment of gay youths to be better students is their guilt over their perceived homosexuality. However, the association between guilt and being a good student was found to hold only among the non-loners. This implies that the loners are better students due to lonerization while the non-loners are better students if they are guilty. Hence, there exist reasons for believing that a fairly large percentage of gay youths

TABLE 5.20

LIKELIHOOD RATIO ANALYSIS OF BEING GOOD STUDENT BY
YOUTHFUL LONER BY DEFEMINIZATION STATUS BY AGE

		Partial Associations			Marginal (0-Order) Associations	
Effect	df	LR Chi-squared	p		LR Chi-squared	p
SY.DA	1	26.91	.001		25.43	.001
SD.YA	2	5.02	.081		8.31	.016
SA.DY	2	9.35	.009		7.52	.023
YD.A	2	36.19	.001		36.45	.001
YA.D	2	16.91	.001		17.17	.001
DA.Y	4	25.21	.001		25.46	.001
SYD.A	2	3.82	.148			
SYA.D	2	0.94	.624			
SDA.Y	4	0.76	.944			
YDA	4	1.08	.897			
SYDA	4	10.17	.038			

Age (A)	Defeminization Status (D)	Youthful Loner (Y)	Percent Good Students (S)	N(100%)
-29	Persistently	Low	29	77
	Effeminate	High	53	138
	Defeminized	Low	44	80
		High	54	217
	Never Effeminate	Low	41	66
		High	49	81
30-39	Persistently	Low	33	46
	Effeminate	High	48	68
	Defeminized	Low	41	78
		High	61	150
	Never Effeminate	Low	51	69
		High	47	69
40+	Persistently	Low	38	24
	Effeminate	High	68	28
	Defeminized	Low	57	60
		High	62	91
	Never Effeminate	Low	42	52
		High	79	29

Source: Compiled by the author.

find an academic and conformist solution to their problems of alienation from adolescent culture appealing.

While a benign conformist solution arising out of guilt over one's homosexuality is something which cannot readily be shared by heterosexuals, it should be noted that such a solution may be adopted by heterosexual youths who have other problems (Gagnon 1979). Hunt (1980) has recently argued that insecurities about their genders felt by boys during childhood give rise to compensatory behaviors to compete and achieve. These behaviors help to explain the high levels of achievement motivation and competitiveness among heterosexual men. Somewhat similar processes may be operative among the Chicago respondents. The defeminized appear to be attempting to overcome their earlier perceived gender deficiencies and to transform themselves from ugly ducklings into beautiful, but still gay, swans.

6

GAYS AND
CRIMINALITY

In the present chapter self-reported measures of criminality are analyzed among both the gay and non-gay respondents. Since age is negatively related to the measures of criminality and is also related to some of the predictors of criminality age is often introduced as a control variable (cf. Table 6.1). Since being a college student versus being a college-age non-student seems modestly negatively related to criminality, comparisons of gays with non-gays are limited to the student groups. Two scales of self-reported criminality are employed. Respondents were asked "How often, if ever, have you engaged in any of the following activities?" A list of criminal behaviors was then provided with the response categories being "Never," "Once or Twice," "Several Times," and "Many Times." The property offenses scale was summed across the items "Forged or Passed Bad Checks," "Stolen a Car," "Shoplifted from a Store," "Stolen Anything From a Person (Face-to-Face)," "Purposely Damaged or Destroyed Other's Private or Public Property," and "Been Armed with or Used a Weapon of Any Kind While Committing a Theft or Robbery." Among the Chicago respondents the property offenses scale has a standardized alpha-reliability of 0.60 while among the heterosexual males reliability is a more modest 0.44. The violent offenses scale consists of the two items "As a teenager did you ever take part in gang fights," and ever "Engaged in Fist Fights." The standardized alpha-reliabilities of this scale are 0.64 among the Chicago respondents and 0.58 among the heterosexual respondents. In the present chapter correlates of criminality among the Chicago respondents are first explored and then gay/non-gay differences in criminality are examined in the light of the analyses among the Chicago respondents.

TABLE 6.1

CRIME-RELATED VARIABLES BY AGE

	-24	25-29	30-34	Age 35-39	40-44	45-54	55-
Percent High on Property Crimes	69	68	58	52	53	33	30
N(100%)	304	419	316	196	111	142	53
	X^2 = 88.95			df = 6		p < .001	
Percent High on Violent Crimes	50	47	48	41	54	47	32
N(100%)	308	419	318	196	110	141	54
	X^2 = 11.41			df = 6		p = .08	
Percent Ever Youthful Loners	64	66	60	57	56	51	52
N(100%)	304	415	318	195	108	142	54
	X^2 = 15.60			df = 6		p < .05	
Percent Good Students	43	49	51	46	62	52	65
N(100%)	297	409	310	191	108	141	52
	X^2 = 18.78			df = 6		p < .01	
Percent Interested in Sports During High School	36	30	34	30	39	34	23
N(100%)	301	412	311	195	109	139	53
	X^2 = 9.08			df = 6		p = ns	
Percent with Pre-Coming Out Guilt	45	51	46	49	49	49	35
N(100%)	309	419	316	196	111	143	52
	X^2 = 7.16			df = 6		p = ns	
Percent High on Psychological Femininity	52	43	44	44	46	46	55
N(100%)	301	416	315	192	110	142	53
	X^2 = 8.81			df = 6		p = ns	

Source: Compiled by the author.

CORRELATES OF CRIMINALITY AMONG GAY MEN

There are a number of reasons why one might expect many gays to be fairly low in criminality. (1) Since many gays tend to be loners and since much crime engaged in by youths is group based (Erickson 1971), one might expect gays to be lower in those forms of criminality which are group-based, e.g., fighting behaviors. (2) To the extent that many gays may adopt the benigh academic solution to their adolescent alienation problems, one might expect them to be lower on criminality since, as several authors have shown (Hirschi 1969; Polk 1969), being a good student during high school is negatively related with juvenile delinquency. (3) To the extent that gays may be somewhat higher on psychological femininity one might expect them to be less criminal since sex is the major predictor of criminality in general and of violent criminality in particular (Simon 1975). (4) To the extent that many gays felt guilty over their incipient homosexuality that guilt may inhibit the expression of anti-social behaviors.

Table 6.2 presents the association of youthful loner with property offenses by defeminization status and age. While youthful loner has no significant zero-order association with property offenses, there is a significant interaction of youthful loner with defeminization status. Being a youthful loner is negatively associated with property offenses among those who were cross-gendered as children but it is positively associated with offenses among those who were not cross-gendered. It seems that youthful loner has a less benign significance among the never effeminate. The suggested interpretation of this is that being a loner among the never effeminate may be indicative of somewhat anti-social motives since the never effeminate appear rather lacking in reasons to be loners. They were not loners due to peer rejection of their effeminacy since they were not effeminate. Also, since they were found to be relatively more interested in adolescent cultural activities such as sports, they also seem lacking in cultural alienation reasons to be loners. The lesser benignity of the youthful loner measure among the never effeminate was hinted at in the data of Table 5.20 where youthful loner seemed to have a less positive effect on being a good student among the never effeminate than among other groups, although the cell for the oldest never effeminate group seemed somewhat out of line. The data of Table 6.2 also show that defeminization status is significantly related to property offenses with the persistently effeminate being the most thieving and the other two groups being approximately equal, although lonerization specifies whether the defeminized or the never effeminate are high on property offenses. Turning to the case of violent offenses, Table 6.3 shows that only youthful loner is related to violent offenses with the youthful loners having engaged in significantly less fighting behaviors. Apparently being a loner reduces both fighting and thieving.

TABLE 6.2

LIKELIHOOD RATIO ANALYSIS OF PROPERTY OFFENSES BY YOUTHFUL LONER
BY DEFEMINIZATION STATUS BY AGE

		Partial Associations		Marginal (0-Order0) Associations	
Effect	df	LR Chi-squared	p	LR Chi-squared	p
PY.MA	1	0.00	.984	1.28	.270
PM.YA	2	31.75	.001	42.56	.001
PA.YM	2	57.98	.001	69.30	.001
YM.A	2	35.89	.001	36.32	.001
YA.M	2	15.26	.001	15.81	.001
MA.Y	4	26.86	.001	27.59	.001
PYM.A	2	15.82	.001		
PYA.M	2	1.45	.485		
PMA.Y	4	3.77	.438		
YMA	4	1.73	.785		
PYMA	4	3.08	.544		

Age (A)	Defeminization Status (M)	Youthful Loner (Y)	Percent High on Property Offenses (P)	N(100%)
-30	Persistently Effeminate	Low	78	79
		High	73	141
	Defeminized	Low	74	83
		High	63	222
	Never Effeminate	Low	54	68
		High	70	83
30-39	Persistently Effeminate	Low	84	45
		High	64	70
	Defeminized	Low	54	80
		High	52	151
	Never Effeminate	Low	40	70
		High	56	70
40+	Persistently Effeminate	Low	54	24
		High	54	28
	Defeminized	Low	42	59
		High	43	94
	Never Effeminate	Low	18	54
		High	37	30

Source: Compiled by the author.

TABLE 6.3

LIKELIHOOD RATIO ANALYSIS OF VIOLENT OFFENSES BY YOUTHFUL LONER
BY DEFEMINIZATION STATUS BY AGE

		Partial Associations		Marginal (O-Order) Associations	
Effect	df	LR Chi-squared	p	LR Chi-squared	p
VY.MA	1	11.24	.001	11.90	.001
VM.YA	2	0.70	.706	1.71	.426
VA.YM	2	0.98	.614	0.72	.699
YM.A	2	36.86	.001	37.18	.001
YA.M	2	14.89	.001	15.20	.001
AM.Y	4	26.04	.001	26.35	.001
VYM.A	2	1.01	.603		
VYA.M	2	0.59	.744		
VMA.Y	4	2.08	.720		
YMA	4	1.38	.847		
VYMA	4	4.90	.300		

Age (A)	Defeminization Status (M)	Youthful Loner (Y)	Percent High on Violent Offenses (V)	N(100%)
-29	Persistently Effeminate	Low	52	80
		High	47	142
	Defeminized	Low	58	83
		High	43	223
	Never Effeminate	Low	54	69
		High	39	83
30-39	Persistently Effeminate	Low	59	46
		High	37	70
	Defeminized	Low	41	80
		High	43	152
	Never Effeminate	Low	53	70
		High	44	70
40+	Persistently Effeminate	Low	52	25
		High	43	28
	Defeminized	Low	45	58
		High	43	94
	Never Effeminate	Low	58	53
		High	43	30

Source: Compiled by the author.

Turning to the hypothesis that those who became good students would have engaged in fewer criminal behaviors, Table 6.4 presents property offenses by having been a good student by youthful loner by defeminization status by age. In this table it was necessary to proceed with a five-variable analysis in order to separate the effects of good student, youthful loner, and age. However, since a five-variable analysis strains the sample size a partial solution was reached by excluding those respondents 40 years of age and older. When retained in the analysis, this age group provides a number of quite small cell frequencies.

Table 6.4 shows that good student is significantly related to lower levels of property offenses at the zero-order and partial

TABLE 6.4

LIKELIHOOD RATIO ANALYSIS OF PROPERTY OFFENSES BY GOOD STUDENT BY
YOUTHFUL LONER BY DEFEMINIZATION STATUS BY AGE[a]

		Partial Associations		Marginal (0-Order) Associations	
Effect	df	LR Chi-squared	p	LR Chi-squared	p
PS.AYM	1	5.28	.002	6.56	.010
PY.SAM	1	0.03	.868	0.00	.959
PM.YAS	1	19.23	.001	23.17	.001
PA.SYM	1	12.37	.001	15.69	.001
SY.AM	1	18.12	.001	19.24	.001
SM.AY	2	4.18	.124	5.93	.052
SA.YM	1	0.63	.428	0.41	.522
YM.A	2	22.84	.001	23.35	.001
YA.M	1	4.58	.032	5.09	.024
MA.Y	2	11.09	.004	11.60	.003
PSY.MA	1	0.45	.504		
PSM.YA	2	0.15	.929		
PSA.YM	1	1.52	.218		
PYM.AS	2	13.33	.001		
PYA.SM	1	0.04	.844		
PMA.SY	2	2.18	.336		
SYM.A	2	4.67	.097		
SYA.M	1	0.09	.761		
SMA.Y	2	0.51	.776		
YMA	2	0.31	.855		
PSYM.A	2	0.11	.946		
PSYA.M	1	1.70	.193		
PSMA.Y	2	1.34	.511		
PYMA.S	2	3.08	.215		
SYMA	2	2.57	.276		
PSYMA	2	1.38	.501		

TABLE 6.4 (continued)

Age (A)	Defeminization Status (M)	Youthful Loner (L)	Good Student (S)	Percent High on Property Offenses (V)	N(100%)
-29	Persistently Effeminate	Low	No	80	54
			Yes	73	22
		High	No	81	64
			Yes	64	73
	Defeminized	Low	No	71	45
			Yes	77	35
		High	No	69	100
			Yes	58	116
	Never Effeminate	Low	No	56	39
			Yes	50	26
		High	No	76	41
			Yes	65	40
30-39	Persistently Effeminate	Low	No	83	30
			Yes	87	15
		High	No	63	35
			Yes	67	33
	Defeminized	Low	No	61	46
			Yes	47	32
		High	No	51	59
			Yes	52	90
	Never Effeminate	Low	No	38	34
			Yes	41	34
		High	No	60	35
			Yes	55	31

[a]Table excludes those over 39 years of age.

Source: Compiled by the author.

levels. We note that the modest association of youthful loner
with age appears to be partially an artifact of the data-gathering
methods employed. Disproportionate numbers of the older
respondents were acquired from the organization for gay men over
40 and old joiners seem less likely to have been loners. The
negative association of age with property offenses present in
Table 6.4 appears to be a generational effect. Tittle (1980, pp.
93-95) has recently shown a negative association between age and
self-reported criminality. He also found that his older
respondents reported knowing fewer people when they were growing
up who got into trouble with the law. As one might expect, he
found the greatest age variation for the offense of marijuana
smoking. The present data also show that marijuana use is among
those criminality items with the strongest associations with age
(data not presented), although there is not much variability in
this item since 89 percent of the Chicago respondents have used
marijuana at least once.

To provide further support for a generational interpretation
of the association of criminality and age, Table 6.5 presents
usage of "other illegal drugs" than marijuana by age and youthful
loner. Table 6.5 shows that drug usage is very strongly
negatively related to age. However, age also specifies the
relationship of drug use and youthful loner. Among the youngest
age group youthful loner is negatively related to drug use while
among the oldest age group it is positively related to drug use.
It thus seems that the significance of being a loner is influenced
by the historical context. Among the youngest age group being a
loner reduces the likelihood that one will acquire the vices of
one's peers. However, among the oldest age group being a loner
seems to make it more likely that one may invent one's own vices.

TABLE 6.5

LIKELIHOOD RATIO ANALYSIS OF ILLEGAL DRUG USE (NON-MARIJUANA)
BY YOUTHFUL LONER BY AGE

Partial (1st Order) Associations				Marginal (0-Order) Associations	
Effect	df	LR Chi-squared	p	LR Chi-squared	p
DL	2	4.12	.128	2.65	.266
DA	2	152.61	.001	151.14	.001
LA	4	8.88	.064	7.41	.116
DLA	4	10.57	.035		

Age (A)	Youthful Loner (L)	Drug Use (D) (Percent)		
		Never	Ever	N(100%)
-24	Low	21	79	104
	Med	32	68	75
	High	37	63	125
	gamma = -0.26			
25-44	Low	43	57	369
	Med	36	64	258
	High	44	56	407
	gamma = -0.01			
45-	Low	88	12	84
	Med	81	19	52
	High	78	22	59
	gamma = +0.25			

Source: Compiled by the author.

Table 6.6 shows that being a good student is also negatively related to violent offenses independently of youthful loner. Since youthful loner appears to have both a direct negative link with violent offenses and an indirect one through good student, it seems to be a rather benign variable leading many gays both into being better students and away from criminality.

Turning to the hypothesis that psychological femininity might be negatively related to criminality, Table 6.7 shows this to be the case. It should be noted that, since the data do not include a measure of psychological femininity for the respondent's adolescence, present femininity is employed. However, the magnitude of the relationship is not impressive. It should be noted that it is psychological femininity, rather than cultural (role) femininity which is negatively related to property offenses. Cultural femininity, as represented by the persistently effeminate, is positively related to property offenses. Psychological femininity proved to have no significant relationship with the violent offenses measure (data not presented). The hypothesis was entertained that, since the actorized have previously been shown to be rather aggressive individuals, femininity and actorization might suppress each other's effects on criminality. Both violent offenses and property offenses were analyzed by femininity by actorization by defeminization status (data not presented). Femininity still showed no relationship with violent offenses while actorization revealed a modest positive association with violent behaviors. For property offenses, the negative relationship of femininity with offenses strengthened while that of actorization with property offenses proved to be moderately positive. However, it should be noted that the effects of both femininity and actorization on property offenses fluctuated wildly across subgroups with there being a significant, and uninterpretable, third-order interaction. Taking up the hypothesis that adolescent guilt over one's homosexuality might inhibit criminality, guilt proved to have no significant associations with either property or violent offenses (data not presented).

TABLE 6.6

LIKELIHOOD RATIO ANALYSIS OF VIOLENT OFFENSES BY GOOD STUDENT BY YOUTHFUL LONER BY DEFEMINIZATION STATUS BY AGE[a]

| Effect | df | Partial Associations | | Marginal (0-Order) Associations | |
		LR Chi-squared	p	LR Chi-squared	p
VS.YMA	1	4.28	.039	6.32	.012
VY.SMA	1	7.85	.005	9.82	.002
VM.SYA	2	0.43	.807	1.34	.511
VA.SYM	1	0.65	.419	0.47	.493
SY.MA	1	18.44	.001	19.66	.001
SM.YA	2	4.83	.089	6.69	.035

TABLE 6.6 (continued)

SA.YM	1	0.60	.440	0.41		.523
YM.A	2	23.87	.001	24.31		.001
YA.M	1	4.57	.032	5.02		.025
MA.Y	2	11.05	.004	11.49		.003
VSY.MA	1	0.38	.539			
VSM.YA	2	2.31	.315			
VSA.YM	1	0.08	.779			
VYM.SA	2	0.42	.812			
VYA.SM	1	0.56	.456			
VMA.SY	2	1.56	.457			
SYM.A	2	5.17	.076			
SYA.M	1	0.05	.817			
SMA.Y	2	0.47	.789			
YMA	2	0.28	.871			
VSYM.A	2	0.15	.929			
VSYA.M	1	0.00	.951			
VSMA.Y	2	2.79	.248			
VYMA.S	2	3.06	.221			
SYMA	2	2.39	.302			
VSYMA	2	4.36	.113			

Age (A)	Defeminization Status (M)	Youthful Loner (Y)	Good Student (S)	Percent High on Violent Offenses (V)	N(100%)
-29	Persistently Effeminate	Low	Low	51	55
			High	59	22
		High	Low	51	65
			High	44	73
	Defeminized	Low	Low	62	45
			High	51	35
		High	Low	44	100
			High	42	117
	Never Effeminate	Low	Low	64	39
			High	41	27
		High	Low	42	41
			High	38	40
30-39	Persistently Effeminate	Low	Low	71	31
			High	33	15
	High	Low	43	35
			High	33	33
	Defeminized	Low	Low	41	46
			High	41	32
		High	Low	41	59
			High	44	91
	Never Effeminate	Low	Low	59	34
			High	50	34
		High	Low	54	35
			High	36	31

[a]Table excludes those over 39 years of age.

Source: Compiled by the author.

TABLE 6.7

LIKELIHOOD RATIO ANALYSIS OF PROPERTY OFFENSES BY PSYCHOLOGICAL
FEMININITY BY YOUTHFUL LONER BY DEFEMINIZATION STATUS

		Partial Associations		Marginal (0-Order) Associations	
Effect	df	LR Chi-squared	p	LR Chi-squared	p
PF.MY	1	6.26	.012	4.42	.036
PY.MF	1	0.18	.669	0.78	.379
PM.FY	2	42.02	.001	40.54	.001
FY.M	1	3.39	.065	2.01	.156
FM.Y	2	9.76	.008	8.38	.015
YM.F	2	39.13	.001	37.74	.001
PFY.M	1	1.95	.162		
PFM.Y	2	3.26	.196		
PYM.F	2	15.75	.001		
FYM	2	0.33	.846		
PFYM	2	0.14	.931		

Defeminization Status (M)	Youthful Loner (Y)	Femininity (F)	Percent High on Property Offenses (P)	N(100%)
Persistently Effeminate	Low	Low	77	69
		High	76	79
	High	Low	73	124
		High	62	111
Defeminized	Low	Low	58	105
		High	59	113
	High	Low	57	253
		High	52	214
Never Effeminate	Low	Low	44	112
		High	35	78
	High	Low	66	111
		High	49	70

Source: Compiled by the author.

The additional hypothesis was tested that an adolescent interest in sports might be facilitative of violent behaviors. The rationale for this hypothesis was that an interest in sports may be conceptualized as an interest in gross or violent bodily movement. Table 6.8 presents violent offenses by adolescent interest in sports by youthful loner by defeminization status. Since the variables of this table are not readily causally orderable, the table simply presents the zero-order associations and the highest-order partials. These data show a fairly strong positive association between interest in sports and violent offenses. Those interested in the socially acceptable form of violence institutionalized in sports are also much more inclined to engage in the anti-social form of violence exemplified in fights. The hypothesis was entertained that the association between sports interest and violent offenses might be explainable by such variables as competitiveness, or dominance or masculinity. Perhaps both sports interests and fighting are alternative expressions of dominance or competitiveness? Table 6.9 tests this possibility by showing violent offenses by adolescent interest in sports by competitiveness by dominance by psychological masculinity. While all of the zero-order associations in this table are positive and significant, the data show that the association between sports interest and violent offenses is only modestly reduced in strength by the controlling for the other three variables. Because sports interest retains a sizable association with violent offenses after the "masculine virtues" have been controlled, those two measures may not be conceptually assimilated to the masculine virtues. Rather, they seem to be indicative of a general propensity to violence in social and anti-social forms.

While masculinity has a significant positive association with violent offenses at the zero-order level that association vanishes when the other variables are controlled. Lower-order partial associations were explored and it was found that the controls for dominance and competitiveness reduce the masculinity/violent offenses relationship to non-significance. The implications of these data are far-reaching. They bear on the "masculinity hypothesis" which has been explored in the criminology literature in recent years. This hypothesis states that since sex is the principal correlate of criminality, and particularly of violent criminality, it is probably masculinity which gives rise to the observed sex differences in criminality. Several authors (Gold and Mann 1972; Norland et al. 1978; Norland and Loy 1981; Cullen et al. 1979) have tested this hypothesis with varying measures of masculinity. The findings on the hypothesis have been somewhat mixed, although they do seem to provide some modest positive support. The data of Table 6.9 suggest a modification of the masculinity hypothesis. It seems that what may predispose males toward violent behaviors more than females is competitiveness

TABLE 6.8

LIKELIHOOD RATIO ANALYSIS OF VIOLENT OFFENSES BY ADOLESCENT
INTEREST IN SPORTS BY YOUTHFUL LONER BY DEFEMINIZATION STATUS

		Partial Associations		Marginal (0-Order) Associations	
Effect	df	LR Chi-squared	p	LR Chi-squared	p
VS.YM	1	45.69	.001	52.00	.001
VY.SM	1	4.54	.033	11.48	.001
VM.SY	2	1.76	.416	2.29	.318
SY.M	1	35.85	.001	49.23	.001
SM.Y	2	54.47	.001	67.85	.001
YM.S	2	24.32	.001	37.77	.001
VSY.M	1	2.59	.107		
VSM.Y	2	0.62	.733		
VYM.S	2	1.37	.505		
SYM	2	2.28	.320		
VSYM	2	0.05	.973		

Defeminization Status (M)	Youthful Loner (Y)	Interest in Sports (S)	Percent High on Violent Offenses (V)	N(100%)
Persistently Effeminate	Low	Low	51	100
		High	62	50
	High	Low	38	185
		High	61	49
Defeminized	Low	Low	43	141
		High	57	76
	High	Low	37	355
		High	60	109
Never Effeminate	Low	Low	44	71
		High	62	117
	High	Low	32	110
		High	59	68

Source: Compiled by the author.

rather than masculinity. Also, interest in sports, conceptualized as a propensity toward violence, may also give rise to the observed sex difference in violent criminality.

Another problem with the masculinity hypothesis is that the currently widely used masculinity scales of Bem (1974) and of Spence and Helmreich (1978) prevent a real testing of that hypothesis since it seems likely that, in fact, they do not measure masculinity. Psychological masculinity has been found to be the best predictor of self-esteem among heterosexual males, heterosexual females, homosexual males and homosexual females (Spence and Helmreich 1978, pp. 50, 66). What justification, then, is there for calling it masculinity? The principal justification for labelling that measure masculinity is the sex difference usually found on the measure. However, that difference may reflect the very strong associations of masculinity with dominance and competitiveness (cf. Table 6.9). If these two measures were controlled, the sex difference on masculinity would certainly weaken and possibly vanish. It may be that the term masculinity is a misnomer and that the variable should be called something more gender-neutral such as "personal efficacy."

Table 6.9 also shows a significant highest-order interaction. While interactions of that order are normally interpretable, a ready interpretation is available. There are four groups in Table 6.9 in which sports interest gives rise to percentage differences of less than 15 percent. These four groups are all ones in which the respondent is low on at least two of the three variables of masculinity, competitiveness, and dominance. Conceptualizing the latter three variables as alternative sources of motivation for translating or generalizing an interest in prosocial violence into anti-social violence, it appears that the respondents must score high on at least two of these three variables for that translation to occur to a substantial degree. Accordingly, sports interest is associated with large percentage differences in violent behaviors only among those groups of Table 6.9 in which the respondents are high on at least two of the three motivational measures. In essence, the interpretation offered assimilates the three variables of masculinity, dominance, and competitiveness to the concept of "motivation" and then interprets the five-variable interaction as one involving only three variables.

TABLE 6.9

LIKELIHOOD RATIO ANALYSIS OF VIOLENT OFFENSES BY ADOLESCENT
INTEREST IN SPORTS BY COMPETITIVENESS BY DOMINANCE BY MASCULINITY

		Partial Associations		Marginal (0-Order) Associations	
Effect	df	LR Chi-squared	p	LR Chi-squared	p
VS.CDM	1	38.30	.001	49.68	.001
VC.SDM	1	9.50	.002	23.90	.001
VD.SCM	1	2.61	.106	10.54	.001
VM.SCD	1	0.26	.610	11.29	.001
SC.MDV	1	14.78	.001	37.34	.001
SD.MVC	1	2.54	.111	5.82	.016
SM.DVC	1	37.00	.001	57.21	.001
CD.MVS	1	52.23	.001	113.25	.001
CM.VDS	1	40.81	.001	114.33	.001
DM.VSC	1	158.98	.001	218.84	.001
VSC.DM	1	0.79	.375		
VSD.CM	1	0.93	.335		
VSM.CD	1	0.51	.474		
VCD.MS	1	0.25	.616		
VCM.SD	1	1.43	.231		
VDM.CS	1	0.46	.498		
SCD.MV	1	0.52	.472		
SCM.DV	1	0.01	.930		
SDM.VC	1	0.22	.638		
CDM.VS	1	0.04	.838		
VSCD.M	1	0.24	.624		
VSCM.D	1	0.00	.963		
VSDM.C	1	0.16	.685		
VCDM.S	1	0.07	.790		
SCDM.V	1	0.15	.670		
VSCDM	1	3.94	.047		

TABLE 6.9 (continued)

Masculinity (M)	Dominance (D)	Competitiveness (C)	Adolescent Sports Interest (S)	Percent High on Violent Offenses (V)	Percent Age Difference	N(100%)
Low	Low	Low	Low	34		312
			High	46	(12)	81
		High	Low	48		93
			High	54	(6)	46
	High	Low	Low	41		112
			High	48	(7)	29
		High	Low	46		89
			High	77	(31)	35
High	Low	Low	Low	41		61
			High	50	(9)	38
		High	Low	40		42
			High	68	(28)	47
	High	Low	Low	41		106
			High	64	(23)	55
		High	Low	44		173
			High	67	(23)	174

Source: Compiled by the author.

Table 6.10 also presents problems for the masculinity hypothesis. It shows that masculinity is _negatively_ related to property offenses. Masculinity, or rather, personal efficacy, seems a more pro-social variable than it has been depicted, once it is pruned of its correlates of competitiveness and dominance. However, it still has a strong association with the more anti-social variable of adolescent sports interest. Although Table 6.10 shows a significant interaction involving property offenses, sports interest, dominance and masculinity that interaction seems uninterpretable and its interpretation is left to those who like to play with Rubik's cubes.

TABLE 6.10

LIKELIHOOD RATIO ANALYSIS OF PROPERTY OFFENSES BY
ADOLESCENT SPORTS INTEREST BY COMPETITIVENESS
BY DOMINANCE BY MASCULINITY

		Partial (1st Order) Associations		Marginal (0-Order) Associations	
Effect	df	LR Chi-squared	p	LR Chi-squared	p
PS.CDM	1	1.55	.214	3.68	.055
PC.SDM	1	0.12	.734	0.37	.544
PD.SCM	1	1.10	.293	0.11	.744
PM.SCD	1	12.47	.001	13.35	.001
SC.DMP	1	19.60	.001	37.50	.001
SD.CMP	1	1.59	.207	6.16	.013
SM.DCP	1	37.65	.001	57.98	.001
CD.MSP	1	54.80	.001	113.36	.001
CM.DSP	1	41.10	.001	113.46	.001
DM.SPC	1	159.83	.001	217.62	.001
PSC.MP	1	0.57	.452		
PSD.MC	1	0.49	.483		
PSM.DC	1	0.00	.973		
PCD.MS	1	1.27	.260		
PCM.DS	1	0.48	.488		
PDM.CS	1	1.00	.318		
SCD.MP	1	0.42	.514		
SCM.PD	1	0.00	.966		
SDM.PC	1	0.11	.736		
CDM.PS	1	0.23	.633		
PSCD.M	1	0.66	.416		
PSCM.D	1	0.08	.783		
PSDM.C	1	4.14	.042		
PCDM.S	1	0.50	.477		
SCDM.P	1	0.04	.843		
PSCDM	1	1.43	.232		

TABLE 6.10 (continued)

Masculinity (M)	Dominance (D)	Competi- tiveness (C)	Adolescent Sports Interests (S)	Percent High on Property Offenses (P)	N(100%)
Low	Low	Low	Low	63	311
			High	56	82
		High	Low	70	93
			High	56	46
	High	Low	Low	60	111
			High	69	29
		High	Low	64	89
			High	71	35
High	Low	Low	Low	48	61
			High	45	38
		High	Low	48	42
			High	57	47
	High	Low	Low	59	105
			High	62	55
		High	Low	58	170
			High	48	145

Source: Compiled by the author.

The above data have shown that several variables may be operating to reduce the levels of criminality among youthful gays. Their massive disinterest in sports seems to impel them away from violent behaviors. Comparing gay and non-gay students, 27 percent of the gays were interested in sports during adolescence as compared with 80 percent of the non-gays. Potentially, their sports disinterest may render them less violent than comparable non-gays. Their propensity to have been loners also seems to steer them away from violent behaviors. Also, their tendency to have been better students seems to reduce their levels of both violent and property offenses. With these hypotheses in mind we now proceed to comparisons between the gay and non-gay students.

GAYS VERSUS NON-GAYS ON CRIMINALITY

Having analyzed the principal correlates of criminality among the Chicago respondents, we now proceed to comparisons on criminality among the gay and non-gay students. Table 6.11 compares these two groups on property offenses with youthful loner included in the analysis. Between-group differences in youthful loner appear to explain away the finding that the non-gays are slightly high on property offenses than the gays. However, the association of youthful loner with criminality seems rather erratic since there is a nearly significant interaction among the three variables of Table 6.11. Hence, the model involving three zero-order relationships among these three variables is not a very good fit to the data. In order to tidy up this state of affairs it was recalled that in preceding analyses there was observed a sizable interaction among youthful loner, property offenses, and defeminization status. Youthful loner was found to be negatively related to property offenses among those cross-gendered as children while being somewhat positively related to property offenses among the approximate quarter of the Chicago respondents who were never effeminate. In the light of this finding, Table 6.11 was rerun excluding those gays who were never effeminate. Never effeminate non-gays were not excluded because the measures of cross-gendering applied to the non-gays seem meaningless and to

TABLE 6.11

LIKELIHOOD RATIO ANALYSIS OF PROPERTY OFFENSES BY YOUTHFUL
LONER BY SAMPLE GROUP

Partial (1st Order) Associations				Marginal (0-Order) Associations	
Effect	df	LR Chi-squared	p	LR Chi-squared	p
PY	1	7.43	.006	10.91	.001
PG	1	1.57	.210	5.05	.025
YG	1	32.55	.001	36.03	.001
PYG	1	2.82	.093		

Sample Group (G)	Youthful Loner (Y)	Percent High on Property Offenses (P)	N(100%)
Gay Students	Low	69	89
	High	65	32
Non-Gay Students	Low	85	79
	High	66	122

Source: Completed by the author.

do so would have excluded most of the non-gays from the analysis. Table 6.12 reveals that the youthful loner measure now behaves in a more civilized manner. The childhood cross-gendered gays seem definitely lower than the non-gays and that difference appears to be due to their propensity for being youthful loners. The excluded never-effeminate gays are quite similar to the non-gays in their level of property offenses. Seventy-five percent of the excluded group are high on property offenses (N=20) compared with 78 percent of the non-gays (N=201). Briefly reporting some non-findings, property offenses were found to be unrelated among the student groups to sports interest, competitiveness, dominance, femininity, and masculinity.

TABLE 6.12

LIKELIHOOD RATIO ANALYSIS OF PROPERTY OFFENSES BY YOUTHFUL
LONER BY SAMPLE GROUP EXCLUDING NEVER EFFEMINATE GAYS

Partial (1st Order) Associations				Marginal (0-Order) Associations	
Effect	df	LR Chi-squared	p	LR Chi-squared	p
PY	1	11.01	.001	15.54	.001
PG	1	1.40	.236	5.93	.015
YG	1	32.95	.001	37.48	.001
PYG	1	0.60	.440		

Sample Group (G)	Youthful Loner (Y)	Percent High on Property Offenses (P)	N(100%)
Gay Students	Low	75	77
	High	61	24
Non-Gay Students	Low	85	79
	High	66	122

Source: Compiled by the author.

Turning to violent offenses, Table 6.13 shows a quite large zero-order difference between the gay and non-gay students in fighting behaviors. At the zero-order level the non-gays are 24 percent more likely to have been involved in violent offenses. The control for adolescent sports interest does not completely eliminate this difference, although it seriously weakens the between-groups relationship. Although the non-gays who were not interested in sports during adolescence are very similar to both gay groups, those interested in sports during adolescence, constituting 80 percent of the non-gays, are very high on violent offenses. Since there is a strong suggestion of an interaction in Table 6.13 further analyses were performed to see why sports interest might be more strongly related to violent offenses among the heterosexuals than among the gays. Two earlier presented

TABLE 6.13

LIKELIHOOD RATIO ANALYSIS OF VIOLENT OFFENSES BY ADOLESCENT
SPORTS INTEREST BY SAMPLE GROUP

Partial (1st Order) Associations				Marginal (0-Order) Associations	
Effect	df	LR Chi-squared	p	LR Chi-Squared	p
VS	1	8.50	.004	21.63	.001
VG	1	4.90	.027	18.03	.001
GS	1	74.63	.001	87.76	.001
VSG	1	2.96	.085		

Sample Group (G)	Adolescent Sports Interest (S)	Percent High on Violent Offenses (V)	N(100%)
Gay Students	Low	45	87
	High	52	33
Non-Gay students	Low	49	41
	High	76	163

Source: Compiled by the author.

findings were recalled. First, it was found in Table 6.9 that sports interest and violent offenses were more strongly related among those higher on the masculine virtues. Second, Table 3.12 suggested that the non-gays might be somewhat higher on competitiveness than the several gay groups of that table. In the

light of these two findings a four-variable analysis of violent
offenses, sports interest, competitiveness, and sample group was
performed (cf. Table 6.14). While this analysis does somewhat
strain the sample sizes of the student groups, it also makes Table
6.13 more comprehensible. The finding of principal interest of
Table 6.14 is that there is a first-order interaction involving
competitiveness, violent offenses, and sports interest. Among the
competitive sports interest is more strongly related to violent
offenses than among the less competitive and among the competitive
heterosexuals this relationship becomes quite strong. Competitive
motivations seem to give meaning to sports interest and to
transform an interest in a social form of violence into anti-
social forms of violence. It seems worth noting that while only
one of the masculine virtues was required in Table 6.14 in order
to produce an interaction all three of the masculine virtues were

TABLE 6.14

LIKELIHOOD RATIO ANALYSIS OF VIOLENT OFFENSES BY ADOLESCENT
INTEREST IN SPORTS BY COMPETITIVENESS BY SAMPLE GROUP

		Partial Associations		Marginal (0-Order) Associations	
Effect	df	LR Chi-squared	p	LR Chi-squared	p
VS.CG	1	8.12	.004	23.21	.001
VC.GS	1	2.65	.104	5.99	.014
VG.CS	1	4.65	.031	18.33	.001
SC.GV	1	5.28	.022	10.56	.001
SG.CV	1	70.18	.001	85.80	.001
CG.VS	1	0.04	.847	3.90	.048
VSC.G	1	4.23	.040		
VSG.C	1	2.72	.099		
VCG.S	1	1.10	.294		
SCG.V	1	0.22	.642		
VSCG	1	0.41	.522		

Sample Group (G)	Competitiveness (C)	Sports Interest (S)	Percent High on Violent Offenses (V)	N(100%)
Gay Students	Low	Low	41	51
		High	38	13
	High	Low	47	34
		High	63	19
Non-Gay Students	Low	Low	56	23
		High	68	65
	High	Low	39	18
		High	82	98

Source: Compiled by the author.

were required in Table 6.9. This suggests that higher levels of the masculine virtues may be required among gays than among non-gays in order for sports interest to be transformed into anti-social violence.

It is worth noting that the data of Table 6.14 probably underrepresent the differences in pugnacity between gays and heterosexual males. Some of the fights that the gays became involved in may have arisen, not because they voluntarily became involved in the fight, but because they were coerced into it by heterosexual males who assaulted them due to their cross-gendering or homosexuality. While heterosexual males may also become involved in fights involuntarily, it is extremely unlikely that they would become so involved because other heterosexual males believed them to be either cross-gendered or gay. Included in the questionnaires for the Chicago respondents only was the item of whether the respondent had "ever been beaten or assaulted by straights because (he) was gay." Among the 88 Chicago students 26 percent reported having been so assaulted while 61 percent of the assaulted were high on violent offenses versus 40 percent of the never assaulted. Although a control for having been assaulted does somewhat reduce the level of pugnacity among the gay Chicago students it should be observed that the association between violent offenses and assault is not statistically significant (X^2=2.98, df=1, p=.08) due to the relatively small size of the Chicago student group.

To explore the impact of the ever assaulted measure on the associations of other variables with violent offenses Table 6.15 presents violent offenses by adolescent sports interest by ever assaulted by defeminization status among all Chicago respondents. The impact of the introduction of the ever assaulted measure is to slightly strengthen the associations of both sports interest and ever assaulted with violent offenses. Having been assaulted is positively associated with having been in fights. Having been assaulted is also associated with defeminization status with 33 percent of the persistently effeminate reporting assault versus 23 percent of the defeminized and 14 percent of the never effeminate. It thus seems that the respondents' heterosexual peers also perceived many of them as cross-gendered in the same ways that the respondents report their own cross-gendering. They then proceeded to punish them for their visible gender deviance. Hence, it seems that a non-trivial part of the fighting incidents in which gays may become involved represent involuntary involvements. Briefly reporting other correlates of violent offenses among the student groups, violent offenses was found to be slightly negatively related to psychological femininity at the zero-order level and to be positively related to dominance, competitiveness, and masculinity.

TABLE 6.15

LIKELIHOOD RATIO ANALYSIS OF VIOLENT OFFENSES BY ADOLESCENT
SPORTS INTEREST BY BEATEN BECAUSE GAY
BY DEFEMINIZATION STATUS

		Partial Associations		Marginal (0-Order) Associations	
Effect	df	LR Chi-squared	p	LR Chi-squared	p
VS.BM	1	52.55	.001	51.27	.001
VB.SM	1	14.78	.001	12.27	.001
VM.BS	2	0.50	.779	2.07	.355
SB.VM	1	2.83	.092	4.38	.036
SM.VB	2	62.40	.001	68.02	.001
BM.SV	2	34.86	.001	39.25	.001
VSB.M	1	1.68	.196		
VSM.B	2	0.49	.783		
VBM.S	2	1.40	.496		
SBM.V	2	1.03	.597		
SBVM	2	0.52	.772		

Defemini- zation Status (M)	Ever Beaten Because Gay (B)	Adolescent Sports Interest (S)	Percent High on Violent Offenses (V)	N(100%)
Persistently Effeminate	Yes	Low	48	101
		High	67	27
	No	Low	40	185
		High	59	71
Defeminized	Yes	Low	51	115
		High	60	43
	No	Low	35	384
		High	58	144
Never Effeminate	Yes	Low	56	27
		High	71	24
	No	Low	33	154
		High	59	161

Source: Compiled by the author.

The above data have shown rather large differences between gay and heterosexual students in the degree to which they are interested in violent activities. These differences may be the major differences between gay and heterosexual males. While heterosexual males appear to be interested in both social and anti-social forms of violence, gay males are interested in neither. Observations of the gay world lead the author to conclude that physical violence is extremely rare in that world and when it occurs it is typically a case of a non-gay male victimizing a gay male (Harry 1982). The pacific nature of the gay world seems to follow from the pacific nature of gay males. Given that the gay disinterest in sports seems to be established during childhood, the pacific nature of gay men may be a very deeply ingrained aspect of their natures. It is also an enduring aspect of their natures since, as reported in the preceding chapter, 50 percent of the DeKalb gay students versus 85 percent of the heterosexual students said that they found sports "fascinating." Given the pacific nature of gays, a sociobiologist might be tempted to speculate that gays are an experiment by nature in an attempt to create a human nature more compatible with the requirements of civil society.

CROSS-GENDERING AND ARRESTS: SOCIETAL REACTIONS

The relationship of cross-gendering to criminality reported above using self-reported measures of criminality is paralleled in the data on arrests. Table 6.16 shows the relationships of childhood and adult cross-gendering with responses to the item "Have you ever been picked up or charged by the police for any non-traffic reason, whether or not you were guilty?" This table shows that only adult cross-gendering is significantly related to arrest. Actually, it more likely shows that only the persistently effeminate differ from the other three categories. There are, of course, strong associations between the self-reported measures of criminality and the arrest measure (data not presented).

It would be useful to know the extent to which the more common arrests of the adult effeminates are due to their having in fact committed more illegal behaviors or the extent to which they may be due to stereotypical discrimination by the police or others. Since the effeminate fit the stereotype of homosexual men their effeminacy makes them more visible as deviant and possibly more definable as suspicious. While it would be useful to see if there is any relationship of adult cross-gendering with arrests after degree of criminality is controlled, our measures are not up to the task. Given that the effeminate seem broadly criminal and that our measure of overall criminality is not exhaustive of all offenses, it would be possible for the effeminate to have been arrested due to their having committed other offenses not included in our scale of overall offenses.

TABLE 6.16

LIKELIHOOD RATIO ANALYSIS OF EVER ARRESTED FOR NON-TRAFFIC
OFFENSE BY CHILDHOOD AND ADULT CROSS-GENDERING

Partial (1st Order) Associations				Marginal (0-Order) Associations	
Effect	df	LR Chi-squared	p	LR Chi-squared	p
EC	1	0.37	.542	2.16	.142
EA	1	11.74	.001	13.53	.001
CA	1	94.14	.001	95.92	.001
ECA	1	2.04	.154		

Adult Cross-Gendering (A)	Childhood Cross-Gendering (C)	Percent Ever Arrested (E)	N(100%)
Some	Some	40	394
	None	29	52
None	Some	29	699
	None	29	381

Source: Compiled by the author.

The data show that the adult cross-gendered are more likely
to receive a variety of negative societal reactions than are other
gay groups.   Table 6.17 shows that having ever "been beat up or
assaulted by straights because (they) were gay" is positively
associated with both childhood and adult cross-gendering.
Apparently the presence of visible gender deviance provokes the
violent propensities of non-gays discussed in the preceding
section.   Miller and Humphreys (1980) have also reported
considerable violent victimization of gays in which groups of
young heterosexual males come to gay neighborhoods to assault
those they perceive to be manifestly gay.

TABLE 6.17

LIKELIHOOD RATIO ANALYSIS OF BEATEN BY STRAIGHTS BECAUSE GAY
BY CHILDHOOD AND ADULT CROSS-GENDERING

		Partial (1st Order) Associations			Marginal (0-Order) Associations	
Effect	df	LR Chi-squared	p		LR Chi-squared	p
BC	1	20.95	.001		31.08	.001
BA	1	13.93	.001		24.06	.001
AC	1	84.30	.001		94.43	.001
BAC	1	0.01	.924			

Adult Cross-Gendering (A)	Childhood Cross-Gendering (C)	Percent Ever Beaten Because Gay (B)	N(100%)
Some	Some	34	392
	None	19	52
None	Some	24	698
	None	14	379

Source: Compiled by the author.

Table 6.18 presents responses to the question "Have you ever been evicted or refusing housing because you were gay?" by childhood and adult cross-gendering. Only adult cross-gendering is significantly related to such experiences since, presumably, not many children go seeking new housing. We also ran responses to the question "Have you ever been fired explicitly because you were gay?" by childhood and adult cross-gendering (data not presented). No significant relationships were found for this item. That no relationships were found emphasizes rather than qualifies the importance of visible conformity to stereotypes as a factor in discriminatory behaviors. It seems likely that, to the extent an employer discriminates on the basis of perceived sexual orientation he would discriminate on the basis of visible effeminacy at the time of initial hiring. Hence, if an effeminate man is initially hired he could then expect to not be fired due to effeminacy since discriminatory employers would have otherwise already weeded him out at time of hiring. Hence, effeminacy can be expected to induce a maximal discriminatory effect at time of initial contact such as in applying for jobs or housing, or in

TABLE 6.18

LIKELIHOOD RATIO ANALYSIS OF EVICTED BECAUSE GAY
BY CHILDHOOD AND ADULT CROSS-GENDERING

Partial (1st Order) Associations				Marginal (0-Order) Associations	
Effect	df	LR Chi-squared	p	LR Chi-squared	p
EC	1	0.27	.605	0.39	.532
EA	1	19.85	.001	19.97	.001
CA	1	94.52	.001	94.64	.001
ECA	1	1.30	.255		

Adult Cross-Gendering (A)	Childhood Cross-Gendering (C)	Percent Ever Evicted (E)	N(100%)
Some	Some	14	393
	None	10	52
None	Some	6	699
	None	7	379

Source: Compiled by the author.

contacts between relative strangers, or in impersonal police encounters, but not later in relationships. In general, these data show that the effeminate bear the brunt of negative societal reaction to gender deviance.

The marginal percentages of the Chicago sample who stated they had experienced a given form of victimization because they were gay are as follows: Fired, 8 percent; Beaten, 24 percent; Evicted, 8 percent; Threatened with extortion, 16 percent. Whether one considers these individual percentages large or small may depend in part on one's political perspectives. However, the percentage of the gay population who report having experienced at least one of these forms of victimization is 39. This latter statistic does not seem small since it means that a large minority of gay men have experienced some form of significant victimization due to their sexual orientation. It should also be noted that even this figure certainly understates the true prevalence of victimization even among the forms of victimization studied. Individuals may be fired or evicted because of their sexual orientations without their knowing that to be the reason. A

number of victimizers may prefer to state other reasons, or none
at all, rather than raise the awkward topic of the victim's sexual
orientation. It should also be noted that, because the question
on employment referred only to firings rather than to original
refusals of employment, the latter form of discrimination is not
included in our statistics. It seems likely that those gay men
who are either out at time of original hiring or conform to
stereotypes would be unlikely to have been hired by discriminatory
employers. Also, they would be less likely to have been fired
simply because they would be less likely to be hired. For these
reasons it sees likely that the extent of victimization of gay men
is higher than that reported above and may include a majority of
the gay population.

7

OCCUPATIONAL AND EDUCATIONAL ATTAINMENTS OF GAYS

In chapter five several variables more characteristic of gays than of non-gays were found to be positively associated with having been better students during high school. These findings lead one to hypothesize that at least some of these measures might be positively associated with higher educational and occupational attainments. The associations of these variables with educational attainments is explored in the following section.

GAYS AND EDUCATIONAL ATTAINMENTS

It was earlier found that having been a youthful loner was positively associated with being a better high school student. The possibility was explored that youthful loner might be positively associated with higher educational attainments in a four-variable analysis involving education, adolescent guilt over homosexuality, youthful loner, and defeminization status (data not presented). Youthful loner was found to have no significant association with years of education at any level. Also not found was the "disablement" interaction between youthful loner and guilt. However, youthful loner is not completely lacking in links to educational attainment since it is indirectly linked to education through good student which, as earlier reported, has a sizable association with education.

The hypothesis was tested that adolescent guilt might have a positive association with education in a four-variable analysis involving years of education, guilt, defeminization status, and age (cf. Table 7.1). Table 7.1 shows positive associations between adolescent guilt and years of education. It seems that young guilty gays may compensate for their negative feelings about their homosexuality through the acquisition of higher education.

TABLE 7.1

LIKELIHOOD RATIO ANALYSIS OF YEARS OF EDUCATION BY ADOLESCENT
GUILT OVER HOMOSEXUALITY BY DEFEMINIZATION STATUS BY AGE

		Partial Associations		Marginal (0-Order) Associations	
Effect	df	LR Chi-squared	p	LR Chi-squared	p
EG.MA	2	7.82	.020	8.48	.014
EM.GA	4	13.42	.009	19.51	.001
EA.GM	4	64.52	.001	67.87	.001
GM.A	2	12.33	.002	12.15	.002
AG.M	2	0.74	.689	0.56	.755
AM.G	4	25.55	.001	25.37	.001
EGM.A	4	1.03	.905		
EGA.M	4	3.81	.432		
EMA.G	8	6.63	.577		
GMA	4	6.30	.178		
EGMA	8	12.87	.116		

Age (A)	Defeminization Status (M)	Adolescent Guilt (G)	(Percent) Years of Education (E)			
			-12	13-16	17+	N(100%)
-29	Persistently Effeminate	Low	18	69	13	125
		High	16	65	19	97
	Defeminized	Low	18	64	18	134
		High	12	60	28	176
	Never Effeminate	Low	13	64	22	90
		High	20	53	27	64
30-39	Persistently Effeminate	Low	24	44	32	59
		High	14	48	38	56
	Defeminized	Low	14	44	43	117
		High	8	39	53	115
	Never Effeminate	Low	17	45	38	82
		High	12	60	28	58
40+	Persistently Effeminate	Low	18	47	35	34
		High	20	45	35	20
	Defeminized	Low	9	50	41	76
		High	14	40	46	76
	Never Effeminate	Low	26	46	28	43
		High	7	43	50	42

Source: Compiled by the author.

Table 7.1 also shows a somewhat stronger association between defeminization status and education with the conformist defeminized having the highest levels of education followed by the never effeminate and the persistently effeminate. Since both feeling guilty over one's homosexuality and being defeminized are characteristics which are very largely unique to gays, these data suggest that special processes are operative among gays to impel them into higher education.

The earlier Detroit data permit a replication of the association between guilt and education since the guilt item is the same for both the Chicago and Detroit studies. Table 7.2

TABLE 7.2

LIKELIHOOD RATIO ANALYSIS OF EDUCATION BY ADOLESCENT GUILT OVER HOMOSEXUALITY BY FATHER'S OCCUPATION (DETROIT DATA)

		Partial (1st Order) Associations			Marginal (0-Order) Associations	
Effect	df	LR Chi-squared	p		LR Chi-squared	p
EG	1	3.85	.049		2.29	.130
EO	1	6.47	.011		4.91	.027
GO	1	8.57	.000		7.00	.008
EGO	1	0.03	.850			

Father's Occupation (O)	Adolescent Guilt (G)	Years of Education (E) (Percent) -12	13+	N(100%)
White Collar	Low	23	77	62
	High	12	88	42
Blue Collar	Low	39	61	46
	High	26	74	65

Source: Compiled by the author.

shows education by adolescent guilt by father's occupational level. (Father's occupation is not available in the Chicago data.) At the zero-order level guilt has no association with education beyond high school while it has a positive partial association with education after father's occupation is controlled. It is clear that father's occupation suppresses the positive association of guilt with education. These data show that those gays raised in blue-collar backgrounds were guiltier than those from white-collar backgrounds. This finding is consistent with national surveys on attitudes toward homosexuality which have shown that persons who are less educated or from lower socioeconomic backgrounds disapprove more of homosexuality (Levitt and Klassen 1974). Also, Duncan and Duncan (1978, pp. 272-275) have found that the less educated, and particularly fathers, believe more in the importance of a boy "acting like a boy." Apparently the adolescent gay male who lives in such a gender-conservative environment is more troubled by negative views of his incipient homosexuality than his white-collar counterpart. It also appears that another response of his is to get out of that environment through acquiring education beyond high school.

The finding that guilty gay youths from blue-collar backgrounds are more likely to obtain higher education than the non-guilty constitutes an indirect replication of a West German study (Reichert and Dannecker 1977). That study compared gay and non-gay university students and found that the gays were from lower status backgrounds than the non-gays. The authors concluded that the blue-collar gays were "compulsively upwardly mobile." Since the concept of "compulsive upward mobility" seems somewhat prejudicial a more neutral description would be that they simply used the educational system to escape a gender-conservative environment. It should be noted that there is some inconsistency between the Chicago and Detroit findings since the guilt/education association in the Detroit data is significant only at the partial level while it is significant in the Chicago data at the zero-order level. However, since the zero-order magnitudes of this association are quite similar in the two sets of data, it seems likely that the difference in significance is due to the very different sample sizes. To establish this point the zero-order cell frequencies for the association of guilt and education in Table 7.2 were multiplied by a factor (6.81) sufficient to equalize the sample sizes of Tables 7.1 and 7.2. A Chi-squared was then computed on these hypothetical data and proved highly significant (X^2=15.98, df=1, p < .001). The Detroit findings also imply that, if it were possible to control for father's occupation in the Chicago data, the guilt/education association would probably strengthen.

It must be noted that the association between education and guilt in the Detroit data does not appear if one employs the cutting point on the education variable of 15 or less versus 16 or more years of education. When this is done it is found that the guilty among respondents from white-collar backgrounds are only 8 percentage points higher on education while among the blue-collar background respondents the guilty are only 5 percentage points higher on education. This implies that, while guilt may get gay youths into college, and particularly those from blue-collar backgrounds, it does not get them out with a degree. On this point Saghir and Robins (1973, pp. 127-128) reported that "A comparison of homosexual and heterosexual men who attended college revealed that homosexual men who started college were more likely to drop out before graduation (X^2=5.01, p < .05)." The reason for this higher dropout rate among gay men may be that, since a disproportionate number of them are from blue-collar backgrounds, they are less well prepared for college than the heterosexuals. This interpretation is not inconsistent with the earlier interpretation that many gays may have been better students during high school. In the earlier presented interpretation many gays may be more likely to go to college because they were better students whereas in the present interpretation many other gays may be more likely to go to college, not because they were better students, but because they were guilty working-class youths who wanted out of a gender-conservative blue-collar culture. These two interpretations simply represent two different reasons why many gays may be more likely to go to college.

In order to further explore the significance of adolescent guilt in the Detroit data, Table 7.3 presents age of coming out by

TABLE 7.3

LIKELIHOOD RATIO ANALYSIS OF AGE OF COMING OUT BY ADOLESCENT GUILT OVER HOMOSEXUALITY BY FATHER'S OCCUPATION (DETROIT DATA)

		Partial (1st Order) Associations		Marginal (0-Order) Associations	
Effect	df	LR Chi-squared	p	LR Chi-squared	p
GA	1	7.89	.005	5.63	.018
GO	1	9.26	.002	7.00	.008
AO	1	6.18	.013	3.92	.048
GAO	1	0.81	.368		

Father's Occupation (O)	Adolescent Guilt (G)	Age of Coming Out (A)[a] (Percent)		N(100%)
		-18 Yrs.	19 Yrs. +	
White Collar	Low	52 (32)	48 (30)	62
	High	26 (11)	74 (31)	42
Blue Collar	Low	63 (29)	37 (17)	46
	High	49 (32)	51 (33)	65

[a]Cell frequencies are in parentheses.

Source: Compiled by the author.

adolescent guilt by father's occupation. The coming out question asked "how old (they) were when (they) first came out." These data show a sizable association between feeling guilty and late coming out. Apparently the guilty delay full acceptance of their homosexuality. Table 7.3 also shows that gay youths from blue-collar backgrounds are a fair amount more likely to come out earlier than their white-collar counterparts despite the fact that they also felt guiltier than those counterparts. The significance of these data is that they help to explain the findings of Table 7.4 which presents years of education by age of coming out by

TABLE 7.4

LIKELIHOOD RATIO ANALYSIS OF EDUCATION BY AGE OF COMING OUT
BY FATHER'S OCCUPATION (DETROIT DATA)

		Partial (1st Order) Associations			Marginal (0-Order) Associations	
Effect	df	LR Chi-squared	p		LR Chi-squared	p
EA	1	8.26	.004		10.58	.001
EO	1	10.42	.001		12.75	.001
AO	1	1.62	.206		3.92	.048
EAO	1	9.27	.002			

Father's Occupation (O)	Age of Coming Out (A)	Education (E) -15 Yrs.	16 Yrs. +	N(100%)
White Collar	-18 Years	42	58	43
	19 Years +	43	57	61
Blue Collar	-18 Years	84	16	61
	19 Years +	46	54	50

Source: Compiled by the author.

father's occupation. In these data late coming out is significantly associated with obtaining a bachelor's degree or more education at the zero-order level. However, it is apparent that all of the effect of age of coming out on educational attainment is confined to those from blue-collar backgrounds. Also, the class difference in education is completely eliminated among the gays from blue-collar backgrounds who came out later. No significance should be attributed to the fact that the age of coming out/father's occupation relationship vanishes in the partial since that partial controls for the outcome variable of education.

These data suggest that adolescent guilt may have benign effects on educational attainment. Guilt is more common among gay youths from blue-collar backgrounds and such youths are more likely to come out earlier. Guilt then partially restrains their propensity to come out earlier. If guilt restrains the propensity of blue-collar gay youths to come out earlier, such delayed coming out seems to eliminate the traditionally found class differences in educational attainments. In short, guilt most helps those most in need of help. Whether all of the effects of guilt on educational attainment are indirect or direct cannot be assessed in the Chicago data since these data do not include measures of age of coming out or of father's occupation.

The finding that an early age of coming out is negatively related to educational attainment is consistent with Gagnon and Simon's (1973, pp. 146, 156) suggestions that "the removal of inhibiting doubts (about one's homosexuality) frequently releases a great deal of sexual activity" and that the effect of that activity on educational or occupational attainments can be quite negative. However, it is not at all clear why the suggested negative effect of coming out should be completely confined to the gays from blue-collar backgrounds. A possible interpretation involves the fact that the association between age of coming out and adolescent guilt appears to differ in its shape by class background. These differing shapes can be best seen in Table 7.3 if one looks at the absolute cell frequencies within parentheses. Among the white-collar group the largest off-diagonal cell is that for the unguilty respondents with late coming out whereas among the blue-collar respondents that cell is the smallest off-diagonal cell. This seems to imply that among the respondents from white-collar backgrounds there are significant reasons for coming out later other than guilt whereas among the blue-collar respondents there are few reasons other than guilt. For the white-collar background respondents these reasons would include plans for investing time and effort in the building of a career while such reasons would be less common among those from blue-collar backgrounds. Given that such other reasons may be more common among those from white-collar backgrounds, they may also serve to suppress among the white-collar youths any negative effects of early coming out on educational attainment. Given the absence of such other reasons among the blue-collar youths, we are left with adolescent guilt as the principal factor restraining early coming out and hence permitting higher educational attainment. This suggested interpretation that higher levels of educational or occupational aspirations among the white-collar youths suppress any negative effects of early coming out, is consistent with the present data and suggested by those data but cannot be proven in those data. Such confirmation will have to await further studies.

The data of the present section strongly suggest that some non-trivial part of the educational differences found in all of the studies comparing gay and non-gay men is real. Gays appear to have been better students during high school, although this may not hold among college students due to the sizable number of blue-collar gay youths fleeing into college from their gender-conservative backgrounds. Being a better high school student is sizably associated with subsequent educational attainment. Adolescent guilt is also positively associated with education and being high on adolescent guilt over one's perceived homosexuality is a characteristic which non-gay males are very unlikely to be high on.

Being defeminized is also positively related to education while being defeminized is a characteristic not many non-gay males can be high on simply because they were never feminized. A possible objection to the suggestion that defeminization may render gays more educated than non-gays would be that being persistently effeminate is negatively related to education and that characteristic, being one on which non-gays are likely to be very low, would render gays less educated. While being persistently effeminate is negatively related to education, it should be noted that the persistently effeminate do not differ on education from the rather gender-conventional never effeminates. The best age group to show this among is those from 30 to 39 years of age since, unlike the younger, most have had sufficient time to complete their education and, unlike the older, their levels of education will not have been strongly affected by generational differences in educational expectations. Among those in their thirties, 35 percent of the persistently effeminate, 48 percent of the defeminized, and 34 percent of the never effeminate have more than 16 years of education. Even among the oldest age group the respective corresponding percentages are 35, 43, and 39. That the persistently effeminates are both lowest in education among those in their twenties, where the respective percentages are 15, 24, and 24, and equal the never effeminate for the older age groups suggests that, with age, the persistently effeminate catch up with the never effeminate while the defeminized surpass the never effeminate. From the above it is rather tentatively offered that the very large numbers of defeminized among gay men helps to elevate their years of education while the smaller numbers of persistently effeminate do not depress years of education. Replication of these findings will be very much needed.

CROSS-GENDERING AND OCCUPATIONAL SITUS

Earlier presented ideas imply that, to the extent a person, gay or non-gay, is committed to a particular gender role or gender culture, that commitment may influence their occupational preferences. Persons committed to traditional interpretations of gender roles may only consider or apply for jobs which have traditionally been gender-typed for their preferred role. It has been well established in the sociological literature that there is massive occupational typing and segregation by gender (Sewell et al. 1980; Oppenheimer 1970, pp. 78-79). Women are disproportionately found in the lower levels of the white-collar stratum, in service occupations, and in selected professional occupations sex-typed as feminine, e.g., teacher, nurse. It also seems clear that the sex typing of occupations in most persons minds is established very early in life. As mentioned earlier, Looft (1971) asked 33 boys and 33 girls of ages six to eight "What do you want to do when you grow up?" and found that the boys listed 18 different occupations while the girls mentioned only nine. The two occupations of teacher and nurse accounted for 25 of the girls' 33 choices while football player accounted for nine of the boys' choices. Reworking data from Nemerowicz's (1979, p. 30) study in which second, fourth and sixth grade boys and girls were asked "What do you want to be when you grow up?" it was found that of 188 boys one percent wanted to be teachers or nurses versus 43 percent of the 156 girls (X^2=94.01, df=1, p < .001). Similarly, two percent of the girls wanted athletic occupations versus 28 percent of the boys (X^2=40.15, df=1, p < .001). Thirty percent of the boys wanted manual jobs versus two percent of the girls (X^2=45.79, df=1, p < .001). Also, one percent of the boys versus five percent of the girls wanted to be "models" or "entertainers" (Fisher's exact two-tailed p=.01). It seems clear from these data that gender typing of occupations and activities occurs quite early in life and reproduces the sex segregation found in the adult labor markets. Such gender typing of occupations may later lead to gender-typing of one's occupational preferences consistent with one's gender-role preference.

This reasoning leads to the hypothesis that those gay men who are cross-gendered during adulthood may also tend to occupy jobs sex-typed for women while the other defeminization status categories would be more likely to be found in more masculine-typed jobs. Bell and Weinberg (1978, p. 278) found some data consistent with this hypothesis in that 10 percent of their white male homosexuals versus 25 percent of the white male heterosexuals were located in "typically masculine fields." The corresponding percentages for blacks were 12 and 36. However, before examining the relationship between gender-typing of occupation and defeminization status, it is necessary to consider the alternative hypothesis that discrimination on the basis of perceived sexual orientation could give rise to such an association. Since the persistently effeminate visibly conform to the common stereotype of male homosexuals, it may be that they are denied jobs in typically masculine fields and by default end up in more feminine-typed occupations.

It is clear from surveys of the general population's attitudes toward homosexuals (Levitt and Klassen 1974) that large segments of the population believe that higher status jobs are inappropriate for homosexuals. Particularly those jobs involving contact with the young (such as teacher), having symbolic functions (such as minister), or involving security work (such as policeperson), are felt to be inappropriate. Levitt and Klassen asked 3,000 persons randomly sampled from the general population if "homosexual men should not be allowed to work in the following occupations." The percentages not allowing in these occupations were: court judge, 77 percent; school teacher, 77 percent; minister, 77 percent; physician, 68 percent; government official, 67 percent; beautician, 28 percent; artist, 16 percent; musician, 15 percent; florist, 13 percent. These data show that large majorities of the general public do not want homosexuals in responsible jobs and would rather relegate them to low-paying and menial positions. They also show that the general public thinks that feminine-typed jobs are more appropriate for male homosexuals. Since large majorities of the general population do not want homosexuals in responsible jobs we must then ask whether and how such preferences may be put into practice. In order to discriminate against gay men it is necessary to be able to identify them. Since most gay men go to some lengths to keep their sexual orientations secret at times of applying for jobs it is principally the visibly effeminate who seem likely candidates for direct discrimination. Data presented earlier showed that the effeminate bear the brunt of discrimination against gay men since they conform to the public stereotypes of male homosexuals. Since the data do not include a measure of direct job discrimination in applying for jobs, it is not possible to explore the extent to which the cross-gendered may have been refused jobs because of their apparent conformity to the stereotypes. Even if the respondents had been asked about such discrimination, there would be the question of the validity of their responses. It seems likely that many employers are unwilling to be so blunt as to inform a gay job applicant that he is being denied a job because he is gay. Rather than create embarrassing situations, other reasons may be typically given. Hence, gay persons may not be in a very good position to know whether they have been discriminated against. Employers are probably a better source of information on such matters.

A variant on the job-discrimination hypothesis is that such discrimination may not occur directly but through anticipation of discrimination. Gays know that it is likely they will be discriminated against if they apply for certain types of higher status jobs or masculine-defined jobs. Hence, in anticipation of such discrimination they may not apply. The occupation of policeperson is a good example of such processes. Most police departments still refuse to hire homosexuals, principally on the pretext that they are blackmailable and secondarily on the basis that it would be bad for the morale or prejudices of heterosexual policepersons. Hence, gays probably rarely apply for such jobs. A further variant on the anticipated job-discrimination hypothesis is that, even if the employer is not discriminatory in hiring, heterosexual employees may make life on the job difficult for the gay man through harrassment or ridicule. Anticipating that his worklife could be made highly and continuously uncomfortable, the gay man may opt for other jobs with less severely masculine cultures. Through discrimination, either direct or anticipated, gay men may end up by default in a variety of jobs which are variously, menial, low-paying, and feminine in nature.

The data permit a test of the hypothesis that gay men, and particularly the cross gendered, have different and particularly feminine jobs more often than do the non-cross-gendered. This is done in several ways. First, comparisons are made of choices as to college major of the DeKalb gay and non-gay students. Such choices should be fairly free of influences of discrimination and speak directly to the hypothesis that cross-gendered gays choose different occupations. Since such choices are probably the major determinants of the types of occupations gay college students later enter, they also speak directly to choices of occupations. Dividing college majors into the two choices of the arts (including such applied arts as graphic design and interior decorating plus the traditional arts) versus all other majors, we find a significant difference between the gay and non-gay students. Of the gay students (N=31) 35 percent were majoring in the arts as compared with 8 percent of the non-gay students (N=200) (Fisher's exact two-tailed p < .001). The largest single group of the heterosexual students were majoring in business. (College major was asked only of the DeKalb respondents.) These data are essentially similar to the findings of Goertzel et al. (1979) who, basing their information on the biographies and autobiographies of eminent males in Euro-American countries, reported that homosexuals attained their eminence disproportionately often in the humanities as opposed to such areas as politics, business, or the military.

A second way in which one may assess whether cross-gendered gay men tend to cluster in particular types of jobs is to see whether cross-gendering is related to type of present occupation. Since cross-gendering is so strongly associated with sexual orientation there would be the strong implication that gay men, in fact, differ from heterosexual men in types of occupations. In order to test these ideas the occupations reported by the Chicago respondents were coded as to their gender-role cultural content. The same categories were used as in the case of ideal occupation (cf. Chapter IV). These were grouped into the seven categories of the arts and acting/entertaining, nurturant occupations (therapists, social workers, nurses, orderlies), teaching, domestic-related (hair and poodle dressing, clothes management, chefs, florists), manual, business and the traditional professions, and other (including travel and "other"). The "other" category consists of a variety of usually lower white-collar, clerical, or service occupations of a fairly nondescript nature (bank teller, insurance adjuster). The acting category was combined with the arts since there were only 21 respondents in the former.

The categorization of occupations in terms of their gender-culture is here termed "occupational situs." The conceptualization and operationalization of occupational situs employed here differs somewhat from those of other writers on situs who typically have defined situses in terms of functions carried on within those situses (Morris and Murphy 1959). The seven categories employed here in the measure of situs range from the two most masculine ones of manual work and business plus the traditional professions to the three somewhat gender-ambiguous categories of other (mostly clerical), teaching, the arts and acting, to the two most feminine ones of nurturant and domestic-related. These categories were created on the basis of the research on the gender typing of occupations by children. The principal difference which would arise between this set of categories and one based on the percentage of employees in a given occupation who are female would involve the arts category. While the arts tend to be dominated by men, children apparently misperceive the arts and rate them as feminine (Stein and Smithells 1969).

Table 7.5 shows the associations among occupational situs, defeminization status, and age. Age is introduced as a control since it is strongly related to situs and moderately related to defeminization status. While the dichotomization of age at under 30 versus 30 and older is a somewhat crude control, the large

TABLE 7.5

LIKELIHOOD RATIO ANALYSIS OF OCCUPATIONAL SITUS BY
DEFEMINIZATION STATUS BY AGE[a]

		Partial (1st Order) Associations			Marginal (0-Order) Associations	
Effect	df	LR Chi-squared	p		LR Chi-squared	p
SM	12	59.28	.001		69.25	.001
SA	6	72.70	.001		82.67	.001
MA	2	9.29	.010		19.26	.001
SMA	12	10.35	.585			

TABLE 7.5 (continued)

STANDARDIZED LAMBDAS FOR PARTIAL ASSOCIATIONS

Defeminization Status (M)	Occupational Situs (S)						
	Arts/ Acting	Teach- ers	Nur- turant	Domes- tic	Man- ual	Bus/ Prof.	Other
Always Effeminate	1.03	-1.87	1.91	2.89	-1.36	-5.22	1.50
Defeminized	0.56	1.29	-1.21	-0.71	-1.23	1.58	0.63
Never Effeminate	-1.34	0.93	-0.61	-1.66	2.57	3.96	-1.81

Age (A)	Occupational Situs (S)						
	Arts/ Acting	Teach- ers	Nur- turant	Domes- tic	Man- ual	Bus/ Prof.	Other
-29	1.88	-5.80	0.13	2.28	0.43	-1.64	3.88
30+	-1.88	5.80	-0.13	-2.28	-0.43	1.64	-3.88

Age (A)	Defeminization Status (M)		
	Always Effeminate	Defeminized	Never Effeminate
-29	2.38	-0.74	-1.58
30+	-2.38	0.74	1.58

Age (A)	Defemi- nization Status (M)	Occupational Situs (S)							
		Arts/ Acting	Teach- ing	Nur- turant	Domes- tic	Man- ual	Bus/ Prof.	Other	N(100%)
-29	Persistently Effeminate	13	2	13	11	8	27	26	180
	Defeminized	13	3	4	6	6	45	22	261
	Never Effeminate	7	4	8	5	9	52	16	128
30+	Persistently Effeminate	11	11	9	8	5	39	17	153
	Defeminized	7	15	8	3	6	50	11	361
	Never Effeminate	6	12	5	1	10	57	8	209

[a]Table excludes the newly effeminate, students, the retired, and the unemployed.

Source: Compiled by the author.

number of situs categories makes this necessary. The cutting point of 30 years of age was chosen because it seems that by that age most males will have had sufficient time to acquire the appropriate skills and education to translate their occupational aspirations into realities or, alternatively, to drift into jobs approximating their aspirations. Hence, the over-30 group may be a somewhat better test of the hypothesis than the under-30 group. However, since Table 7.5 reveals no significant interaction and the patterns of association appear quite similar for both the younger and older age groups, we turn to an examination of the lambdas which are easier to read than the percentages in a table with so many cells. The data show that the persistently effeminate are significantly over-represented in the domestic-related category of occupations and much under-represented in the business/traditional professions category. Correspondingly, the never effeminate are significantly over-represented in the two masculine categories of manual work and business/traditional professions. These two groups differ significantly from each other in all seven occupational categories. The defeminized are between the other two groups on five of the seven occupational categories. It thus appears that gender-role preference is related to the gender-typedness of occupations.

As one might expect, there are large differences in educational level among the occupational situses. The percentages having 16 or more years of education are: the arts, 67; teaching, 95; nurturant, 65; domestic-related, 19; manual, 21; business/professions, 64; other, 31. Can these educational differences explain the association of defeminization status and situs? Unfortunately, the data do not permit a simultaneous control for both age and years of education. Fortunately, however, this control is not needed in order to see whether there is an association between defeminization status and situs. Even if all of the association between these two variables were explained by education, this would simply provide a mechanism showing how defeminization statuses eventuate in differing occupational situses. As a further exploration of the relationship between cross-gendering and occupational situs occupational situs was run by self-reported masculinity/femininity by age. The results replicate the preceding analyses (data not presented). Those describing themselves as "A little" or "Quite" feminine were found to be severely under-represented in the two masculine categories while being moderately over-represented in the domestic and nurturant categories. There thus appear to be sorting processes operative which guide the visibly effeminate into feminine-typed occupations and away from masculine-typed ones.

While it has been shown that those who differ on defeminization status also differ on the gender-typing of their occupations, it has not yet been shown whether the occupational differences are voluntary or whether they arise out of either direct or anticipated discrimination. However, several parts of our data suggest that these occupational differences are, at least in part, voluntary and arise out of differences in gender-role commitments. First, it was shown that the DeKalb gay and heterosexual students differed significantly on their chosen majors. Such differences seem in large part voluntary since discrimination in choosing college majors seems unlikely to occur in higher education to any extensive degree and particularly at larger state-supported, non-south, non-religiously-affiliated schools. Secondly, it will be remembered that it was earlier shown how ideal occupations were significantly related to childhood and adult cross-gendering. Such choices of the ideal seem unlikely to be due to discrimination.

Thirdly, we now show how the gay and non-gay students differ in their visions of an ideal occupation. Table 7.6 presents detailed listings of the occupational ideals of the respondents for the gay non-students, the gay students, and the non-gay students. For purposes of statistical analysis these occupations are grouped into the six broader categories shown in that table and the gay and non-gay students were compared. There is a large and significant relationship between sexual orientation and occupational ideals (X^2=39.65, df=5, p < .001). The associated standardized lambdas show that the gay students were considerably more likely to choose both the arts and the feminine/domestic category while the heterosexual students were much over-represented in the sports category. Most of those choosing sports-related occupations wanted to be professional athletes. Apparently the childhood visions of masculine and athletic glory which Nemerowicz (1979, p. 130) found persist well into adulthood among heterosexual males. The heterosexual students were 20 times more likely to choose athletic ideals than were the gay students to whom the vision of being "Saturday's Hero" had little appeal. The latter more often idealized artistic and feminine occupations.

The above differences between gay and non-gay students in chosen majors, differences between gay and non-gays students in ideal occupations, and the differences by defeminization status in both ideal and real occupations collectively strongly suggest that cross-gendered gay men do, in fact, have different visions of preferred occupations. These ideals seem to be formed during childhood and, for the persistently effeminate, are carried forward into adulthood. During adulthood they serve as criteria for the selection of occupations within which the individual can

TABLE 7.6

IDEAL OCCUPATIONS BY SAMPLE GROUPS (PERCENT)

Ideal Occupations	Sample Groups		
	Gay Non-Students	Gay Students	Non-Gay Students
The Arts/Acting			
Arts	24.2	24.8	11.9
Acting	5.8	5.3	1.0
Entertaining	6.6	8.8	5.7
Opera-Singer	0.6	0.0	0.0
Feminine/Domestic			
Teaching	5.6	4.4	2.1
Nurturant	7.2	10.6	3.1
Grooming	1.6	1.6	0.0
Home & Food	1.3	0.0	0.0
Floristry	0.7	0.0	0.0
Sports			
Sports	0.8	2.7	16.1
Manual/Masculine			
Military	0.1	0.1	1.0
Law Enforcement	0.3	0.0	1.0
Manual	2.2	0.1	1.0
Agricultural/Outdoor/Animal	1.9	2.7	5.2
Business/Professions			
Science/Technology	2.6	6.2	11.4
Business	13.0	5.3	13.0
Political	2.2	0.1	2.6
Religious	1.8	1.8	0.5
Traditional Professions	11.9	11.5	13.0
Other			
Travel	5.0	6.2	4.7
Other	4.6	5.3	6.7
N(100%)	1250	113	193

Source: Compiled by the author.

feel psychologically or culturally comfortable. Such visions may consist of the two correlated but partially independent criteria of aversion to stereotypically defined masculine occupations and of attraction to stereotypically defined feminine occupations.

The magnitude and consistency of these sets of differences were somewhat surprising given the fact that a decade to a half-century intervened between present real or ideal occupations and childhood cross-gendering phenomena. The particular type of job one has or wants to have is subject to a large number of strong labor-market influences such as availability of jobs, discrimination, seniority, skills, and qualifications. Also, in the course of growing up the individual is exposed to a variety of new influences which familiarize him with new occupational possibilities. Individuals often change their preferred occupations a number of times during their pre-adult and youthful years, e.g., college students changing their majors several times.

The data presented strongly suggest that later factors which might influence a person toward entering or considering an alternative line of work are filtered through the criteria provided by gender-role culture and associated gender ideals. For example, a cross-gendered gay man exposed to professional athletics is not effectively invited to become a professional athlete since he defines that role as not consistent with his ideals for self. The process of filtering out possibilities seems identical to the situation of the young heterosexual who watches a drag show. He simply discounts the occupation of female impersonator as not consistent with the self. Similarly, most females probably never consider the possibility of becoming a prostitute or proctologist.

The filtering-out and attraction-to processes which seem to be operative among gay men as they choose and drift into or out of occupations seem to be the same ones which guide heterosexual males and females into differing types of gender-typed jobs. Males and females learn gender-roles and associated proper and improper occupations at quite early ages (Nemerowicz 1979). Girls learn that women are not scientists and boys learn that men are not usually artists, or at least "real" men are not artists. These early laid down definitions of gender culture are carried forward to adult periods largely intact. For example, because of such gender-cultural internalizations females are considerably less interested in science by early high school (Keeves 1973). Later, when and if they entertain the possibility of jobs in science, they also discover that either it is too late to change or they are considerably behind in preparation. They then learn that the bus for science goes by only once in a lifetime and that was decades ago; if they persist they must walk. If the influences of gender culture are so powerful among heterosexual men and women one should also expect them to be of considerable importance in the lives of gay men.

The relationships shown above between defeminization status and present occupation may somewhat understate the strength of the relationship between gender culture and occupation. It was earlier observed that in the course of the defeminization process gay men discontinue the more obviously and visibly feminine of their activities while focusing on or retaining more subtle aspects of femininity. Thus, while otherwise behaving gender-conventionally, they may involve themselves in the arts which to them symbolize a feminine-culture identification. To the extent they define art as feminine and find it rewarding their identification with feminine culture is rewarded. To the extent that some gay men are able to perceive selected aspects of a given occupation as expressive of feminine culture or identification they may be able to define that occupation as consistent with their gender-ideals even though it otherwise contains little of feminine culture. Such selective redefining of the nature of a given occupation permits the individual to involve himself in the occupation out of private motives which may be considerably different from the motives or character conventionally attributed to persons incumbent in such jobs.

Within the data a likely example of the operation of such private definitions of jobs involves the occupational category of outdoor/agriculture/animal-related. Twenty-six (1.9 percent) of the Chicago respondents mentioned such job as ideal occupations compared with 10 (5.2 percent) of the heterosexual respondents. Such occupations are conventionally, although not always, defined as masculine in nature. However, among the particular occupations in that overall category mentioned by the gay and non-gay respondents there was not much overlap in choices. Seven of the 26 gays mentioned "veterinarian" while none of the 10 heterosexuals did. An additional gay also mentioned "zoo attendant" while two others named "horse trainer." Choices such as veterinarian suggest the strong possibility that individuals may see such jobs as outlets for nurturant propensities toward animals in the same way that the occupation of nurse has evident nurturant qualities for humans. It is noted that three of the 10 heterosexuals also mentioned occupations involving animals: "fish farmer," "fish and game warden," "fish and wildlife management." Such choices, however, seem less suggestive of nurturant interests. The nature of these differences between the gay and non-gay respondents suggests that the gender-culture ideals operating at the gross level of sorting gay men of differing degrees of cross-gendering into gender-different jobs also operate at finer levels of discrimination to sort gays into different subspecialties within a given occupation. Thus, within the profession of medicine we would hypothesize gays to be over-represented in psychiatry and pediatrics, more arguably in gynecology, and under-represented in surgery. As a final observation on such selective definings of the gender-nature of given occupations it is interesting to note that there was one person among the Chicago respondents whose real occupation was in the outdoor/agriculture/animal-related category; he was a "manager of a pet shop." The selection of such jobs seems to involve a process whereby certain aspects--in the present instance pets--of the occupation are put to special psychological uses such that they are the symbolic miniaturizations of that vast cultural complex called the feminine gender role.

In further exploration of the gender-symbolic properties which particular occupations or aspects of occupations may have

for individuals, the cases where the respondents mentioned as
ideal occupations sports or sports-related jobs were examined.
Thirteen gay men from the three gay sample groups mentioned such
jobs as compared with 31 of the non-gay respondents. While the
relative frequency of mentioning sports-related ideal occupations
has been shown above to be much higher among the heterosexuals,
the types of athletic occupations mentioned also seem to differ by
sexual orientation. Firstly, only one of the gays mentioned being
a team player in sports such as football, hockey, or baseball
("baseball player") as compared with ten of the 31 heterosexual
respondents (Fisher's exact two-tailed p=0.13). This trend is
similar to Saghir and Robins' (1973, p. 176) finding that gay men
were less interested in sports than heterosexual men and those
sports that interested them tended to be individual rather than
team ones.

A second way in which the athletic occupations mentioned by
the gay and non-gay respondents differed was in degree of
specificity with which they described their particular interests.
While one might anticipate that, since the heterosexuals have been
shown to be vastly more interested in sports they would have
responded in greater detail, it was the gays who were more
specific. None of the 13 gays as compared with 11 of the 31
heterosexuals used such general descriptions as "professional
athlete," "star athlete," "athlete," or "professional sports"
(Fisher's exact two-tailed p=.02). From this difference it is
inferred that the heterosexuals had a general identification with
that most masculine of activities, athletics, while the gays were
only willing to identify with those particular aspects of
athletics which are not excessively symbolic of male gender
culture and which may permit the introduction of feminine
elements.

The gender significance of physical objects may not be apparent to many people because these objects are almost always employed in gender-appropriate ways. The situation is similar to
that of the fish who doesn't know he is swimming in water. However, the gender significance of objects becomes intensely apparent when those objects are employed in a gender-deviant manner.
An otherwise masculine appearing male who is carrying a purse is
the object of widespread notice and suspicion since the object is
being employed deviantly. This appears to explain why, for example, while purses for men have occasionally been manufactured,
they have never succeeded. They were gender-deviant products and
products which violate the norms of gender culture rarely succeed,
except perhaps among gender deviants. Similarly, when first
introduced in the 1960s, long hair on men aroused intense
suspicion of the motives of the wearers of that hair. In more
recent years, even very long hair on men became more accepted, as
long as it was unkempt and/or dirty. However, if it is clean and
too well kept it arouses suspicions of gender deviance.

The suggested process of symbolic miniaturization of the
immensely elaborate feminine gender-role into certain aspects of
an occupation is similar to Stoller's (1979, pp. 165-175) process

of "microdotting." To him, microdotting involves the representation and therefore evocation of erotic scripts by almost anything capable of serving as a symbol. Typically, the erotic microdots are bodily parts (ankles or penises) or clothes or gestures exhibited by potential sexual partners. For fetishists or sado-masochists the fetishized object symbolizes a sequence of anticipated erotic activities. Stoller acknowledges the existence of non-erotic microdots but develops his ideas in terms of the erotic. In the present usage of the term miniaturization it is intended that a particular activity or object involved--in the present instance in an occupation--can symbolize the whole set of activities and paraphernalia associated with feminine gender culture. Such private symbolizations, typically secret from other persons, permit the introduction of feminine identification into otherwise unfeminine activities. They permit the cross-gendered gay man to feel feminine and, therefore, psychologically at ease in the course of carrying out occupational activities conventionally defined as either masculine or gender-neutral.

Miniaturizations differ from Stoller's erotic microdots in that, although both are symbolic compounds of many other things, microdots seem more unique and less substitutable for other symbols serving the same function. For example, some individuals are sexually excited by feet or toes which for them symbolize whole sequences of erotic activities; ankles or hair or elbows won't do. In contrast, the feminine gender role is capable of an immense number of possible alternative and motivationally effective miniaturized symbolizations. A lab smock can represent a gown for a technician. A shoulder bag can represent a purse for an airline steward. Pets can represent children--or pets--for a pet shop manager. The large number of alternative ways in which the feminine gender role can be symbolically miniaturized seems to derive from the fact that gender roles have been so immensely elaborated in many cultures that thousands of activities or objects are associated with one gender or the other and can, therefore, stand for a gender. Femininity is symbolically present in occupations dealing with furs, drapes, hair, food, pets, antiques, art, tablecloths, serving others, serving food, setting a table, jewelry, flowers, entertaining men, designing household objects, and children. Because individuals come into contact with such embodied femininity in so many different ways, there are as many alternative and common ways in which it can be surreptitiously symbolized. In contrast, the attachments of individuals to erotic microdots seems considerably more fixed due to the limited number of ways in which one experiences the erotic. Erotic complexes have been considerably less culturally elaborated and woven into all aspects of public life than have gender roles.

To the extent that cross-gendered gay men tend to be concentrated in jobs which have been traditonally defined as "womens' work," they may have suffered some of the income discrimination encountered by women. If one examines income by occupational situs by age in the Chicago data, one finds very large income differences by situs with the feminine situses being among the lowest paid (data not presented). However, one should separate out two different components of such income discrimination. One reason for the low pay received by many gay men, particularly the cross-gendered, is that they entered occupations of low skill and hence low pay, e.g., orderly, bank teller, sales. A second reason for their low pay is that the occupations they have entered have been defined as women's occupations and, for that reason, these occupations have been given lower pay. Employers have at times paid "women's occupations" less under the assumptions that, either women didn't need as much income as men because they would be shortly quitting their jobs to get married or because they had husbands to support them (Sawhill 1974). Several studies (Simmons et al. 1975; Wolf and Fligstein 1979) have reported that men of a given level of education working in women's occupations are paid less than if they were working in men's occupations. Thus, to the extent that there has been operative such discrimination against "women's occupations" gay men have probably shared in that discrimination.

It is important to note that the question of whether cross-gendered gay men enter female-typed occupations due to discrimination versus voluntarily is not the question of whether there is occupational discrimination against cross-gendered gay men. Since there is occupational sex discrimination against both women and female-typed jobs the "voluntarism" question becomes one of which form of discrimination cross-gendered gay men experience. Do they enter female-typed jobs due to sexual orientation discrimination and subsequently become the victims of sex discrimination against those jobs, or do they voluntarily enter female-typed jobs and subsequently become the victims of discrimination against those jobs. The data presented above strongly suggest the latter to be the case for cross-gendered gay men while the former might be more operative among non-cross-gendered gay men.

The present chapter has attempted to document in a variety of ways that gay men have high levels of education, that they are highly concentrated in the white-collar segment of the labor force, and that their different occupational distribution arises out of childhood commitments to feminine culture, aversion to masculine culture, and benign effects of adolescent guilt over their homosexuality. While some of the data supporting these ideas have been direct, e.g., the relationships between cross-gendering and occupational situs, others have been indirect. Of course, the most direct evidence on the differing educational and occupational locations of gay men would be straightforward comparisons of large representative samples of gay and heterosexual men. Although there is always the question of the representativeness of a sample of gay men, documented educational differences between gay and heterosexual men exist in the literature in abundance. However, they have been ignored. That researchers have been able to show there are no or only minor differences on psychological measures such as self-esteem or masculinity does not prove that there are no cultural differences. We hope to have shown above that there are large differences in gender culture between gay and non-gay men and that these differences have many and major effects.

The present chapter has attempted to show through both the Chicago and Detroit samples that gay men are upwardly mobile in terms of education. The motivations for this upward mobility appear to be a complex of adolescent characteristics involving social isolation, alienation from heterosexual adolescent culture, and guilt over their incipient homosexuality. This complex of feelings may be strongest among working-class gay youths who live in a cultural environment which more strongly disapproves of gender-deviant behavior. While working-class gay youths seem to have the greater problems surrounding their homosexuality, they also may put those problems to the best use through efforts to compensate for their felt differentness and inferiority. To the extent that such youths become upwardly mobile, at least across the blue-collar/white-collar line, there is the implication that the population of adult gays, while an excessively educated group, also contains a disproportionate segment of persons from blue-collar backgrounds. This question must be left for others to explore.

A RETURN TO QUESTIONS OF SAMPLING

The finding that adolescent guilt over one's homosexuality is positively associated with obtaining higher education among gay men has two implications for the student samples. First, it implies that gay graduate students should have been guiltier than gay undergraduate students. Second, it implies that graduate students should constitute a large percentage of gay students than they constitute among non-gay students. Table 7.7 tests the first implication by comparing gay graduate and gay undergraduate students on all the major variables of the present work. The most notable finding of Table 7.7 is that the gay graduate students are 30 percent more likely to have been guilty as adolescents than the undergraduates. This finding once more indicates the importance of adolescent guilt in fostering upward mobility. The only other significant differences between the two gay student groups is that the gay graduate students were better students during high school and are lower on violent offenses than the gay undergraduates.

TABLE 7.7

ALL MAJOR VARIABLES BY STUDENT STATUS AMONG GAY STUDENTS
(Percent High)

Variable	Undergraduate Students	Graduate Students	X^2	p
Adolescent Guilt	42	72		
N(100%)	81	40	10.00	.003
Adolescent Sports Interest	32	18		
N(100%)	81	39	2.64	.159
Interest in Arts	80	92		
N(100%)	81	40	3.04	.140
Youthful Loner	72	78		
N(100%)	81	40	0.48	.489
Self-Esteem	56	54		
N(100%)	80	39	0.06	.804
Masculinity	46	50		
N(100%)	80	40	0.15	.698
Femininity	53	46		
N(100%)	79	39	0.51	.474
Dominance	60	64		
N(100%)	80	39	0.19	.666
Competitiveness	51	35		
N(100%)	79	40	2.62	.106
Property Offenses	69	62		
N(100%)	81	39	0.68	.408
Violent Offenses	54	32		
N(100%)	80	40	4.84	.028
Good High School Student	40	62		
N(100%)	80	40	5.41	.020
Adolescent Interest in Girls	51	45		
N(100%)	81	40	0.34	.561
Frequent Adolescent Dates	48	52		
N(100%)	81	40	0.20	.652
Actorization	64	72		
N(100%)	77	40	0.93	.335
Childhood Cross-Gendering	78	87		
N(100%)	81	39	1.50	.220
Adult Cross-Gendering	34	33		
N(100%)	77	39	0.00	.963

Source: Compiled by the author.

The second implication was also confirmed. The data show
that 34 percent (N=122) of the gay students are graduate students
compared with 7 percent (N=204) of the non-gay students (X^2=38.93,
df=1, p < .001). This suggests that gay undergraduates may be
more likely to go on to graduate or professional school than the
non-gays if they succeed in obtaining a bachelor's degree. Only

the DeKalb groups were asked about their plans to attend graduate or professional school. The data show a strong trend for the gay students to be more likely to plan on graduate or professional school ($X^2 = 3.31$, df=1, p=.07). Of the 22 gay DeKalb undergraduates, 59 percent said that they were "definitely" or "probably" going to attend graduate or professional school compared with 39 percent of the 190 non-gay undergraduates. From these findings it is inferred that the data consistently show a greater propensity for gay men to acquire higher education. It should be noted that some of the reported differences between the several student groups would probably not replicate when studying students at a school which is largely inaccessible to youths from blue-collar backgrounds due to either reasons of income or academic entrance standards or which lacks programs that might appeal to many gays.

The finding that the gay students included a larger percentage of graduate students than did the non-gay students raises the question of whether the differences and non-differences found between the gays and non-gays in the preceding chapters were due to the presence of the larger percentage of graduate students among the gay students. Does a control for graduate versus undergraduate student status alter the findings of the present work? This question, asked in general, is largely meaningless. Unless one has a particular hypothesis that student status should be related to a gay/non-gay difference on a particular variable partials by student status would be quite meaningless and without rationale. Hence, the zero-order gay/non-gay differences and non-differences already presented are more meaningful than would be partials by student status.

In the particular case of having been a good student during high school, there is a rationale for examining the gay/non-gay partials while controlling for student status. It will be remembered that guilty gay youths from blue-collar backgrounds were found more likely to enter college but that, presumably due to their inferior high school preparation compared to white-collar gay youths, they were also more likely to drop out of college. This implies that the gay/non-gay difference in having been a good high school student may be reduced or vanish if one examines that difference only among the undergraduates. Table 7.8 compares gay and non-gay undergraduate students on having been better high school students and finds that the gay/non-gay difference has vanished. This lack of difference is consistent with earlier interpretations. Comparisons among the graduate students are not possible since the data include only 14 non-gay graduate students.

Table 7.8 also shows gay/non-gay comparisons among the undergraduates on all of the other principal variables of the present work for the reader who might be interested in these partials. With three exceptions, all differences and non-differences are the same as the zero-order ones. The gay undergraduates are now higher on self-esteem than the non-gay

TABLE 7.8

ALL MAJOR VARIABLES BY SAMPLE GROUP AMONG UNDERGRADUATE STUDENTS
(Percent High)

Variable	Gay Students	Non-Gay Students	X^2	p
Good High School Student	40	36		
N(100%)	80	190	0.43	.513
Adolescent Sports Interest	32	82		
N(100%)	81	190	62.68	.001
Interest in Arts	80	58		
N(100%)	81	190	11.88	.001
Youthful Loner	72	39		
N(100%)	81	188	24.34	.001
Self-Esteem	56	40		
N(100%)	80	190	6.01	.014
Masculinity	46	43		
N(100%)	80	187	0.20	.658
Femininity	53	28		
N(100%)	79	187	15.63	.001
Dominance	60	51		
N(100%)	80	187	1.69	.193
Competitiveness	51	59		
N(100%)	79	190	1.57	.210
Property Offenses	69	77		
N(100%)	81	190	1.78	.182
Violent Offenses	54	71		
N(100%)	80	190	7.50	.006
Adolescent Interest in Girls	51	90		
N(100%)	81	190	51.72	.001
Frequent Adolescent Dates	48	70		
N(100%)	81	190	11.70	.001
Actorization	64	62		
N(100%)	77	189	0.07	.791
Childhood Cross-Gendering	78	30		
N(100%)	81	189	52.07	.001

Source: Compiled by the author.

undergraduates. A possible interpretation of this puzzling difference is that, since adolescent guilt is sizably related to adult self-esteem and being a gay graduate student is related to guilt, the exclusion of the graduate students from these comparisons excluded many of those with lower self-esteem. While this interpretation has some appeal, the very minimal difference in self-esteem between the gay graduate and undergraduate students renders this explanation unlikely. A second case in this table where the gay/non-gay partial relationship differs from the zero-order one is that of property offenses. While the non-gays remain higher on property offenses than the gays, the difference is no longer significant. This appears to be due to the reduced sample size of this table, to the fact that the gay graduate students are somewhat lower on property offenses, and to the fact that the zero-order gay/non-gay difference on property offenses was never very big to begin with. The remaining case where the gay/non-gay partial differs from the zero-order relationship is that the difference in competitiveness has become non-significant. This seems to be due to the gay graduate students being somewhat lower on competitiveness than the gay undergraduate students.

Since the gay/non-gay comparisons of the present work were very largely limited to student populations, the question arises as to whether generalizations of the findings should be limited to student populations or, more broadly, to those with at least some college education? It seems that the appropriate population to which one might reasonably attempt to generalize would be those males with at least some college education, of which students are a subset. This means that the gay/non-gay findings reported above may not hold if one were to compare blue-collar gays and non-gays or less educated gays and non-gays. However, it should be noted that this limitation does not seem to be a major one. If, as argued above, the cell including either blue-collar gays or gays with no college education is a rather small cell, then the limitation is minor.

8

AGING,
GAY LIAISONS, AND
EROTIC PREFERENCES

DECISION MAKING AND AGE DIFFERENCES AMONG GAY COUPLES

We now attempt to assess the extent to which age and age preferences serve as criteria influencing the selection of sexual/romantic partners among gay males. We also explore whether age differences and similarities between partners structure power and decision making among couples.

Gender-structured Relationships. There appear to be three major forms into which homosexual pairings have been structured in various historical cultures. Carrier (1977, 1971) has reported that heterosexual gender roles appear to have served as the models for structuring homosexual pairings in a Latin American tradition of homosexuality, although that tradition is not limited to Latin American countries. Within this tradition participants in homosexual encounters roughly model their behaviors around heterosexual roles and thereby tend to contrast differences between partners. In these cases gender-role determines dominance in the relationship. The case of the berdache among American Indians is another instance in which heterosexual roles have informed homosexual pairings (Kessler and McKenna 1978, pp. 24-25).

While earlier writers on the topic of homosexuality such as Bieber et al. (1962, pp. 232-234) or Socarides (1968, pp. 73-76) have suggested that contemporary gay male couples tend to model their relationships on heterosexual gender roles, the research on this question has found little support for such a formulation. Westwood (1960, p. 119) reported extremely little patterning of attractions among English homosexuals such that more masculine and feminine men were mutually attracted to each other. Rather, the very large majority found masculinity attractive. While Haist and

Hewitt (1974) were able to classify their gay male respondents into insertors and insertees, their questions obliged the respondents to choose only one or the other of these activities but not both or neither. Saghir and Robins (1973, pp. 74-75) found that the large majority of gay persons do not pattern their relationships on an approximation to a husband-wife model. Bell and Weinberg (1978, p. 93) also reported "very little evidence of a 'masculine/feminine' sex-role dichotomy in the performance of household tasks." While a rather small minority of gay male couples may, like male transexuals (Kando 1973, pp. 23-24), organize their relationships around the traditional gender role dichotomies, the evidence seems fairly clear that gender roles do not seem to inform the large majority of pairings of gay men in Western non-Latin societies.

Age-Inegalitarian Relationships. A second cultural pattern which has sometimes structured homosexual relationships among males is that in which an older adult male establishes a relationship with an adolescent or pre-adolescent male. The most widely known case of this pattern is that from ancient Greece in which the older male assumed a dominant mentor relationship with a pre-adult male (Dover 1978, pp. 84-87). In this pattern age, rather than gender, appears to define dominance in the relationship. This form of institutionalized homosexuality also occurs in a number of primitive societies such as among several groups in New Guinea (Herdt 1980, pp. 318-320). While age differences in this pattern, rather than gender, serve as a principal criterion around which homosexual liaisons are structured, such liaisons seem to be ideologically linked to the obtaining system of gender roles through the rationale that during the liaisons the younger partner benefits from the older in a number of ways which will enhance his future masculinity as an adult heterosexual.

The findings on the extent to which such age differences structure homosexual liaisons in Western societies are mixed but suggest that while pairings between partners of significant age differences are not rare, they do not constitute the majority case. Cotton (1972) reported age differences in a majority of the sexual partners in his study of demographic differences between gay male partners. However, his sample was small and it was not indicated in that study just what constituted an age difference. His data did indicate greater demographic similarity between close friends than between sexual partners. This suggests that parties to a relationship, sexual or social, can be expected to be similar on demographic characteristics, including age, to the extent that the relationship is emotionally close. However, sexual relationships may or may not involve emotional closeness. Since very few of the sexual relationships reported by Cotton (1972) involved living together one may suspect that most of his sexual partners were not particularly close. It thus seems that one may need to specify whether one is talking about close relationships versus temporary sexual encounters when describing differences and similarities between partners since there probably is a greater democracy in bed than in marriage.

Bell and Weinberg (1978, p. 319) reported that 48 percent of their white gay males involved in a current affair differed from their partners by no more than five years, suggesting some tendency for partners to be of similar ages. Similarly, Westwood (1960, p. 117) reported no marked tendency for gay males to either have affairs with or be attracted to persons outside their own age group. Harry and DeVall (1978, p. 124) found that those in their early 20's preferred older men as sexual partners; those from 25 to 34 preferred same-age partners while those over 35 preferred younger or same-age partners. Their data also showed that a preference for younger partners was associated with a preference for being dominant in a relationship in terms of decision making while a preference for older partners was associated with a preference for subordination. Although these data suggest the possibility that age differences may structure decision making among gay couples, almost half of their respondents preferred same-age partners and the association between decision making and age preference was not particularly strong (gamma=0.22). It is also unknown from the Harry/DeVall data just how large age differences must be to affect decision-making since their respondents were simply asked if they preferred sexual partners younger, the same age, or older than themselves but were not asked about specific age differences.

Age-Egalitarian Relationships. The above rather mixed findings on age preferences in gay relationships suggest that there may be two age-structured patterns. The first may be a rough approximation to the Greek pattern in which the older and younger find each other mutually attractive, although it is unclear just which age groups may be attracted to each other and whether older means five or twenty years. The other pattern, constituting the third common structuring of gay relationships described in the present work, appears to also be one in which age affects attraction and decision making in a relationship but does so in such a way as to create pairings among persons of approximately equal age which are also egalitarian in decision making. This pattern of attraction and egalitarianism among persons of equal ages appears to be largely lacking, or invisible, in those cultures which have structured homosexual relationships around the Greek pattern (Dover 1978, pp. 86-87; Herdt 1980). The pattern of egalitarianism seems to be the form of gay relationship which is found more commonly in modern societies which tend to emphasize individual happiness and egalitarianism in intimate relationships. These gay relationships may resemble contemporary heterosexual pairings in which there occurs great homogamy as to demographic characteristics (Kerckhoff 1974), but also differ from heterosexual pairings in that neither age nor gender differences operate to bring about the common inegalitarianism found in the latter.

Table 8.1 presents the relationship of age to preferred age of sexual partner. The question on preferred age was "My usual

TABLE 8.1

PREFERRED AGE OF SEXUAL PARTNER BY AGE

Preferred Age of Sexual Partner	Age				
	-24	25-29	30-34	35-39	40+
-24	20	8	11	12	9
25-29	46	41	28	20	15
30-34	25	34	40	35	26
35-39	7	13	17	20	27
40+	2	3	4	13	23
N(100%)	276	344	265	161	243

$$X^2 = 223.29 \qquad df = 16 \qquad gamma = 0.36$$

Source: Compiled by the author.

preferred age for the man I like to relate sexually to is:". A scale of response categories with five year intervals ranging from 10 to 75 or older was provided the respondents. Respondents were also provided the alternative response category of "Age is not important to me." Of our 1,556 respondents 19.6 percent indicated that age was not important. Since viewing age as unimportant is also useful information we introduce these responses into the analysis subsequently.

In broad outline the data of Table 8.1 support the idea that the partner preferences of gay men are for persons of ages similar to their own since as age increases preferred age increases. The preference for age-similar partners is more pronounced among those from 25 to 34 years of age. However, it is also apparent that preferred partner's age does not increase in a one-to-one ratio with age. The preference for somewhat older partners exhibited by those in their early 20's changes to a preference for persons of the same age among those from 25 to 34 and subsequently to a preference for younger partners among those over 35. The propensity of those over 40 to prefer younger men does not change if we break down the over 40 group more finely. The data suggest that both age egalitarian and age inegalitarian preferences are

quite common and that preferences for age inequality are most
common among the oldest and youngest age groups. However,
preferences for age different partners do not often reach beyond
five to ten years with the median difference for the sample as a
whole being 4.9 years. Hence, while choices of age different
partners are common, such choices do not conform very closely to
the Greek model in which age differences between partners were
apparently quite large with the younger partner most always being
an adolescent or pre-adolescent. Indeed, less than two percent of
our respondents mentioned preferred ages of less than 20 years.

Since the data of Table 8.1 are based on stated preferences,
one may wonder about the extent to which these preferences are
realized. Age groups attracted to a given age group may not have
their attractions reciprocated. In order to see the age
differences in actual relationships, Table 8.2 exhibits the age of

TABLE 8.2

AGE OF CURRENT PARTNER BY RESPONDENT'S AGE

Partner's Age	Respondent's Age				
	-24	25-29	30-34	35-39	40+
-24	36	17	18	21	8
25-29	28	35	28	15	7
30-34	18	27	27	30	16
35-39	10	13	17	18	13
40+	7	8	10	16	56
N(100%)	135	214	163	95	118
	X^2 = 195.51		df = 16		p < .001

Source: Compiled by the author.

current sexual partners against the respondent's own age. A
relationship was operationalized as having a "current lover or
sexual partner with whom you are going or living." We note that,
among all respondents, 51 percent had current relationships, 38
percent had had past relationships, while the remaining 11 percent
reported that their sexual encounters had been too brief to
include any which might be called a relationship. The median age
difference among current partners is 5.0 years. Table 8.2 reveals

a substantial association between the ages of current partners.
Approximate similarity of ages appears to be the dominant trend,
as among the preferences data, although the older tend to be
paired with somewhat younger, but not very young, partners. We
note that the 56 percent of those over 40 who also are paired with
others over 40 is an artifact of our groupings of respondents
since many of the 56 percent are paired with persons younger than
themselves.

Table 8.3 shows more clearly than Table 8.1 that preferences
for persons of significantly different ages from oneself are
concentrated among those over 35 and also those under 25. While

TABLE 8.3

DIFFERENCE BETWEEN RESPONDENT'S AGE AND PREFERRED AGE OF
SEXUAL PARTNER BY AGE (Percent)

Age-Preferred Age Difference	Respondent's Age					
	Under 24	25-29	30-34	35-39	40+	Total %
Partner's Age is:						
Over 10 Years Older	12	4	1	1	0	4
6 to 10 Years Older	29	14	4	4	1	11
1 to 5 Years Older	47	38	21	9	2	26
0 to 5 Years Younger	12	39	43	38	11	28
6 to 10 Years Younger	1	6	23	20	21	13
Over 10 Years Younger	0	0	8	27	65	17
N(100%)	276	344	265	161	243	1289

$X^2 = 940.18$ df = 20 p < .001

Source: Compiled by the author.

only 12 percent of those under 25 prefer partners more than ten years different from themselves in age, 65 percent of those over 40 do. A possible interpretation of this pattern is that increasing age symbolizes maturity and dominance such that the very young who lack these traits desire them in partners while the older who possess these traits also seek a complementary partner. Another possible interpretation is that the older desire the younger for their physical attractiveness. However, this interpretation would not explain why those under 25 find older men attractive or why so few of the older men find those under 25 attractive. A possible third interpretation of why older men may be interested in persons ten or more years different from themselves is that age differences of a given magnitude may have differing significances for persons of varying ages. While a five year difference between a 20 year old and a 25 year old may be sufficient to establish inegalitarianism in a relationship, the same difference between a 40 and 45 year old probably has little significance. Some support for the declining significance of smaller age differences with increasing age is provided by the finding that age is positively associated with responding that "Age is not important to me" in a sexual partner (X^2 = 14.15, df = 4, p. < .01). The percentage so responding among those under 25 is 13 percent which gradually increases to 24 percent among those over 40. While combinations of these three interpretations are likely to be true we pursue below the age-difference inegalitarianism hypothesis.

While we have above shown that there is a positive association between age and the preferred age of one's erotic partners and interpreted this in terms of changing age tastes with age, a considerably different, although not contradictory, interpretation is possible. The data of Table 8.1 show that men under 25 like men about 30, those 25 to 35 like men about 30 and those over 35 like men in their 30's. This suggests that, while preferred partner age increases with age, it increases at a glacial rate. Figure 8.1 shows this slow increase in the form of a scattergram and regression line. The correlation coefficient of age with preferred age is 0.34 while the slope (B) of this line is a very gradual 0.22. The standard deviation for preferred age is 6.1 years (X=29.4) and that for age is 9.7 (X=32.4). The implication of this gradual slope is that people age considerably faster than their erotic visions. While one may grow old and wrinkled one's erotic ideal remains forever embalmed in eternal youth.

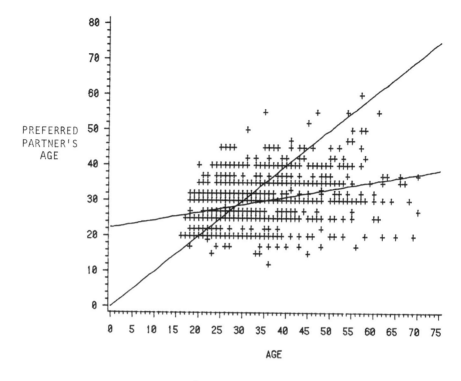

FIGURE 8.1 PREFERRED PARTNER'S AGE BY AGE

These data suggest that views of physical attractiveness remain relatively constant throughout life. This may also occur among heterosexual males and explain the often suggested propensity of older men to like younger women. However, it should be noted that, under this interpretation, older men do not later in life come to find young women attractive; they always liked young women. Pietropinto and Simenauer (1977, Table 32) have reported that with increasing age men are increasingly averse to sex with older women. In response to the question "How would you feel about having sex with older women" 9 percent of those 18 to 29 years of age versus 35 percent of those 55 to 65 years of age responded that the woman must be the respondent's age or younger. While these data do not necessarily show that older men like younger, as opposed to same-age, women, they are consistent with those found among our gay respondents. Hite (1981, p. 107) also recently reported that most men prefer younger women.

There is some evidence that standards of physical attractiveness are fairly widely shared within a given culture. In one experiment facial pictures of males and females of ages 7, 12, 17 and of adults in their 30's were shown to groups of subjects of ages 7, 12, 17 and to adults of an average age of 36. All age groups agreed that the 17-year-olds were most attractive (Cross and Cross 1971). These findings that persons in their late teens or early twenties are felt most attractive are also consistent with the fact that the very large majority of prostitutes are also in this age range (Davis 1981). While there is certainly a need for more research on the question of preferred ages of erotic, as compared to marital, partners, the data seem to suggest that heterosexual males eroticize females around 20 but that their age preferences also probably increase with age as we found among our gay men. We note that the data on age differences between husbands and wives are only indirectly relevant to our questions here since they depend on both supply and demand and we are here principally interested in demand preferences.

Although there seems to be a general similarity between the erotic age preferences of gay and non-gay males, one difference does stand out. In our data we found that males under 25 like those five to ten years older. It seems unlikely that there is a corresponding pattern for heterosexual males under 25, but rather that heterosexual males of all ages prefer women the same age or younger. A consequence of this difference appears to be that the average preferred age of erotic partners for gay men is about 30 while that for heterosexual males may be nearer 20. Why there may be this difference is unclear but the social norms that males should not be interested in women significantly older than themselves may eliminate most cases where heterosexual males might be interested in older women.

Age Difference and Decision Making While approximate similarity of ages among partners both actual and preferred is the dominant trend, the also common preference for partners of differing ages invites examination since it suggests that age differences may serve as a factor around which relationships inegalitarian in dominance or decision making may be organized. In order to explore the extent to which preferences for age different partners are also preferences for more or less dominant partners, Table 8.4 presents a log-linear analysis of preferred dominance in "the man to whom I like to relate sexually" by preferred age by age. The measure of dominance here employed was a five-point rating scale running from "Dominant" to "Compliant." It should be noted that for all age and age-preference groups a large majority preferred non-dominant partners. This is consistent with Peplau and Cochran's (1982) finding that 92 percent of their gay respondents said that both partners in a relationship should have "exactly equal say." Table 8.4 reveals that the younger are more likely to prefer dominant partners. Also, those who prefer older partners are more likely to prefer them dominant. These associations of age and age preferences in

TABLE 8.4

LIKELIHOOD RATIO ANALYSIS OF PREFERRED PARTNER DOMINANCE
BY PREFERRED AGE BY AGE

Partial (1st Order) Associations				Marginal (0-Order) Associations	
Effect	df	LR Chi-squared	p	LR Chi-squared	p
DP	3	24.92	.001	13.78	.003
DA	4	26.16	.001	15.03	.005
PA	12	191.92	.001	180.78	.001
DPA	12	13.49	.335		

Age (A)	Preferred Age (P)	Preferred Dominance(D) (Percent)		N(100%)
		Low	High	
-24	-24	70	30	53
	25-29	72	28	120
	30-34	67	33	66
	35+	64	36	25
25-29	-24	93	7	27
	25-29	84	16	135
	30-34	70	30	116
	35+	63	37	51
30-34	-24	93	7	28
	25-29	86	14	72
	30-34	78	22	99
	35+	68	32	57
35-39	-24	78	22	18
	25-29	94	6	32
	30-34	70	30	53
	35+	65	35	52
40+	-24	80	20	20
	25-29	89	11	37
	30-34	81	19	58
	35+	83	17	118

Source: Compiled by the author.

partners seem to indicate that the relatively visible characteristic of age may be taken by potential parties to a relationship as one indicator of the expectable dominance structure in that relationship. Hence, it can serve as a sorting mechanism helping persons identify candidates for both egalitarian and inegalitarian relationships.

In order to assess the extent to which age differences between actual parties to a relationship influence dominance or decision-making structures, Table 8.5 presents reported decision-making differences by age differences by whether the relationship in question is a current or past one. The measure of decision-making was "In our relationship I make (made) the decisions: Always, Mostly, Half and Half, Occasionally, Never." Not included in this table are the 11 percent of respondents who said their sexual encounters had been too brief to include any which might be described as a relationship. Table 8.5 shows that older partners in both past and present relationships are reported to make decisions more often. Hence, age differences or their lack seem a significant factor around which dominance and decision making is structured in gay relationships. It is worth noting that there appears to be a measure of asymmetry in the association between decision making and age differences. While the percentage differences presented in Table 8.5 are of modest to moderate magnitudes, those predicting from decision-making to age differences are much larger. Among current relationships 30 percent of those respondents saying they made the decisions had older partners versus 74 percent of those with partners who made the decisions. The corresponding percentages for past relationships are 27 and 70 percent. Hence, if a gay relationship is inegalitarian in decision making it is likely to be a relationship among age different persons while age differences predict less well to decision making.

Table 8.5 also shows that current relationships differ significantly from past ones in decision making. This difference is largest for the egalitarian category and minimal for the others. Such an association is consistent with the notion that inegalitarian relationships may be more fragile than egalitarian ones, although there are other possible interpretations.

The data presented above have shown that age seems to be a major criterion serving to define pools of potential erotic and romantic partners among gay men and also serving to define the expectable dominance structure in a relationship. However, it should be cautioned that since our measures of preference were in terms of "the man I like to relate sexually to," somewhat different findings might appear when asking about a partner with whom they would be interested in having a more significant or enduring relationship. It may be that in the case of enduring relationships, as opposed to sexual encounters, selection criteria favoring similarity on age and other variables operate with greater force and hence age different pairings or preferences

TABLE 8.5

LIKELIHOOD RATIO ANALYSIS OF DECISION MAKING BY COUPLE'S AGE
DIFFERENCE BY CURRENT VERSUS PAST RELATIONSHIPS

Partial (1st Order) Associations				Marginal (0-Order) Associations	
Effect	df	LR Chi-squared	p	LR Chi-squared	p
DA	4	90.35	.001	90.09	.001
DC	2	17.65	.001	17.39	.001
AC	2	0.51	.774	0.25	.882
DAC	4	1.95	.745		

Relation-ship (C)	Age-Difference (A)	Decision Making (D)[a] (Percent)			
		I Made Decisions	Half & Half	He Made Decisions	N(100%)
Current	Respondent 3 or More Years Younger	16 (30)	69 (44)	15 (74)	339
	Zero to 2 Years Age Difference	24 (24)	72 (25)	4 (12)	184
	Respondent 3 or More Years Older	32 (46)	64 (29)	4 (14)	255
Past	Respondent 3 or More Years Younger	18 (26)	60 (46)	22 (67)	243
	Zero to 2 Years Age Difference	28 (23)	62 (26)	9 (19)	141
	Respondent 3 or More Years Older	44 (50)	50 (29)	5 (14)	190

[a]Column percentages within categories of the relationship variable
are within parentheses.

Source: Compiled by the author.

would be less commonly found than among our data. However, since the patterning of age differences among our respondents with current actual relationships strongly resembled those among the preference data, we would expect no great differences in findings.

While there appear to be some similarities between the age different pairings found in our data and the Greek model of same sex relationships, the differences seem at least as great as the similarities. The Greek model involved liaisons with between adolescent or pre-adolescent youths and adult males. However, an interest in adolescent males was found to be virtually non-existent in our data. Of course, there do exist adult gay men who are principally or exclusively interested in adolescents (Silverstein 1981, ch. 8). They do not appear to exist in sufficient numbers to be detectable in most surveys of gay males.

Our data suggest that homosexual relationships in modern societies differ substantially from both the gender-role defined form found in the Latin American model and that found in the Greek model. The latter two forms of relationships seem severely inegalitarian while in the modern model the large majority of gay men believe in decision-making equality in the relationship, whatever the actual practice may be. Such egalitarianism in gay relationships seems to be economically facilitated by the rarity with which there occur cases in which one party to a relationship financially supports the other. Harry (1979, p. 623) found only one percent of his respondents were economically supported by another man and we found none at all in the present data. Since both parties to a gay relationship typically are employed total financial dependency is a basis for inequality in a relationship does not arise.

We do not here intend to depict dominance as being the only, or even the principal characteristic attributed to older males. Other characteristics such as emotional stability or masculinity may make older males attractive to other males of whatever age. For example, 53 percent (N = 419) of our respondents who had current or past partners three or more years younger than themselves found masculinity attractive in the "man I like to relate sexually to" versus 62 percent (N = 305) of those with partners no more than two years different in age versus 72 percent (N = 444) of those whose partners were three or more years older than themselves (X^2 = 33.64, df = 2, p. < .001). Masculinity thus appears to serve as an additional characteristic which serves to allocate potential partners.

HOMOSEXUAL EROTIC OBJECT CHOICE AS EGO IDEAL

It was earlier noted that formulations of gay liaisons in terms of "butch-fem" pairings have received little support in the research literature. In contrast to such formulations, Tripp (1975, pp. 75-79) developed the alternative hypothesis that what appeals most to the large majority of homosexual males is masculinity. This attraction is part of an idealization of masculinity which has become eroticized. The ego ideal has also become the erotic ideal. Under this hypothesis gay men who most value masculinity in themselves should also value it in their erotic partners and less masculine males should also be interested in less masculine males.

Table 8.6 tests this hypothesis by showing the associations among age, preferred masculinity in erotic partner, and the item "It is very important to me to look masculine." We find a quite strong association between preferred partner masculinity and self-valued masculinity. Those who value masculinity in the self also value it in erotic partners. We note that the partial associations of this table are somewhat stronger than the zero-order ones since age is positively associated with self-valued masculinity but negatively associated with desired partner masculinity. The adoration of masculinity in others declines with age while a desire to be gender-conventional increases with age, suggesting again that some defeminization may continue throughout adulthood.

The data of Table 8.6 suggest that the "butch-fem" hypothesis concerning gay liaisons was maximally misleading. Rather, they suggest that what may be more common are "butch-butch" and "fem-fem" liaisons, and that there is homophily in erotic object choice according to relative masculinity. This interpretation assumes, however, that those who value masculinity in themselves are also masculine while those who value masculinity less are less masculine. Table 8.7 tests this interpretation by examining "important to look masculine" by childhood and adult cross-gendering. We find that only adult cross-gendering has a significant and sizable association with "important to look masculine". The adult non-cross-gendered value masculinity in themselves more than the cross-gendered. The remaining question of whether the adult non-cross-gendered also prefer more masculine partners is also answered affirmatively in Table 8.8. Adult cross-gendering has moderate significant negative zero-order and partial associations with preferred partner masculinity while childhood cross-gendering has only a small positive partial association of borderline significance. We also note that the association of adult cross-gendering with preferred partner masculinity vanishes when "important to look masculine" is controlled (data not presented), thus indicating the importance of gender ideals for the self as criteria for choosing erotic others.

TABLE 8.6

LIKELIHOOD RATIO ANALYSIS OF PREFERRED PARTNER MASCULINITY BY
"IMPORTANT TO LOOK MASCULINE" BY AGE

Partial (1st Order) Associations				Marginal (0-Order) Associations	
Effect	df	LR Chi-squared	p	LR Chi-squared	p
PI	1	155.22	.001	142.90	.001
PA	6	23.23	.001	10.90	.092
IA	6	33.64	.001	21.31	.002
PIA	6	8.74	.189		

Age (A)	Importance of Looking Masculine (I)	Preferred Partner Masculinity (Percent)		
		Low	High	N^a(100%)
-24	Low	52	48	126
	High	19	81	166
25-29	Low	58	42	149
	High	20	80	231
30-34	Low	59	41	102
	High	27	73	201
35-39	Low	56	44	52
	High	29	71	130
40-44	Low	80	20	30
	High	29	71	80
45-54	Low	55	45	38
	High	38	62	96
55-	Low	77	23	13
	High	44	56	36

[a]Respondents had the option of indicating masculinity was not
important. Hence, these Ns are reduced.

Source: Compiled by the author.

TABLE 8.7

LIKELIHOOD RATIO ANALYSIS OF "IMPORTANT TO LOOK MASCULINE"
BY CHILDHOOD AND ADULT CROSS-GENDERING

Partial (1st Order) Associations				Marginal (0-Order) Associations	
Effect	df	LR Chi-squared	p	LR Chi-squared	p
IC	1	1.13	.287	0.81	.367
IA	1	63.55	.001	63.23	.001
CA	1	96.23	.001	95.91	.001
ICA	1	1.50	.220		

Adult Cross-Gendering (A)	Childhood Cross-Gendering (C)	Importance of Looking Masculine (I) (Percent)		
		Low	High	N(100%)
Some	Some	53	47	393
	None	48	52	52
None	Some	29	71	697
	None	33	67	381

Source: Compiled by the author.

TABLE 8.8

LIKELIHOOD RATIO ANALYSIS OF PREFERRED PARTNER MASCULINITY BY
CHILDHOOD AND ADULT CROSS-GENDERING

Partial (1st Order) Associations				Marginal (0-Order) Associations	
Effect	df	LR Chi-squared	p	LR Chi-squared	p
PC	1	3.91	.048	1.22	.269
PA	1	14.53	.001	11.84	.001
CA	1	88.97	.001	86.29	.001
PCA	1	0.46	.498		

Adult Cross-Gendering (A)	Childhood Cross-Gendering (C)	Preferred Partner Masculinity (P) (Percent)		
		Low	High	N^a(100%)
Some	Some	44	56	355
	None	46	54	48
None	Some	32	68	664
	None	39	61	364

[a]Respondents had the option of indicating masculinity was not
important. Hence, these Ns are smaller than others.

Source: Compiled by the author.

The associations of "important to look masculine" with
defeminization status, in addition to helping validate the
measures of defeminization status, indicate that differing gender
ideals guide the behaviors of our defeminization status groups.
The effeminate groups are less impressed with masculinity either
as a personal ideal or in an erotic partner. We also anticipated
that the actorized would be similarly less impressed with the
importance of looking masculine. We ran preferred partner
masculinity by "important to look masculine" by defeminization
status by actorization and found that actorization was
significantly negatively related to "important to look masculine"
at both the zero-order and second-order partial levels (data not
presented). Since, as suggested much earlier, the actorized
apparently view femininity as an achievement, their disinterest in
looking masculine is understandable. They were not found to

differ significantly from other groups on preferred partner masculinity at either the zero-order or partial levels. These data suggest that degree of masculinity serves as an assortative criterion in the gay world whereby persons of similar degrees of masculinity and cross-gendering choose each other. It is probably visible cultural role masculinity that is the operative criterion influencing choices rather than psychological masculinity which is not readily assessable in first encounters.

If erotic partner ideals are also ego ideals we may ask whether there are similarities between the two ideals on aspects other than masculinity. Do persons who eroticize young men also believe it is important to look youthful? Table 8.9 tests this

TABLE 8.9

LIKELIHOOD RATIO ANALYSIS OF "IMPORTANT TO LOOK YOUTHFUL" BY PREFERRED AGE OF SEXUAL PARTNER BY AGE

Partial (1st Order) Associations				Marginal (0-Order) Associations	
Effect	df	LR Chi-squared	p	LR Chi-squared	p
IP	4	42.77	.001	32.44	.001
IA	5	16.76	.005	6.42	.267
PA	20	225.38	.001	215.05	.001
IPA	20	24.76	.211		

Age (A)	Important to Look Youthful (I)	Preferred Partner Age (P)				
		-24	25-29	30-34	35-39	40-
-24	Percent Agreeing	56	41	29	40	20
	N(100%)	54	126	69	20	5
25-29	Percent Agreeing	55	55	37	39	9
	N(100%)	29	141	117	44	11
30-34	Percent Agreeing	70	53	40	35	18
	N(100%)	30	53	105	46	11
35-39	Percent Agreeing	42	59	59	27	38
	N(100%)	19	32	56	33	21
40-44	Percent Agreeing	100	55	73	42	33
	N(100%)	5	20	22	26	33
45-	Percent Agreeing	50	53	48	40	30
	N(100%)	16	17	42	40	40

Source: Compiled by the author.

hypothesis by presenting responses to the item "It is quite important to me to look youthful" by preferred age of sexual partner by age. We find here fairly strong associations between preferred partner age and feeling it is important to look youthful. These data are consistent with the hypothesis of erotic ideals as also ego ideals, although we should note some curvilinearity in the association of preferred partner age with important to look youthful among the older age groups. It may be that when there is a very large age difference between the respondent and his preferred erotic partner viewing one's erotic partner as also an ego ideal becomes untenable.

At this point we take up certain psychiatric hypotheses (Ovesey 1965; Hatterer 1970, pp. 36-37) with which the above presented data, particularly those of Table 8.6, have some apparent consistency. Although there are variants on these hypotheses, they basically argue that many homosexual males feel inadequate as males. Because of this self-perceived inadequacy, they engage in homosexual acts as a reparative mechanism for restoring their diminished self-esteem and psychological masculinity. Through incorporating the masculinity of other men, both physically and symbolically, they reassure themselves about their own perceived competence as males. These hypotheses imply that desires for masculine partners should be associated with diminished self-esteem and masculinity. We tested these implications by running self-esteem and psychological masculinity against preferred partner masculinity and found no hint of a relationship of the latter measure with either self-esteem (X^2=0.87, df=2, p=ns) or with masculinity (X^2=1.80, df=2, p=ns). We also tested the related hypothesis that a feeling that it is "important to look masculine" might be expressive of feelings of low self-esteem or lessened masculinity. "Important to look masculine" was not significantly associated with either self-esteem (X^2=1.07, df=2, p=ns) or psychological masculinity (X^2=4.32, df=2, p=ns). We also examined the associations of preferred partner masculinity and "important to look masculine" with self-esteem and psychological masculinity while controlling for childhood cross-gendering, defeminization status, and actorization. Under none of these conditions did any significant relationships appear between self-esteem or masculinity and partner masculinity or self-valued masculinity. Hence we find no support for the hypothesis of homoerotic behaviors as symbolically reparative acts. To idealize and eroticize masculinity in other men does not necessarily imply that one perceives oneself as deficient in the qualities one eroticizes.

THE GAY SOCIAL PARTICIPATION CAREER AND THE CRISIS OF AGING

Gagnon and Simon (1973, pp. 149-151) have posited the existence of a crisis of aging which occurs among gay men during their late 30's. They suggested that the gay world is essentially a singles world centered around the acquisition of sexual partners. Within that world a great emphasis is placed on physical appearance and youthfulness. As the gay man approaches forty he becomes less desirable and must eventually come to face the future prospect of diminishing sexual and social rewards from other gays. Unlike many heterosexuals, he also must often face aging alone without the supports of a wife, children or other relatives. Knowledge of the existence of such problems associated with aging seems common among gay men. Saghir and Robins (1973, pp. 174-176) reported common concerns over aging among their gay respondents.

Although aging is a concern among many gays it is important not to overdramatize its seriousness. Weinberg (1970) did find that gay men over 45 were more likely than younger gay men to live alone, to associate less with other gay men, to associate more with heterosexuals, and to experience less sex. However, he also found that this declining gay social and sexual activity was not accompanied by increased feelings of loneliness or depression, or other psychological problems. Rather, the older gay men were found to be somewhat better off psychologically than younger gay men. They evidently had adequately adapted to their lower levels of gay social participation. The Weinberg data also showed that those under 25 had the most psychological problems and resembled the oldest age group in having fairly low levels of social and sexual participation in the gay world. Apparently, the youngest were still in the process of coming out and disaffiliating from the heterosexual world.

Weinberg's (1970) data and Gagnon and Simon's (1973, pp. 149-151) ideas suggest that for some gay men the crisis of aging may constitute a turning point in the adult gay social participation career. The first stage in this career consists of coming out which typically occurs during late adolescence or during one's early 20's. During this stage one comes to accept one's gay identity and to adjust to the gay world (Dank 1971; Harry and DeVall 1978, pp. 65-67). One also disaffiliates from relatives and comes to focus one's friendships among other gays. The second stage, lasting until approximately 40 or 45, constitutes the period of active social and sexual involvement with other gay men. During this period most of one's close friends are other gays and one may acquire a, or several, lovers with whom one may live. Toward the end of this period there develops the crisis of aging which occurs due to declining sexual and social rewards from other gays. From the Weinberg (1970) data it would appear that a common solution to this crisis is a measure of social withdrawal from the gay world and a return to associating with heterosexuals as one did during the pre-coming out period. The crisis of aging may thus serve as a means for redirecting the older gay man's social energies toward alternative social relationships. Of course, the return to heterosexual associations need not be the only solution to the aging crisis and other solutions are possible within the context of the gay social world.

Several authors (Gagnon and Simon 1973, pp. 149-151; Friend 1980) have suggested that gay men undergo an "accelerated aging" process which occurs earlier in their lives than in the lives of heterosexual males. The reason for this early aging is that the gay social world is importantly a sexual world in which youthful beauty is emphasized. With the passage of youthful looks one's sociosexual value is sharply diminished and the prospects for a rewarding life decline. In contrast the period of life during which looks are emphasized among heterosexuals is largely restricted to the 20's when they are actively involved in courtship behaviors. While similar physical aging also occurs among heterosexual males the period during which those changes become evident is one in which physical attractiveness is no longer emphasized to such an extent. Encapsulated by involvement with their families during their 30's and 40's, these physical aging changes may go by largely unnoticed and not acquire the great social significance they seem to have in the gay world.

In discussing the possibility of accelerated aging among gay men it is important to distinguish two conceptually different aging changes which have been observed in the literature on aging. One change appears to be from a state of viewing oneself as "middle-aged" to viewing oneself as "old" (Harris and Associates 1975). Passing through this transition gives one the self definition of an old person or senior citizen. A second aging change is that of going through a mid-life crisis (Levinson et al. 1978; Gould 1972) which commonly occurs during one's early 40's. It is important to note that the contents of these two transitions differ considerably. The transition to old age is one in which the individual comes to see his active life of achieving or accomplishing things as largely over. However, the mid-life transition appears to be one during which the individual realizes that the remaining time for doing this is growing limited and he questions the direction of his life or lack thereof. He spends time thinking of the meaning of his life and either may redirect it or reaffirm its present direction. The central question of the mid-life crisis appears to be what to do with one's remaining life rather than whether there is any active life remaining. One senses the finitude of remaining time as the rising moon of death begins to glow beyond the now not so distant horizon.

The concept of accelerated aging seems to imply that gay men go through aging changes similar to those of heterosexual men but do it earlier. If this is so, one must ask whether this early aging refers to an early growing old or to an early mid-life crisis? The literature on this question is inconsistent. Kimmel (1978) has attempted to identify early aging with Levinson et al.'s mid-life crisis although his sample was only 14. Friend

(1980) seems to identify early aging with the transition beyond middle age. However, his data consisted only of self-identified "older" gay men and he lacked a control group of either heterosexual males or younger gay men or older not "older" identified gay men. It may be that the aging crisis observed by Gagnon and Simon (1973, pp. 149-151) may for some gay men be a mid-life crisis in which they redirect their lives to new activities and relationships while for others it may constitute the transition beyond an active middle age. It is also possible that which crisis is at hand among gay men approaching forty may only be answerable after examining the outcomes of that crisis. In this possibility the solution or adaptation reached may define the nature of the crisis. It is also possible that the crisis through which many gay men pass around age 40 is somewhat unique to gay men and that the analogies to heterosexual aging crisis are misleading. Below we attempt to get a purchase on the nature of the gay crisis of aging by examining its correlates and some of the conditions under which it is more and less likely to occur.

Our principal measure of concerns about aging is the Likert item "The thought of growing old bothers me." As Table 8.10 shows, those in their early 40's are more concerned about growing old than both the younger and the older respondents. Until approximately age 40, there is very little variation in response to this item. Also, those over 55 seem to have resolved their concerns about aging since they are the least likely of all age groups to be worried about growing old. Another manifestation of an apparent crisis of aging in Table 8.10 is the age patterning of responses to the item "It is quite important to me to look youthful." Looking youthful is of most concern to those from 40 to 44 years old and less for other age groups. That concern over looking youthful is a part of the crisis of aging is shown by that item's very strong relationship with worries about aging. Among those not worried about aging, 27 percent think it important to look youthful (N=966) as compared with 69 percent among those concerned about aging (N=580), (X^2=258.77, df=1, p. < .001). We should note that while here we are interpreting the "important to look youthful item" as expressing concerns over aging we earlier interpreted that item as indicative of a youthful emphasis component of the ego ideal. However, both of these interpretations are easily assimilable to the same concept of identification with youth or disidentification with age. While the "important to look youthful" item expresses a positive idealization of youth the "growing old" item expresses the negative side of this concept. We note the existence of the problem in data from one-time surveys that it is difficult to distinguish phenomena due to aging from those which are generational differences. However, in the present case this difficulty seems minimal due to the fact that the greatest concern about aging is found among males who are neither the oldest nor the youngest. The observed relationship of aging concerns with age would be somewhat difficult to assimilate to a generational interpretation since it would require that only those born between 1933 and 1938 should be especially concerned about aging.

Table 8.10 also reveals that self-esteem seems to take a dip during the early 40's and thereafter recovers. However, it recovers to a moderate but not high level as indicated by the

TABLE 8.10

WORRIES ABOUT AGING, SELF-ESTEEM, COUPLE STATUS,
SEXUAL ORIENTATION OF FRIENDS AND IMPORTANT TO
LOOK YOUTHFUL BY AGE (Percent)

		-24	25-29	30-34	35-39	40-44	45-54	55+
					Age			
Percent Worried								
About Aging		37	36	36	40	50	38	24
N(100%)		306	420	318	195	111	144	53
x^2 = 12.61				df = 6			p < .05	
Self-	Low	31	31	26	29	40	24	18
Esteem	Med	42	44	46	43	40	57	52
	High	27	25	28	28	21	19	30
N(100%)		305	417	318	195	111	144	54
x^2 = 21.38				df = 12			p < .05	
Percent Coupled		47	56	55	53	43	45	32
N(100%)		308	419	318	195	110	144	54
x^2 = 20.86				df = 6			p < .01	
Percent With Mostly Gay								
Friends		44	50	54	50	52	43	34
N(100%)		308	420	316	194	111	144	53
x^2 = 14.16				df = 6			p < .05	
Important to Look Youthful (Percent								
Agreeing)		39	44	43	46	53	45	28
N(100%)		307	418	319	196	111	144	54
x^2 = 13.04				df = 6			p < .05	

Source: Compiled by the author.

large percentages of respondents in the two oldest age groups who are in the medium self-esteem category. This moderate recovery supports the suggestion by Weinberg (1970) that one common adaptation to aging involves a decrease in both very negative feeling states and very positive feeling states. There occurs a measure of resignation or acceptance together with some lowering of expectations.

Table 8.10 also shows a number of other age-related changes which seem to parallel the changes in concerns about aging and indicate the timing of the gay social participation career. Having "a current lover or sexual partner with whom (they) are going or living" is most likely for respondents 25 through 39 and lower for the other age groups. This pattern supports the earlier suggested idea of there being both an early coming out phase during which the person affiliates with the gay world and a later aging phase during which there occurs a measure of disaffiliation. The data in Table 8.10 on the extent to which most of the respondent's close friends are gay or heterosexual again suggest a two-transition phasing of the gay social participational career. While the data of Table 8.10 show that a decline in self-esteem and an increase in worries about aging both occur in the same age groups they do not necessarily show that lessened self-esteem is directly associated with worries about growing old. However, Table 8.11 does show a sizable negative association of self-esteem with worries over aging. The crisis of aging thus appears to be one in which the gay man experiences doubts about himself.

Having established the existence of Gagnon and Simon's (1973, pp. 149-151) crisis of aging, although somewhat later than they suggested, we now must examine how it may articulate with the gay social participational career. Are differing forms of gay social participation more or less likely to be accompanied by aging difficulties? Table 8.12 presents worries about aging by age by whether the respondent has a current lover or sexual partner. We find that those with a current lover are somewhat less likely to be concerned over aging. Apparently their current success in coupling prognosticates for them a more benign aging process. The significant interaction effect shown in Table 8.12 indicates that the crisis of aging seems very largely confined to those not currently coupled. Among the uncoupled, the crisis of aging appears to be more common, to occur earlier, and to last longer than among the coupled. It thus appears that the existence and timing of the crisis of aging is conditioned by the social context within which it occurs and the individual's success in that context. The successful--the coupled--appear to anticipate little difficulties with aging.

While one's success or lack thereof in the sociosexual activities of the gay world appear to clearly influence the likelihood that one will experience a mid-life crisis, one's own standards defining success are also important. If one defines success in terms of activities or persons which are either scarce or not readily available to a person of one's own age the

TABLE 8.11

LIKELIHOOD RATIO ANALYSIS OF SELF-ESTEEM BY AGE
BY WORRIES ABOUT AGING

Partial (1st Order) Associations				Marginal (0-Order) Associations	
Effect	df[a]	LR Chi-squared	p	LR Chi-squared	p
SA	6	13.05	.042	15.52	.017
SW	2	67.83	.001	70.30	.001
AW	3	6.63	.085	9.09	.028
SAW	6	8.69	.192		

Worries About Aging (W)	Age (A)	Self-Esteem (S) (Percent)			N(100%)
		Low	Med	High	
Yes	-24	44	37	19	113
	25-29	37	46	17	149
	30-34	40	42	18	112
	35-39	44	36	20	78
	40-44	49	29	22	55
	45-54	40	42	18	55
	55+	38	46	15	13
No	-24	22	46	32	191
	25-29	27	43	30	268
	30-34	18	49	33	205
	35-39	19	47	34	116
	40-44	30	50	20	56
	45-54	15	66	19	89
	55+	12	55	32	40

[a]While the data are presented using seven age categories in order
to show the lack of variation among the three youngest groups, in
the significance tests we have combined the three youngest and two
oldest age groups.

Source: Compiled by the author.

TABLE 8.12

LIKELIHOOD RATIO ANALYSIS OF WORRIES ABOUT AGING
BY AGE BY COUPLE STATUS

Partial (1st Order) Associations				Marginal (0-Order) Associations	
Effect	df[a]	LR Chi-squared	p	LR Chi-squared	p
WA	3	8.32	.040	8.62	.03
WC	1	6.66	.002	6.96	.01
AC	3	12.17	.007	12.47	.01
WAC	3	8.22	.042		

Couple Status (C)	Age (A)	Worries About Aging (W) (Percent)		N(100%)
		No	Yes	
Coupled	-24	62	38	144
	25-29	67	33	233
	30-34	64	36	174
	35-39	67	33	103
	40-44	60	40	47
	45-54	74	26	65
	55+	88	12	16
Not Coupled	-24	64	36	161
	25-29	61	39	186
	30-34	66	34	143
	35-39	52	48	91
	40-44	44	56	63
	45-54	52	48	79
	55+	70	30	37

[a]While the data are here presented using seven age categories in
order to show the lack of variation among the youngest age
groups, in the significance tests we have combined the three
youngest and two oldest age groups.

Source: Compiled by the author.

likelihood of success seems considerably reduced. In the context of the gay sexual marketplaces, men who define success in terms of considerably younger men may go unrewarded and experience concerns over aging rather early. As a means of taking into account the individual's own standards of success, we examined worries about aging by preferred age of sexual partners by age (see Table 8.13).

TABLE 8.13

LIKELIHOOD RATIO ANALYSIS OF WORRIES ABOUT AGING BY
PREFERRED AGE OF SEXUAL PARTNER BY AGE

Partial (1st Order) Associations				Marginal (0-Order) Associations	
Effect	df	LR Chi-squared	p	LR Chi-squared	p
WP	4	46.22	.001	34.65	.001
WA	5	22.57	.001	11.01	.051
PA	20	223.48	.001	211.91	.001
WPA	20	14.05	.828		

Age (A)	Worries About Aging (W)	Preferred Age of Sexual Partner (P)				
		-24	25-29	30-34	35-39	40+
-24	Percent Yes	40	41	36	25	0
	N(100%)	55	125	69	20	5
25-29	Percent Yes	55	45	34	22	9
	N(100%)	29	141	118	45	11
30-34	Percent Yes	47	48	29	30	9
	N(100%)	30	73	104	46	11
35-39	Percent Yes	68	53	46	28	24
	N(100%)	19	32	56	32	21
40-44	Percent Yes	100	60	54	54	27
	N(100%)	5	20	22	26	15
45+	Percent Yes	50	29	48	32	26
	N(100%)	16	17	42	40	39

Source: Compiled by the author.

These data show that those interested in the young as sexual partners are considerably more likely to experience concerns over aging than are those interested in same-age or older men. Showing the combined effects of both age and preferred age, the percentage concerned about aging rises to 100 percent among those few men in their early 40's who like men under 25 and falls to zero percent among those few under 25 who like men over 40. These data suggest that for the gay world the crisis of aging is often, although not necessarily exclusively, formulated in terms of intimate relationships. The rewards one obtains or does not obtain in those relationships plus the standards one brings to intimate or sexual relationships create the conditions giving rise to an aging crisis and may provide the terms in which that crisis is worked out.

While the data of Table 8.13 show that those interested in considerably younger partners are more concerned about aging, we may also ask whether those concerns are justified? Do those interested in the younger experience less social and sexual rewards than other men of similar ages? Table 8.14, which presents couple status by the age difference between one's preferred partner and oneself by age seems to answer this question. Those interested in men more than five years younger than oneself are less likely to be in a coupled state than other men of the same age while those interested in older men are the most likely to be coupled. While we found that those interested in younger men are more likely to be concerned over aging and less likely to be coupled, we also found no significant association between being interested in younger men and number of sexual partners in the last year with age controlled (data not presented). It thus seems that concerns over aging are not primarily influenced by success or its lack in the sexual marketplaces of the gay world but rather by more intimate and meaningful attachments.

The above data appear to show that age preferences in partners play an important role in defining the terms through which an aging crisis is worked out. The increasing shift with age toward a preference for considerably younger partners places many gay men in a disadvantaged state since their attractions for younger men are often not reciprocated. A further outgrowth of this situation is that those attracted to the younger are more likely to be uncoupled and, as we saw earlier, it is among the uncoupled that a crisis of aging occurs most commonly. It thus appears that it is the youth orientedness of the gay world, and particularly the extent to which that youth orientedness exists in older gay men, which sets the stage for an aging crisis and defines what is to be considered a crisis.

While our data thus far suggest that it is declining sexual and intimate rewards which may precipitate the aging crisis, other data show that the aging crisis should not be perceived simply in sexual terms. Table 8.15, presenting number of sex partners during the last year by age by couple status, shows that the years during which the aging crisis most commonly occurs are also the

TABLE 8.14

LIKELIHOOD RATIO ANALYSIS OF COUPLE STATUS BY DIFFERENCE
BETWEEN AGE AND PREFERRED PARTNER AGE BY AGE

Partial (1st Order) Associations				Marginal (0-Order) Associations	
Effect	df	LR Chi-squared	p	LR Chi-squared	p
CD	2	19.84	.001	21.15	.001
CA	5	16.43	.006	17.74	.010
DA	10	605.80	.001	607.11	.001
CAD	10	7.35	.692		

Age (A)	Couple Status (C)	Preferred Age Difference (D)		
		Partner 6 or More Years Younger	Partner 5 Years Younger to 5 Yrs. Older	Partner 6 or More Years Older
-24	Percent Coupled	33	38	58
	N(100%)	3	161	144
25-29	Percent Coupled	47	54	60
	N(100%)	19	264	136
30-34	Percent Coupled	55	52	62
	N(100%)	82	168	68
35-39	Percent Coupled	43	53	71
	N(100%)	76	77	42
40-45	Percent Coupled	41	39	50
	N(100%)	63	23	24
46+	Percent Coupled	38	55	51
	N(100%)	144	9	45

Source: Compiled by the author.

TABLE 8.15

LIKELIHOOD RATIO ANALYSIS OF NUMBER OF SEX PARTNERS
DURING LAST YEAR BY AGE BY COUPLE STATUS

Partial (1st Order) Associations				Marginal (0-Order) Associations	
Effect	df	LR Chi-squared	p	LR Chi-squared	p
NA	6	25.31	.001	22.01	.001
NC	1	41.04	.001	37.75	.001
AC	6	21.56	.002	18.26	.006
NAC	6	3.80	.704		

Couple Status (C)	Age (A)	Number of Sex Partners (N) (Percentages)		N(100%)
		0-14	15-	
Coupled	-24	58	42	141
	25-29	55	45	215
	30-34	58	42	163
	35-39	51	49	100
	40-44	54	46	44
	45-54	79	21	62
	55-	47	53	17
Not Coupled	-24	44	56	154
	25-29	40	60	173
	30-34	38	62	133
	35-39	33	67	87
	40-44	34	66	59
	45-54	57	43	76
	55-	51	49	35

Source: Compiled by the author.

years during which the gay man experiences the largest number of
sexual partners. Hence, declining sexual rewards do not seem to
be an immediate cause of the aging crisis (cf. Figure 8.2).
However, anticipations of declining rewards may contribute to that
crisis since the uncoupled gay man in his early forties may be
less able to perceive a satisfying projection of his present
lifestyle into the future than a coupled gay man of comparable
age.

Couple attachments seem to influence the development of aging
crises while sexual involvements have little effect. Indeed,
we found that, controlling for couple status, number of sex partners
has a modest _positive_ association with worries over aging, again
suggesting that it may be difficult to project into the future a

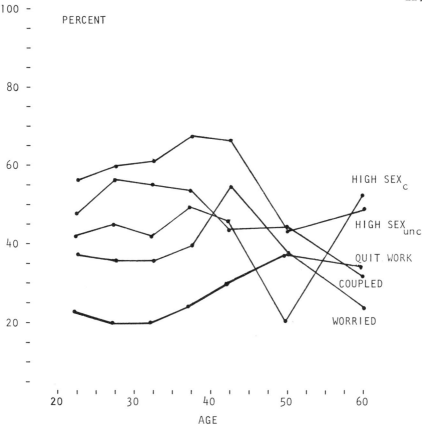

FIGURE 8.2 PERCENT WITH SELECTED CHARACTERISTICS BY AGE

satisfying lifestyle involving many sexual encounters (data not presented). That couple status contextualizes aging crises while number of sex partners is of minor significance suggests that it may be useful to distinguish between psychological attachments and sexuo-behavioral involvements. While psychological attachments typically give meaning and direction to one's life, behavioral activities do not intrinsically carry with them their own meanings and hence may or may not have significance for other aspects of one's life or provide indications as to the nature of one's future. As Hirschi (1969) found in the context of delinquency research, psychological attachments to others are of major significance in guiding one's behavior whereas simple physical involvement in various conventional activities such as sports is of little importance. In the present research, it appears that one may engage in sexual encounters with many or few other men but those encounters have little significance for other aspects of one's life. As Simon and Gagnon (1967) pointed out, it is hazardous to attribute intrinsic meanings to sexual behaviors and to define individuals in terms of their sexual behaviors.

In describing the mid-life crisis, Levinson et al. (1978) shows that it may be manifested in diverse spheres of one's life depending on the structures in which the individual is imbedded. It may be worked out in an occupational context in which the person evaluates how far he has come and whether it is still possible for him to attain further achievements. It may also be worked out in terms of marital or domestic attachments in which a man comes to realize his marriage is empty and dissolves it in pursuit of more rewarding relationships. The data thus far presented appear to indicate that for gay men the mid-life crisis is played out in terms of intimate and sexual attachments. Table 8.16 further supports this hypothesis of the "intimatization" of the mid-life crisis among gay men. We find that those who deem age an important criterion in erotic partners are more concerned over aging than those who responded that "Age is not important to me." Partner preferences once more seem to give meaning to the mid-life crisis. In these data using age as a criterion defining desirable partners may render one's own age salient and problematic since, if one is older, that criterion may also define oneself as undesirable.

While it is clear that many gay men seem to undergo aging crises which are framed in romantic/erotic terms one may also wonder whether gay men also experience aging crises defined through other aspects of one's life. Since Levinson (1978) describes many cases where the aging crises of heterosexual men are occupationally framed there should probably also occur similar experiences among gay men. Do gay men in their early forties also experience doubts about the directions their careers have been going and about the worthwhileness of their occupational attachments? In order to explore this possibility, we examined responses to the item "If you were to get enough money to live as comfortably as you would like for the rest of your life, would you continue to work or would you stop working?" by age and worries about aging (cf. Table 8.17). We interpret this item as indicating job or work attachment. Excluded from Table 8.17 are the retired. We see in these data that there is a significant interaction effect such that the crisis of aging occurs more prominently among those who would quit working. We note that the association of quit working responses with age, while specifying the relationship of age with worries over aging, cannot in any sense explain away the latter relationship. While worries over aging peak in the age period of 40 to 44 years, the quit working response shows little variation until 45 years of age and then increases for the oldest two age groups, presumably reflecting anticipations of retirement.

TABLE 8.16

LIKELIHOOD RATIO ANALYSIS OF WORRIES ABOUT AGING BY
IMPORTANCE OF PARTNER'S AGE BY AGE

		Partial (1st Order) Associations		Marginal (0-Order) Associations	
Effect	df	LR Chi-squared	p	LR Chi-squared	p
WI	1	10.49	.001	9.15	.002
WA	5	18.71	.002	17.37	.004
IA	5	22.09	.001	20.75	.001
WIA	5	3.01	.699		

Age (A)	Partner's Age Important (I)	Worries About Aging (W) (Percent) No	Yes	N(100%)
-24	No	69	31	39
	Yes	62	38	266
25-29	No	76	24	79
	Yes	62	38	340
30-34	No	71	29	66
	Yes	63	37	249
35-39	No	73	27	41
	Yes	56	44	154
40-44	No	64	36	22
	Yes	45	55	86
45-	No	72	28	53
	Yes	63	37	144

Source: Compiled by the author.

TABLE 8.17

LIKELIHOOD RATIO ANALYSIS OF WORRIES ABOUT AGING
BY AGE BY QUIT WORKING

Partial (1st Order) Associations				Marginal (0-Order) Associations	
Effect	df	LR Chi-squared	p	LR Chi-squared	p
WA	6	9.78	.134	10.25	.115
WQ	1	29.51	.001	29.98	.001
AW	6	19.03	.004	19.50	.003
WAQ	6	13.80	.032		

Would Quit Working (Q)	Age (A)	Worries About Aging (W) (Percent)		N(100%)
		Low	High	
No	-24	65	35	231
	25-29	65	35	325
	30-34	72	28	250
	35-39	63	37	142
	40-44	57	43	77
	45-54	68	32	90
	55-	73	27	30
Yes	-24	55	45	69
	25-29	60	40	84
	30-34	35	65	63
	35-39	47	53	45
	40-44	34	66	32
	45-54	52	48	50
	55-	73	27	15

Source: Compiled by the author.

The data of Table 8.17 indicate that attachment to work inhibits
the development of a mid-life crisis in the same way that
attachment to a current partner inhibited it.   Apparently
significant attachments to a variety of things provide meaning for
the individual and restrain propensities to question the meaning
and direction of one's life and future.   These data strongly
suggest that the mid-life crisis is a crisis of meaning which
occurs when the psychological hold of one's environment has
weakened.   In such cases the individual may continue to be
involved in activities such as sexual encounters or occupations
but not be very psychologically attached to them.   The mid-life
crisis appears to differ from other transitional crises in that it

occurs while one is within a stable life structure. In contrast, the rethinkings of the meaning and direction of one's life which occur during early adulthood and near retirement take place when one is in transition from one set of institutional structures to another. During the mid-life crisis, the psychological hold of the obtaining life structure on the individual seems to weaken without corresponding changes in the structure. The individual is behaviorally involved but not committed. Theoretically, persons in mid-life crises appear to resemble Merton's (1968, pp. 203-207) anomic ritualists who follow conventional rules but are not particularly committed to the goals for which those rules are designed.

Our data provide considerable support for Hirschi's (1969) control theory according to which psychological and moral attachments, but not behavioral involvements, restrain the individual from departing from conventional routines. Intimate attachments and work attachments provide meaning and interest for the individual. They assure him of the significance of the activities within which he is involved. When they evaporate avenues open up for changes in lifestyle. During such usually quiet crises the individual casts about for either new directions or new attachments to give significance to his life. Mid-life crises seem to occur as crises of meaning while one is involved in the stable life structure one has created during the period of early middle age. Usually in the course of building that structure some needs or interests were given priority while other less compelling ones were denied fulfillment. As the psychological hold of the environment weakens during the mid-life crisis, those older denied interests may cry for fulfillment before it is too late. The crisis then may involve a dialectic between one's met but no longer rewarding needs and those never met and possibly never meetable.

Since it has been shown that attachments to both work and other persons inhibit the mid-life crisis one may wonder whether these are separate effects or whether attachment is a general factor. Is meaning manifested in one area of one's life sufficient to give meaning to other areas? We examined worries about aging by age by couple status by the quit working measure (data not presented). The quit working/worries/age interaction remained significant while the couple status/worries/age interaction dropped below statistical significance. However, this result appears to be due to a third interaction between couple status, age, and quit working (cf. Table 8.18). The association between age and quit working responses seems completely confined to the uncoupled. Therefore, coupledness seems to inhibit the development of psychological disengagement from work during one's forties and later. However, coupledness does not appear to have this effect during earlier stages of life since there do not seem to be any strong propensities toward disengagement during those years. Indeed, there is a hint in the data that the coupled may be somewhat more disengaged from work during the earlier years,

TABLE 8.18

LIKELIHOOD RATIO ANALYSIS OF QUIT WORKING
BY AGE BY COUPLE STATUS

Partial (1st Order) Associations				Marginal (0-Order) Associations	
Effect	df	LR Chi-squared	p	LR Chi-squared	p
QA	6	19.37	.004	19.33	.004
QC	1	0.06	.802	0.02	.883
AC	6	19.07	.004	19.03	.004
QAC	6	13.85	.031		

Couple Status (C)	Age (A)	Percent Would Quit Working (Q)	N(100%)
Coupled	-24	26	143
	25-29	23	226
	30-34	22	172
	35-39	25	100
	40-44	19	47
	45+	26	77
Uncoupled	-24	20	158
	25-29	18	182
	30-34	18	141
	35-39	23	87
	40-44	38	61
	45+	41	109

Source: Compiled by the author.

perhaps because being coupled may provide a psychological distraction from work. That coupledness and work attachment are associated for the later years of life seems to explain the drop in the significance of the age/worries about aging/couple status interaction once quit working is controlled. Since attachment seems to be something of a general factor for the later years of life a control for either couple status or work attachment is partially a control on alternative measures of attachment.

Since couple status and work attachment appear to be important in influencing the advent of the mid-life crisis it would be useful to know what variables contribute to coupling and work attachment. While quit working responses have no significant association with either income or education they are related to occupational level. Of our upper white-collar respondents 16 percent (N=298) gave quit working responses; lower white collar, 24 percent (N=740); blue-collar respondents, 20 percent (N=78);

service workers, 33 percent (N=241); and among students the percentage was 19 (N=83); (X^2=21.97, df=4, p. < .001). This association between work attachment and occupational level is quite consistent with the many other studies on work attachment or job satisfaction (Hall 1969, pp. 47-48). It also provides a link between the psychological phenomenon of a mid-life crisis and the encompassing social structure. Being currently coupled has no significant relationships with education, income, or occupational level.

Returning to the question of whether the above presented crisis of aging among gay men is Levinson's famous mid-life crisis, we feel a fairly definite affirmative answer to this question is appropriate. Rather than being a special gay aging crisis, the phenomena observed seem to be part of the general aging crisis among males. Had our aging crisis been framed only in terms of sexual success in the gay marketplaces, we would have probably inferred that we were observing a special case. However, we found only a slight positive association of number of sex partners in the last year with concerns about aging. Alternatively, had concerns over aging been only influenced by couple status we would have also inferred the presence of a special gay aging crisis. However, since the aging crisis observed was found to be influenced by both work attachment and couple attachment the aging crises apparent among our gay respondents seem to assume both intimate and occupational forms and therefore resemble those reported by Levinson. If this is true, it means that the crisis of aging observed by Gagnon and Simon among gay men 15 years ago was an early discovery of the mid-life crisis.

While the data presented show a fairly benign resolution of the crisis of aging among the gay respondents, a methodological caution is in order. If some gay men withdraw from the gay world during their forties this means that, when one samples gays from that world, one will disproportionately acquire respondents who have resolved their aging concerns within that world and remained in that world. Hence, those gay men who found other, non-gay-world, solutions to their aging crises may appear rather different from those obtainable from the gay world. This problem arises out of the fact that students of homosexuality remain forever haunted by questions of whether their results are due to their sampling methods.

9

CONCLUDING
INTERPRETATIONS

CROSS-GENDERING AND SOCIAL CLASS

A question not dealt with above is that of the relationship between childhood cross-gendering and parental occupational level. Data on the socioeconomic backgrounds of the parents of homosexuals seem non-existent in the literature. This seems to arise because the researchers are interested in creating samples of comparable gays and non-gays and therefore attempt to match on parental occupational level or on current occupational level of their respondents. However, to control for occupational level of respondents is to indirectly control for parental levels (cf. Saghir and Robins 1973, p. 12 and Siegelman 1972). Hence, there seems to be no empirical evidence on the question of the relationships of either cross-gendering or homosexuality to parental occupational level.

Kinsey et al. (1948, pp. 438-439) have published data by both respondent's and parent's occupations on the incidence of homosexuality among single males. However, these data seem useless for purposes of assessing the relationships of homosexuality or cross-gendering with parental social class. As Gagnon and Simon (1973, pp. 131-132) have reported, those individuals classified by Kinsey as homosexual include more persons with only incidental adolescent homosexual experience than they include those who by some more stringent standard could be called continuingly homosexual.

Farrell and Morrione (1976) have reported that gay men who conform most to the popular stereotypes of homosexuals have lower socioeconomic levels than other gays, although their measure of stereotype conformity seems to be a mixture of cross-gendering items (e.g., cross-dressing) and those measuring simple participation in the gay world (e.g., uses homosexual slang). These data replicate the above presented relationship between adult cross-gendering and occupational level. Still, if it is true that gay men from parental blue-collar backgrounds are disproportionately upwardly mobile across the blue-collar line, data on the current occupational levels of gays are a very poor substitute for data on their parents' levels.

Despite the lack of evidence that there is a relationship between parental occupational level and childhood cross-gendering a number of comments are in order since such a relationship would modify some of the interpretations of the preceding chapters. If there is a relationship which would prove some of the above findings spurious it is that working-class backgrounds produce effeminate homosexuals while middle-class parental backgrounds produce less effeminate ones. This would be consistent with Farrell and Morrione's (1976) findings that the effeminate occupy lower status jobs. It would also be consistent with Leznoff and Westley's (1956) findings to the effect that more "overt" homosexuals are both younger and have lower status and more stereotypical jobs than more "covert" ones. Such a relationship, however, would not alter the findings on defeminization. It would explain the tendency of the non-effeminate to be more conformist in school participation, to be more educated, and to be less criminal. It would not explain the effects on conformity which are due to being a youthful loner since youthful loner is positively associated with cross-gendering during childhood and with various measures of conformity. Indeed, since most of the measures of conformity were shown to have stronger associations with being a loner than with childhood cross-gendering, introducing parental class into the analysis would probably strengthen the associations of loner, guilt, etc. with conformity.

The brief explorations of the relationships of parental background with other measures in the Detroit data provided some evidence that homosexuality, and perhaps cross-gendering, may have more or larger effects among gay youths of working-class parental backgrounds. Cross-gendered gay youths are more visibly gender-deviant in working-class culture due to the emphasis in that culture on masculinity. Hence, their rejection and alienation may be greater. Such greater alienation could conceivably explain the above discussed tendency for working-class gay youths to be more upwardly mobile in terms of education. It would also provide a further rationale as to why working-class cross-gendered gay youths may avoid entering their fathers' manual occupations, as they otherwise might be expected to, and to find jobs in some other sector. For these reasons, it is not anticipated that further, and much needed, research on the relationship of parental class and cross-gendering will substantially negate the findings. That relationship will be explored by the author in his next research project.

DEFEMINIZATION STATUS AND MALLEABILITY

It may seem in the above analysis that excessive emphasis has been given to the continuities in gender culture between childhood and adulthood exhibited by gay men and that more recent and contemporaneous influences have been underplayed. It may be felt that humans are more malleable than they have been represented. However, malleability is itself variable between persons. While many people are quite influenceable, others seem to be living rebukes to learning theory. The persistently effeminate are a good example of such individuals who seem able to pursue their private visions of the good and the beautiful despite tremendous, although intermittent, pressures to defeminize. In contrast are the defeminized who conform, although belatedly, to conformist pressures. The formulation of four types of homosexuals defined according to defeminization status brought malleability into the analysis as a variable, rather than treating it as a constant across all respondents.

The greatly differing degrees of malleability shown by the four defeminization status groups partly arises out of the substantive criteria used to define these groups. Defeminization status was defined in terms of degrees of childhood and adult commitments to gender culture. Gender identity, sexual orientation, and, to a lesser degree, gender role are among the most enduring cultural phenomena as psychiatrists attempting to "cure" deviations in these phenomena have found. Transexualism and homosexuality are viewed by virtually all psychiatrists as among the most difficult aspects of an individual to change through therapeutic means. (Briefly disputing Masters and Johnson's (1979) claims to have transformed homosexuals into heterosexuals, it is noted that 83 percent of their "cures" constituted making bisexuals more heterosexual in behavior.) Rigidity in gender phenomena seems particularly strong among males. Because defeminization status was defined in terms of gender-role commitments one would expect less malleability exhibited than if one had created a similar typology out of (say) past and present aggressiveness or self-esteem.

Gender as an ideal appears to be established in most people at very early ages and remains substantially immutable for most of their lives, although the content of those ideals may be somewhat more variable with age. People, particularly males, rarely question the ideal nature of gender ideals. Rather, they more commonly question the adequacy with which they or others approximate those ideals. Many seem indignantly proud of their loyalty to those ideals and question the gender-adequacy of persons who question gender ideals. Questioning gender ideals is often viewed as gender deviance. An effect of this is that gender ideals are infrequently reflected upon and intelligence becomes virtually inoperative in the area of gender.

It was found that those who were persistently effeminate were more cross-gendered as children than those who defeminized. This implies that earlier extreme commitments to a gender-role culture are less reversible than less extreme ones. Those who depart greatly from gender-role conformity early in life are less able to reverse or mute earlier commitments when social pressures make it expedient. This may occur because, at the extreme of a gender-role commitment, a role preference becomes an identity through which the basic self is defined or self-reified and repudiation of such commitments is felt to be a threat to the core self. Qualifying Money and Higham's (1976, p. 115) description, "gender identity is the private experience of gender-role," but only at the extreme of a gender-role preference. Transexuals are the best example of an extreme gender-role commitment being transformed into an identity which is retained throughout life at considerable personal cost to the individual. For those less committed to a feminine gender role that role is perceived as a preference or an option which may be put on and off as circumstance and mood permit. Hence, defeminization is possible and is not equivalent to the death of the self. Conformity to gender-role standards is also possible without violating a basic sense or self. Broadly generalizing, malleability in gender-significant behavior is reduced to the extent that role and identity have been fused.

It should be noted that there are differences in the psychologies of transexuals and of the actorized persistently effeminate. The former have fused role and identity whereas for the latter femininity remains only a role which may be detached from the self. That the actorized persistently effeminate retain a distinction between role and gender identity means that the idealized feminine gender role remains for them an object of aggressive striving whereas the fusion of role and identity in the transexual has eliminated the need for such strivings and the attendant showy displays of the feminine role. The transexuals have managed to integrate their ideals and selves and hence direct their energies to other tasks, usually the attainment of a sex-reassignment operation so as to create a further measure of integration. The integration of gender identity and gender role attained by transexuals may explain the earlier found differences in the psychologies of the actorized persistently effeminate and the quasi-transexuals. The aggressiveness of the former derives from their pursuit of femininity while the lack of aggressiveness of the latter derives from their attainment of femininity in both role and identity, although their solution gives rise to the problem of having a body with which they can not identify.

It is useful to entertain the question of the extent to which social pressures toward gender-role conformity are the source of the fairly general conformity found among the defeminized? Are the positive traits of the defeminized such as less criminality and being better students only due to social pressure to conform? Would these virtues vanish if there were less rigidly defined gender roles? On this question, partial answers seem possible.

To the extent that a general conformity is due to an alienation from youthful culture rather than directly due to defeminization one might expect that their general conformity would persist even in the absence of rigidly defined gender roles. Youthful alienation seems to arise out of a lack of appeal of the activities defined as appropriate for males. One of the major activities so defined is an interest in the opposite sex. Absent adolescent homosexuals becoming heterosexuals, it seems that a considerable measure of alienation would remain although it might be reduced somewhat if activities such as sports were more incorporated into the feminine role. It is noted that, while a conformist solution was found to be more common among the defeminized, it was not limited to them. Hence, pressure to defeminize need not be the only source of a conformist solution to alienation even though the defeminized are the best candidates for such a solution since they have already started on the road to general conformity.

The reader committed to a social interactionist perspective may feel that the gay youth has been excessively depicted as a person whose gender-role preference was formed during childhood and then remained largely unmodified throughout adolescence. Even among the defeminized that preference may have simply gone into hiding until adulthood while not being greatly changed and only became more muted and indirect in its expression. Such a representation of the childhood to adulthood evolution of the gay youth and his role preference is substantially what is here intended. However, that represented evolution is not in conflict with social interactionist principles. It appears from the published literature that the effeminate boy learns by age five or six that many persons, particularly males, do not approve of his role preference. Hence, he learns to suppress expressions of that preference on many occasions. He also learns to substitute more subtle expressions of a feminine role preference for such grosser ones as cross-dressing. To the extent that he is able to largely or completely conceal from others his role-preference and his incipient homosexuality (which he almost always conceals), he avoids interactions which focus on his feminine role preference; his preference goes un-noticed or commented on. To the extent that this occurs interaction which substantially modifies that preference cannot occur for he has too quickly learned to hide his interests. A basic principle of the social interactionist perspective is that the behaviors and attitudes of parties to a relationship are modified in the course of continuing interaction. However, when interaction does not occur (as in the case of loners) or centers on things other than the gay youth's role preference (as in the case of the defeminized), that interaction is irrelevant to the basic modification or elimination of a feminine role preference. Thus, partial defeminization prevents further defeminization. The case of defeminization of gay youths does not contradict the social interactionist perspective but only confirms it by pointing out the circumstances in which its principles governing conventional interaction cannot be expected to operate. In order to operate there must occur interaction and that interaction must be relevant.

The partial defeminization process here described is logically similar to the evolution of the subconscious in psychoanalytic theory. Within that theory the contents of the subconscious are not available to consciousness and are thereby not readily modifiable by the individual. In the present schema a feminine gender-role preference, while very largely available to consciousness, is not easily available to social interaction and cannot be as readily modified in the course of interaction as other less highly disapproved phenomena. Also, since a feminine gender-role preference is available to consciousness, the gay youth, knowing it to be disapproved, attempts to express it principally in those settings in which it will not be disapproved. He is thereby able to consciously subvert the principles of the social interactionist perspective. Returning to the analogy with psychoanalytic theory, the gay youth's early hiding of his role-preference in order to prevent its further modification would be called resistance, but in this case a very conscious resistance.

If partial defeminization forestalls further defeminization how does one explain the case of the persistently effeminate whose effeminacy must be more visible and thereby available to social interaction? In part, this is to be explained by partial defeminization on the part of the persistently effeminate. Even those who were extremely effeminate during childhood have reduced somewhat the levels of their effeminacy. However, the major explanation of their persistent effeminacy is that they simply had more invested in the feminine gender role during childhood and thereby had more to lose psychologically through relinquishing it. To the extent that the feminine gender role early became a basic part of their identities, as in the extreme case of transexuals where role and identity have been fused, they were simply less malleable and, in effect, told social interactionist theory to go to hell as they determinedly pursued their dreams of the good and the beautiful. As shown above, many of the persistently effeminate seem to be rather strong-willed persons able to withstand negative feedback.

It has been observed above that gender identity, sexual orientation, and gender role seem substantially unchangeable with gender role being more changeable. The present work is concluded with a hypothesis as to the reasons for that immutability. It is offered that the reason for the immutability of the basic components of gender, and particularly of gender identity, is that gender identity is established during the second and third years of life as Money and Ehrhardt (1972) have shown, and that period of one's life falls within the period of infantile amnesia. The phenomenon of infantile amnesia is that apparently no one can remember back into their childhood earlier than the fourth year of life (Campbell and Spear 1972). For some individuals the period of infantile amnesia may extend to the eighth or ninth year. The reasons for infantile amnesia, which is found in both humans and rats, appear to be several. A biological reason is that the central nervous systems of infants and children are still immature and throughout childhood there occurs the depositing of myelin in those systems which increases the ability of the system to transmit larger amounts of information. A second and psychological reason for infantile amnesia is that the systems for coding and filing information employed by infants and children are quite primitive and much information is misfiled or lost. For example, a coding system in which objects are categorized as either large or small and human or non-human would shortly make accurate retrieval of information impossible. A search in the large-nonhuman category could come up with a giraffe or the Empire State Building. Combinations of the biological and psychological interpretations of infantile amnesia are quite possible. A third reason offered for infantile amnesia is that children's later environments and modes of relating to their environments change sufficiently that earlier experienced events are no longer adequately evoked by their new different environments. Some evidence for this interpretation is available in rat experiments in which it is found that, if rats are placed into the same environment in which they once learned but subsequently forgot certain behavior, the relearning of those behaviors is enhanced.

Because of infantile amnesia the criteria employed by young children to reach conclusions about gender identity and gender role are not available to them or to others during later life. Hence, conclusions reached about one's own gender cannot be later corrected, disputed or modified. More importantly, the reasons for those conclusions cannot be disputed because they are no longer available. This statement must be qualified by observing that, if the conclusions and the criteria for those conclusions concerning one's gender remain constant over the years, it may be possible to modify earlier conclusions. However, it appears that in most cases, while the conclusions about one's gender remain the same, the reasons for getting to those conclusions change. Children typically do not employ the same criteria for labeling one's gender during early childhood as do adults, i.e., genitalia. Prior to age four children typically employ a wide variety of criteria other than genitalia to define gender (Kohlberg 1966; Kessler and McKenna 1978, pp. 103-109). These include height, hair length, clothes, whether the person works, whether the person likes or engages in various gender-typed activities, and how the parents have labeled the child. However, by ages six to eight there is a generally established agreement among children that the principal criterion of gender is genitalia.

Because the criteria for assessing gender often change between the period during which one is deciding on one's own gender and later years, it is hazardous to assume that very early gender-significant decisions can be modified through therapies or social influences. The most famous case of such an assumption was Freud's claim that genitalia were of over-riding significance in the eyes of children for the establishment of gender. Freud apparently needed this adultocentric speculation as to the importance of genitalia during early childhood in order to develop his concepts of castration anxiety and of penis envy. Even when children are aware of genital differences they may not use them as criteria of gender (Kohlberg 1966). While there are self-evident reasons for adults to consider genitalia very significant, young children seem to consider other phenomena at least as important or interesting; they must be taught that genitalia are important.

If children must be taught that genital differences are the major criterion distinguishing the sexes, the isolation of the genitalia as of primary importance seems to constitute an instruction in the teleology of the sexes and of sexuality. The primacy of genitalia implies that the sexes are designed for sexuality in general and heterosexuality in particular. Through such instruction an importance is given to sexual activities which they otherwise wouldn't have. Through such instruction children learn that sexuality is supposed to be a central focus of their lives, although the biological energies heightening that sexuality are not to arrive until puberty. We are not here denying the existence of sexuality during early childhood. Rather, it is suggested that the importance of that sexuality has been exaggerated.

The hypothesis here offered also explains why gender roles seem more malleable than gender identities. Although gender identities seem to be established during the second and third years of life, gender roles are learned later and over a more extended period. During the second and third years of life gender roles seem to have only minimal content and are largely gender labels. Their contents during that period seem to consist largely of physical differences and a few gross activities such as fathers doing things outside of the house while mothers do things inside the house. Toward the end of the period of infantile amnesia children begin to rapidly learn the immense degree to which gender roles have been elaborated and articulated with the larger economic and political structures such that they can rather accurately anticipate whether many occupations are gender-typed for men or for women (Nemerowicz 1979, pp. 67, 70). An easily testable implication of the amnesia hypothesis is that there should occur greater rigidity in gender-role typing to the extent that the individual's period of infantile amnesia lasts longer or is broader in scope.

The hypothesis here offered may also help to explain the phenomenon of those individuals who become transexuals late in life without a history of prior cross-gender interests. Such individuals are puzzling since neither a cross-gender role or gender identity appear to have prepared them for a transexual transformation. However, if they may have acquired a cross-gender identity during the period of infantile amnesia but acquired a same-gender role immediately after the amnesia period they would then be more prepared for their transexual transformations.

Subsequent events encountered during their adult years before their transexual tranformations may trigger the earlier internalized cross-gender identities in a manner similar to the way in which rats relearn previously forgotten behaviors when placed in environments similar to the ones in which they originally learned those behaviors. The later pre-transformational environmental events may trigger a reorganization of the archaic gender identity and their current gender role so as to bring them into greater concordance. Such individuals may fall in the two vacant columns of Figure 1.1 (columns 5 and 6) which had previously been left empty.

The implications of the gender identity/infantile amnesia hypothesis for sexual orientation are less clear. The lack of clarity arises out of the question of the extent to which gender identity versus gender role versus other factors are the principal determinants of sexual orientation. The case of never cross-gendered gay men who appear to have both masculine gender identities and gender roles suggests that neither identity nor role may be determinative of sexual orientation. Similarly, most cross-gendered gay men appear to have a conscious masculine gender identity. However, if it is possible for the early learned but forgotten gender identity to not be concordant with the later learned gender role, then the forgotten gender identity may be determinative of sexual orientation. In these cases the forgotten gender identity may be discordant with, but not necessarily conflictful with, the adult gender identity which arises as an inference from one's role behaviors. In this scenario the forgotten gender identity informs the individual's sexual behaviors while adult gender role informs his non-sexual behaviors. The two sets of phenomena may then constitute separate non-conflicting domains of the person's life. If this is the case with gay men, then the homosexual groups of Figure 1.1 would have to be reclassified into the right half of that figure.

It was earlier suggested that gender is teleologically defined for children in terms of their potential for future sexuality. Although children may come to conclusions as to their own gender identities using a wide variety of criteria, by middle childhood their gender identities are redefined such that gender and gender identities are significant primarily because of their potential for sexuality. Such a linking of gender identities with sexuality seems to make the early learned gender identities determinative of sexual orientation. In contrast, gender roles seem less defined in terms of sexuality and hence may be less important influences on one's adult sexual orientation.

The gender identity/infantile amnesia hypothesis introduces elements of the unconscious into the present analysis of gender. However, the unconscious here suggested is not Freud's subconscious. His dark, demonic, and melodramatic subconscious is created out of repressions and filled with fears and forbidden desires. The unconscious here suggested is a much more benign one. It is simply a dusty old attic containing abandoned toy preferences, childish ideas and ideals, and an identity or two. Whether it is a purely cognitive unconscious, unlike Freud's, or whether it has affective motivating aspects remains for future research. However, even if it is very largely a cognitive unconscious it may have potential for guiding the behaviors of individuals. Cognitions of the physical or essential natures of men and women are certainly consequential for the individual's subsequent behaviors.

An implication of the gender identity/infantile amnesia hypothesis is that research into the origins of gender identity is not possible when asking adults to recall their childhoods. Respondents can not remember the circumstances surrounding the establishment of their gender identities, although they can remember considerable material from the slightly later period when they were learning gender roles. This has implications for the conclusions reached by Bell et al. (1981a) in their recent book on the origins of sexual orientation, Sexual Preference. They found that a large number of measures of parental and peer influences on adult sexual orientation were quite poor predictors of adult sexual orientation. Their measures were largely derived from the many psychiatric theories on the origins of homosexuality. Finding that none of these theories were confirmed, they concluded that the origins of sexual orientation are probably biological. Of course, the form of their argument is one of default. It assumes that one has tested and eliminated all possible or feasible environmental hypotheses. While these researchers did test and eliminate a large number of environmental hypotheses, they did not eliminate all. They did not test hypotheses deriving from the establishment of gender identities. Moreover, they could not test such hypotheses since their data were derived from interviews of adults recalling their childhood characteristics and environments. For these reasons their conclusions on the biological origins of sexual orientation must be held in abeyance, although the biological hypothesis does have some support.

Another implication of the gender identity/infantile amnesia hypothesis is that the interpretations by some psychiatrists of homosexuality as being due to preoedipal conflicts should be seen as claims without evidence. In his 1978 reformulation of his theories on the origins of homosexuality Socarides described four forms: variational, situational, oedipal, and preoedipal. The situational and variational forms are of little interest here since they are due to temporary or adult environmental influences. The oedipal form is also of lesser interest since oedipal homosexuals seem similar to Ovesey and Wood's (1980) pseudo-homosexuals who are basically heterosexuals having a homosexual panic, plus a few other refugees from heterosexuality. Of major interest is the preoedipal form which purports to depict most gay men. In Socarides description preoedipal homosexuals are characterized by a "primary feminine identification, as a result of the inability to traverse the separation-individuation phase (from one-and-a-half to three years)," "fear of engulfment" by the mother, "remembering (being) often replaced by acting out," and "castration fear" (Socarides 1978, pp. 92-94).

The major problem with this analysis of male homosexuality is that all of the explanatory concepts or events derive from the period of infantile amnesia and events during that period are unavailable both to the gay patient and his therapist. Socarides appears to be admitting this when he says that "remembering is often replaced by acting out." If the gay patient can not remember back into the period of infantile amnesia we arrive at the situation where understanding of contributory events occurring during that period is based on the therapist's interpretations of the homosexual patient's post-period behaviors. Since the interpretation of the significance of post-period behaviors for events occurring during the period of infantile amnesia requires the assumptions of psychoanalytic theory, we arrive at a situation where a theory validates itself. By any scientific criteria this is nonsense.

Between his 1968 and 1978 volumes on homosexuality Socarides appears to have become aware of the need for more direct evidence on his theories of the preoedipal origins of homosexuality. "In this volume I have attempted a clear differentiation between data and theory, utilizing direct infant observations by child analysts whose investigations delineated the early maturational failures and vicissitudes of child development" (1978, p. 77). This sentence is then followed by a list of references to works by child analysts since, as is by now apparent, direct observations of children or reports by their parents appear to be the only credible means of studying children during the period in question. However, the child analysts whom he relies on for evidence do not make a clear differentiation between theory and data. For example, Galenson and Roiphe (1973), theorizing on the basis of one three year old child whom they observed in a nursery for many months, repeatedly state that indicators of "castration anxiety" were often observed in this child. However, not once do these authors state what observables or behaviors or verbalizations are being taken as indicators of castration anxiety. Again, theory appears to be validating itself.

A final implication of the gender identity/infantile amnesia hypothesis is that it may explain the nearly universal failure of psychiatry in general and psychoanalysis in particular in their attempts to change transexuals and homosexuals into gender conformists (Tripp 1975, pp. 236-239). If the events surrounding the establishment of gender identity and, more arguably, sexual orientation are unavailable to the patient and his psychiatrist, both are left in the dark as to the possible origins of those phenomena. If they assume that they are available when they are not, failure is virtually guaranteed. The failure of psychoanalytically informed psychotherapies to change transexuals and homosexuals into gender conformists seems especially telling for theories which from their inception have placed gender and the components of gender at the very core of their theories.

It is hoped that future research will take up the hypothesis here offered linking childhood amnesia, gender identity, and sexual orientation. In particular, longitudinal studies are needed to explore the link between gender identity and sexual orientation, given the inability of recall studies to reach back into the period of infantile amnesia. Richard Green (1980) is currently conducting such a longitudinal study of effeminate boys whom he first began observing during the middle 1960s. Within a few years it should be possible to assess many of these boys adult sexual orientations. However, given the phenomenon of infantile amnesia, it should be cautioned that observations of the gender typing of boys during middle childhood may not adequately represent the characteristics of those boys during early childhood. Green's study appears to be able to circumvent this problem since, although most of his observations of the boys seem to come from middle childhood, he also has available the mothers' reports about the boys for early childhood.

It is hoped that the concept of the unconscious here developed will be used by future researchers with greater caution and evidence than the Freudian subconscious has been used. Psychoanalytically informed theories have placed into that subconscious numerous constructs such as separation-individuation conflicts, penis envies, multiple identities, castration anxieties, and repressions. The observable bases for the creation of such constructs are typically not described. Subsequently, the constructs are pulled out of the subconscious to explain the phenomena from which they were derived. It is hoped that future researchers will not begin to populate the mind of the child during the period of infantile amnesia with similar Ptolemaic epicycles.

APPENDIX

Very shortly before the present work was to go to press the volume <u>Sexual</u> <u>Preference:</u> <u>Statistical</u> <u>Appendix</u> was published (Bell et al. 1981b). The data in many of the tables of that work are similar to the data of the present work. In particular, that work contains numerous gay/non-gay comparisons which are also examined in the present work. Hence, a brief comparison of the findings of the present work with those of the work by Bell et al. is in order. Since there are no instances in <u>Sexual</u> <u>Preference</u> where their findings do not replicate the findings of the present work, only the replications are explored below.

The data of <u>Sexual</u> <u>Preference</u> reveal sizable gay/non-gay differences in childhood gender-typed interests and behaviors. Sixty-eight percent of their white homosexual males (WHMs) (N=575) reported that they were "Not at all" or "Very little" interested in "boys' activities (e.g., baseball, football)" during grade school compared with 11 percent (N=284) of the white heterosexual males (WHTMs). The comparable percentages for black males (BHMs) were 37 (N=111) and 4 (BHTMs) (N=53). The percentages ever cross-dressing during grade school were 32 (WHMs; N=574), 10 (WHTMs; N=284), 36 (BHMs; N=111), and 8 (BHTMs; N=53). In response to the question "To what extent did you enjoy specifically girls' activities (e.g., hopskotch, playing house, jacks?" the percentages responding "Somewhat" or "Very Much" were 46 (WHMs; N=575), 12 (WHTMs; N=284), 56 (BHMs; N=111), and 10 (BHTMs; N=53). Other items on childhood cross-gendering show similar differences.

Their data also replicate the gay/non-gay differences in being a loner. In response to the question for grade school, "to what extent were you a loner?," the percentages responding "Somewhat" or "Very Much" were 71 (WHMs; N=575), 50 (WHTMs; N=284), 61 (BHMs; N=111), and 41 (BHTMs; N=53). Their data also show persistence in the loner characteristic. In response to the question for high school, "to what extent were you a loner" the percentages responding "Some" or "Very Much" were 70 (WHMs; N=575), 53 (WHTMs; N=284), 55 (BHMs; N=111), and 38 (BHTMs; N=53). Responses in the expectable directions during high school were also found on a number of items measuring alienation from peers. These items include "How often did you feel left out?", "How popular were you with kids your own age?", "Would you say you had more, as many as, or fewer friends during those years than other kids your own age?", and "During this time period, to what extent do you think you were different from the other (same-sex peers) your age?" As a follow-up question to the last question, their respondents were asked "In what ways do you think you were different?" Sizable differences between the gay and nongay males were reported for "Amount of interest in sports" and "Homosexual interests and/or lack of heterosexual ones." The Bell et al. data also report that the median age at which gay respondents label themselves homosexual appears to be about 18 or 19 (p. 83).

In the present work, it was argued that guilt over one's perceived homosexuality is a characteristic which is virtually unique to gays and one which is unlikely to be found among heterosexuals. Some of the Bell et al. data bear on this point (p. 83). Only their heterosexual respondents were asked "During the time that you were growing up, did you ever feel that you were sexually different?" Only 12 percent of the WHTMs (N=284) and 4 percent of the BHTMs (N=53) responded yes. Of those who responded yes, 22 percent of the whites and zero percent of the blacks mentioned "homosexual interests or behaviors."

The Bell et al. data also bear on the defeminization status categories employed in the present work. In the present work, the percentages of respondents in these categories were: persistently effeminate, 26 percent; newly effeminate, 3 percent; defeminized, 46 percent; never effeminate, 25 percent. In the Bell et al. study, the interviewers rated the respondents on their apparent masculinity or femininity. The percentage rated "Very feminine (effeminate)" or "Somewhat feminine (effeminate)" was 29 percent among the WHMs and 30 percent among the BHMs. The numbers in these groups correspond quite closely to the combined 29 percent in our combined persistently effeminate and newly effeminate categories. The respective percentages of the WHMs alnd BHMs who were rated "Somewhat masculine" or "Very masculine" were 23 and 29. These percentages correspond closely to the 25 percent of the respondents in the present study who were categorized as never effeminate. The rest of the male homosexual respondents in the Bell et al. study were placed in a category labeled "Neither especially feminine nor especially masculine." The respective percentages of the WHMs and BHMs placed in this category were 48 and 41. It is worth noting that, while it is occasionally claimed that there are a fair number of effeminate heterosexual men, the respective percentages of WHTMs and BHTMs described as "Very feminine (effeminate)" or "Somewhat feminine (effeminate)" in the Bell et al. study were 1 and 0.

BIBLIOGRAPHY

Albini, Joseph. 1971. The American Mafia: Genesis of a Legend. Boston: Appleton-Century.

Astin, Alexander. 1972. "College Dropouts: A National Profile." American Council on Education Research Monographs 7(1).

Bakwin, Harry. 1968. "Deviant Behavior in Children: Relation to Homosexuality." Pediatrics 41(3):620-629.

Barr, R. F., B. Raphael, and Norma Hennessey. 1974. "Apparent heterosexuality in two male patients requesting change-of-sex operation." Archives of Sexual Behavior 3(July):325-330.

Bates, J. E., and P. M. Bentler. 1973. "Play activities of normal and effeminate boys." Developmental Psychology 9(July):20.

Bates, J. E., P. M. Bentler, and S. Thompson. 1973. "Measurement of deviant gender development in boys." Child Development 44(September):591-598.

Bell, Alan. 1969. "The Scylla and Charybidis of psychosexual development." Journal of Sex Research 5(May):86-89.

Bell, Alan, and Martin Weinberg. 1978. Homosexualities. New York: Simon and Schuster.

Bell, Alan, Martin Weinberg, and Sue Hammersmith. 1981a. Sexual Preference. Bloomington, Ind.: Indiana University Press.

_____. 1981b. Sexual Preference: Statistical Appendix. Bloomington, Ind.: Indiana University Press.

Bem, S. L. 1974. "The measurement of psychological androgyny." Journal of Consulting and Clinical Psychology 42(April):155-162.

Bergler, E. 1956. Homosexuality: Disease or Way of Life? New York: Hill and Wang.

Bernard, Jessie. 1981. The Female World. New York: Free Press.

Berzins, J., M. Welling, and R. Welter. 1978. "A new measure of psychological androgyny based on the Personality Research Form." Journal of Consulting and Clinical Psychology 46(February):126-138.

250

Bieber, I., H. J. Dain, P. R. Dince, M. G. Dreelich, H. G. Grand, R. H. Gundlach, M. W. Kremer, A. H. Rifkin, C. W. Wilber, and T. B. Bieber. 1962. Homosexuality: A Psychoanalytic Study. New York: Basic Books.

Blumstein, Philip, and Pepper Schwartz. 1977. "Bisexuality: Some social psychological issues." Journal of Social Issues 33(2):30-45.

Bochman, Jerald. 1970. Youth in Transition: The Impact of Family Background and Intelligence on Tenth-Grade Boys, v.II. Ann Arbor, MI: Survey Research Center, Institute for Social Research.

Brown, Daniel. 1956. "Sex-role preference in young children." Psychological Monographs, 70(14).

Brown, Daniel. 1957. "Masculinity-femininity development in children." Journal of Consulting Psychology 21(June):197-202.

Brown, M. D. (ed.). BMDP Biomedical Computer Programs. Berkeley: University of California Press, 1977.

Burton, Roger, and John Whiting. 1961. "The absent father and cross-sex identity." Merrill-Palmer Quarterly 7(January):85-95.

Campbell, Byron A., and Norman E. Spear. 1972. "The ontogeny of memory." Psychological Review 79(May):215-236.

Carrier, Joseph. 1977. "Sex-role preferences as an explanatory variable in homosexual behavior." Archives of Sexual Behavior 6(January):53-65.

_____. 1971. "Participants in urban Mexican male homosexual encounters." Archives of Sexual Behavior 1(4):279-291.

Cavan, Sherri. 1966. Liquor License: An Ethnography of Bar Behavior. Chicago: Aldine.

Cohen, Albert. 1955. Delinquent Boys. New York: Free Press.

Cole, Nancy, and Gary Hansen. 1973. "An analysis of the structure of vocational interests." In The Vocational Interests of Young Adults, ed. Gary Hansen and Nancy Cole, pp. 57-72. Iowa City: American College Testing Program.

Coleman, James. 1961. The Adolescent Society. New York: Free Press.

Cotton, Wayne L. 1972. "Role-playing substitutions among male homosexuals." Journal of Sex Research 8(November):310-323.

Cross, J. F., and J. Cross. 1971. "Age, sex, race, and the perception of facial beauty." Developmental Psychology 5(3):433-439.

Cullen, Francis, Kathryn Golden, and John Cullen. 1979. "Sex and delinquency: A partial test of the masculinity hypothesis." Criminology 17(November):301-310.

Daley, Nelda. 1981. "Are 'Little Women' really 'Little Men'? Stereotyping or androcentric bias in the contemporary American novel. Paper presented at the meetings of the American Sociological Association. Toronto, August. Mimeographed.

Dank, Barry. 1971. "Coming out in the gay world." Psychiatry 34(May):180-197.

Datesman, Susan, Frank Scarpitti, and Richard Stephenson. 1975. "Female delinquency: An application of self and opportunity theories." Journal of Research in Crime and Delinquency 12(July):107-123.

Davis, Nannette. 1981. "Prostitutes." In Deviance, ed. Earl Rubington and Martin Weinberg, pp. 305-313. New York: MacMillan.

Delph, Edward. 1979. The Silent Community. Beverly Hills: Sage.

DeVall, William. 1979. "Leisure and lifestyles among gay men." International Review of Modern Sociology 9(July-December):179-195.

Diamond, John T. 1977. "On the Social Structure of Imagery." Unpublished Ph.D. dissertation, Ohio State University.

Dion, K. 1977. "The incentive value of physical attractiveness for young children." Personality and Social Psychology Bulletin 3(Winter):67-70.

Dion, K., E. Berscheid, and E. Walster. 1972. "What is beautiful is good." Journal of Personality and Social Psychology 24(December):285-298.

Doidge, William, and Wayne Holtzmen. 1960. "Implications of homosexuality among air force trainees." Journal of Consulting Psychology 24(February):9-13.

Dover, K. J. 1978. Greek Homosexuality. London: Duckworth.

Drake, Charles, and Daniel McDougall. 1978. "Effects of the absence of a father and other male models on the development of boys' sex-roles." Developmental Psychology 13(September):537-538.

Duncan, Beverly, and Otis Dudley Duncan. 1978. Sex Typing. New York: Academic Press.

Edelbrock, Craig, and Alan Sugawara. 1978. "Acquisition of sex-typed preference in pre-school aged children." Developmental Psychology 14(November):614-623.

Ehrhardt, Anke. 1979. "The interactional model of sex hormones and behavior." In Human Sexuality, ed. H. Katchadourian, pp. 150-160. Berkeley: University of California Press.

Elliott, Delbert, and Harwin Voss. 1974. Delinquency and dropout. Lexington, MA: Heath.

Erickson, Maynard. 1971. "The group context of delinquent behavior." Social Problems 19(Summer):114-129.

Evans, Ray. 1972. "Physical and biochemical characteristics of homosexual men." Journal of Consulting and Clinical Psychology 39(August):140-147.

Fagot, Beverly. 1977. "Consequences of moderate cross-gender behavior in pre-school children." Child Development 48(September):902-907.

Farrell, Ronald, and Thomas Morrione. 1974. "Social interaction and stereotypic responses to homosexuals." Archives of Sexual Behavior 3(September):425-442.

Farrell, Ronald, and James Nelson. 1976. "A causal model of secondary deviance: the case of homosexuality." Sociological Quarterly 17(Winter):109-120.

Feinbloom, D., M. Fleming, V. Kijewski, and M. Schulter. 1976. "Lesbian/feminist orientation among male-to-female transsexuals." Journal of Homosexuality 2(Fall):59-71.

Fenichel, Otto. 1945. The Psychoanalytic Theory of Neurosis. New York: Norton.

Freund, Kurt. 1974. "Male homosexuality." In Understanding Homosexuality, ed. J. A. Loraine, pp. 25-81. New York: Elsevier.

Freund, Kurt, Ernest Nagler, Ronald Langevin, Andrew Zajac, and Betty Steiner. 1974. "Measuring feminine gender identity in homosexual males." Archives of Sexual Behavior 3(May):249-260.

Freund, Kurt, R. Langevin, J. Satterberg, and B. Steiner. 1977. "Extension of the gender identity scale for males." Archives of Sexual Behavior 6(November):507-519.

Friend, Richard. 1980. "Gayging: Adjustment and the older gay male." Alternative Lifestyles 3(May):231-248.

Gagnon, John. 1979. "The interaction of gender roles and sexual conduct." In Human Sexuality, ed. H. Katchadourian, pp. 225-245. Berkeley: University of California Press.

_____. 1973. "Scripts and the coordination of sexual conduct." In Nebraska Symposium on Motivation, ed. James Cole and Richard Diensbier, pp. 27-59. Lincoln: University of Nebraska Press.

Gagnon, John, and William Simon. 1973. Sexual Conduct. Chicago: Aldine.

Galenson, E., and H. Roiphe. 1973. "Object loss in early sexual development." Psychoanalytic Quarterly 42(January):73-90.

Gibbs, Leonard. 1974. "Effects of legal procedures on juvenile offenders' self-attitudes. Journal of Research in Criminology and Delinquency 11(January):51-55.

Goertzel, Mildred, Victor Goertzel and Ted Goertzel. 1979. "Coping with sexual divergency: Experiences of eminent homosexuals." Paper presented at the Meetings of the American Sociological Association, August, New York. Mimeographed.

Goffman, Erving. 1961. Asylumns. Garden City, N.Y.: Doubleday.

Gold, Martin, and David Mann. 1972. "Delinquency and defense." American Journal of Orthopsychiatry 42(April):463-479.

Gould, Robert. 1972. "The phases of adult life." American Journal of Psychiatry 129(November):521-531.

Green, Richard. 1980. "Patterns of sexual identity in childhood." In Homosexual Behavior, ed. Judd Marmor, pp. 255-256. New York: Basic Books.

_____. 1979. "Biological influences on sexual identity." In Human Sexuality, ed. H. Katchadourian, pp. 115-133. Berkeley: University of California Press.

_____. 1976. "One-hundred ten feminine and masculine boys: Behavioral contrasts and demographic similarities." _Archives of Sexual Behavior_ 5(September):425-446.

_____. 1974. _Sexual Identity Conflict in Children and Adults._ New York: Basic Books.

Green, R., M. Fuller, B. R. Rutley, and J. Hendler. 1972. "Playroom toy preferences of fifteen masculine and fifteen feminine boys." _Behavior Therapy_ 3(July):425-429.

Green, Richard, and John Money, eds. 1969. _Transsexualism and Sex Reassignment._ Baltimore: John Hopkins University Press, 1969.

_____. 1966. "Stage-acting, role-taking, and effeminate impersonation during boyhood." _Archives of General Psychiatry_ 15(November):535-538.

Greenberg, J. S. 1973. "A study of self-esteem and alienation of male homosexuals." _Journal of Psychology_ 83(January):137-143.

Grosser, George. 1951. "Juvenile Delinquency and Contemporary American Sex Roles." Ph.D. dissertation. Cambridge, Mass.: Harvard University.

Haist, Mark, and Jay Hewitt. 1974. "The butch-fem dichotomy in male homosexual behavior." _Journal of Sex Research_ 10(February):68-75.

Hall, Richard. 1975. _Occupations and the Social Structure_, 2nd ed. Englewood Cliffs, N.J.: Prentice-Hall.

Harris, Anthony. 1977. "Sex and theories of deviance." _American Sociological Review_ 42(February):3-16.

Harris, L., and Associates. 1975. _The myth and reality of aging in America._ Washington, D.C.: National Council on Aging.

Harry, Joseph. 1982. "Derivative deviance: The cases of fag-bashing, blackmail, and shakedown of gay men." _Criminology_ 19(February):in press.

_____. 1979. "Bisexuality and psychological well-being in men." Paper presented at the Meetings of the Society for the Study of Social Problems. Boston, August.

Harry, Joseph, and William DeVall. 1978. _The Social Organization of Gay Males._ New York: Praeger.

Hart, Maureen, Howard Roback, Bennett Tittle, Larry Weitz, Barbara Walston and Embry McKee. 1978. "Psychological adjustment of nonpatient homosexuals: Critical review of the research literature." Journal of Clinical Psychiatry 39(July):27-31.

Hatterer, Lawrence. 1970. Changing Homosexuality in the Male. New York: McGraw-Hill.

Heilbrun, Alfred. 1973. "Parent identification and filial sex-role behavior." In Nebraska Symposium on Motivation, ed. J. Cole and Richard Diensbier, pp. 125-194. Lincoln: University of Nebraska Press.

Heilbrun, Alfred, and Norman Thompson. 1977. "Sex-role identity and male and female homosexuality." Sex Roles 3(February):65-79.

Herdt, Gilbert. 1981. Guardians of the Flutes. New York: McGraw-Hill.

Heston, L., and J. Shields. 1968. "Homosexuality in twins: A family study and a registry study." Archives of General Psychiatry 18(February):149-160.

Hindelang, Michael. 1976. Criminal Victimization in Eight American Cities. Cambridge, MA: Ballinger.

Hirschi, Travis. 1969. The Causes of Delinquency. Berkeley, CA: University of California Press.

Hite, Shere. 1981. The Hite Report on Male Sexuality. New York: Knopf.

Hoffman, Martin. 1968. The Gay World. New York: Basic Books.

Holeman, R. E., and G. Winokur. 1965. "Effeminate homosexuality: A disease of childhood." American Journal of Orthopsychiatry 35(January):48-56.

Hooker, Evelyn. 1958. "Male homosexuality in the Rorschach." Journal of Projective Techniques 22(March):33-54.

_____. 1957. "The adjustment of the male overt homosexual." Journal of Projective Techniques 21(March):18-31.

Humphries, Laud. 1971. "New styles in homosexual manliness." Transaction 8(March/April):38-46.

Hunt, Janet. 1980. "Sex stratification and male biography." Sociological Quarterly 21(Spring):143-156.

Jones, Warren, Mary Chernovetz, and Robert Hansson. 1978. "The enigma of androgyny." Journal of Consulting and Clinical Psychology 46(April):298-313.

Kallman, F. J. 1952. "Twin sibships and the study of male homosexuality." American Journal of Human Genetics 4:136-146.

Kameny, Franklin. 1972. "Gay liberation and psychiatry." In The Homosexual Dialectic, ed. J. McCaffrey, pp. 182-194. Englewood Cliffs, N.J.: Prentice-Hall.

Kando, Thomas. 1974. "Males, females, and transsexuals." Journal of Homosexuality 1(1):45-64.

_____. 1973. Sex Change: The Achievement of Gender Identity Among Feminized Transexuals. Springfield, IL: Charles C. Thomas.

Karlen, Arno. 1978. "Homosexuality: The scene and its students." In The Sociology of Sex, ed. J. Henslin and E. Sagarin, pp. 223-248. New York: Schocken.

Karlen, Arno. 1971. Sexuality and Homosexuality. New York: Norton.

Karr, Rodney. 1978. "Homosexual labeling and the male role." Journal of Social Issues 34(3):73-83.

Keating, Walter. 1961. "Scholarship of participants in high school football." The Athletic Journal 41(February):11ff.

Keeves, John. 1973. "Differences between the sexes in mathematics and science courses." International Review of Education 19(1):47-63.

Kelly, James. 1979. "The aging male homosexual: Myth and reality." In Gay Men, ed. M. Levine, pp. 253-262. New York: Harper & Row.

Kelly, Jeffrey, and Judith Worell. 1977. "New formulations of sex-roles and androgyny: A critical review." Journal of Clinical and Consulting Psychology 45(December):1101-1115.

Kerckoff, A. 1974. "The social context of interpersonal attraction." In Foundations of Interpersonal Attraction, ed. T. Huston, pp. 61-78. New York: Academic Press.

Kessler, Suzanne, and Wendy McKenna. 1978. Gender: An Ethnomethodological Approach. New York: Wiley.

Kimmell, Douglas. 1978. "Adult development and aging: A gay perspective." Journal of Social Issues 34(3):113-130.

Klockars, Carl. 1974. The Professional Fence. New York: Free Press.

Kinsey, Alfred, Wardell Pomeroy, and Clyde Martin. 1948. Sexual Behavior in the Human Male. Philadelphia: W. B. Saunders.

Kinsey, A. C., W. Pomeroy, C. Martin, and P. Gebhard. 1953. Sexual Behavior in the Human Female. Philadelphia: W. B. Saunders.

Kohlberg, Lawrence 1966. "A cognitive developmental analysis of children's sex-role concepts and attitudes." In The Development of Sex Differences, ed. Eleanor Maccoby, pp. 82-173. Stanford, CA: Stanford University Press.

Kohlberg, Lawrence, and Edward Zigler. 1967. "The impact of cognitive maturity on the development of sex-role attitudes in the years 4 to 8." Genetic Psychology Monographs 75(February):89-165.

Lavin, David. 1973. "Sociological determinants of academic performance." In The School in Society, ed. S. Sieber and D. Wilder, pp. 78-98. New York: Free Press.

Lebovitz, P. S. 1972. "Feminine behavior in boys." American Journal of Psychiatry 128(April):1283-1289.

Lehne, Gregory. 1976. "Homophobia among men." In The Forty-Nine Percent Majority, ed. D. David and R. Brannon, pp. 66-88. Reading, MA: Addison-Wesley.

Lemert, Edwin. 1967. Human Deviance, Social Problems, and Social Control. Englewood Cliffs, N.J.: Prentice-Hall.

Levine, Robert A. 1979. "Anthropology and sex: Developmental aspects." In Human Sexuality, ed. H. Katchadourian, pp. 309-319. Berkeley: University of California Press.

Levine, Edward, Charles Phaiova, and Miodrag Mihailovic. 1975. "Male to female: The role transformation of transexuals." Archives of Sexual Behavior 4(March):173-185.

Levinson, Daniel, Charlotte Darrow, Edward Klein, Maria Levinson, and Braxton McKee. 1978. The seasons of a man's life. New York: Knopf.

Levitt, E. E., and A. D. Klassen. 1974. "Public attitudes toward homosexuality." Journal of Homosexuality 1(1):29-43.

Leznoff, Maurice, and William Westley. 1956. "The homosexual community." Social Problems 3(April):257-263.

Lief, Harold. 1977. "Current thinking on homosexuality." Medical Aspects of Human Sexuality 11(November):110-111.

Linton, Ralph. 1936. The Study of Man. New York: Appleton-Century-Crofts.

Lockwood, Daniel. 1980. Prison Sexual Violence. New York: Elsevier.

Looft, William. 1971. "Sex differences in the expression of vocational aspirations." Developmental Psychology 5(September):366.

Lynn, D. B., and W. L. Sawrey. 1959. "The effects of father-absence on Norwegian boys and girls." Journal of Abnormal and Social Psychology 59(September):258-262.

Maccoby, Eleanor, and Carol Jacklin. 1974. The Psychology of Sex Differences. Stanford, CA: Stanford University Press.

McCauley, E. A., and A. A. Ehrhardt. 1977. "Role expectations and definitions: A comparison of female transexuals and lesbians." Journal of Homosexuality 3(Winter):137-147.

Margolese, M. S., and O. Janziger. 1973. "Androsterone/etiocholanolone ratios in male homosexuals." British Medical Journal 3(July):207-210.

Masters, William H., and Virginia Johnson. 1979. Homosexuality in Perspective. Boston: Little-Brown.

Matza, David. 1964. Delinquency and Drift. New York: Wiley.

Merton, R. K. 1968. Social Theory and Social Structure. New York: Free Press.

_____. 1957. Social Theory and Social Structure. New York: Free Press.

Meyer-Bahlburg, Heino. 1977. "Sex hormones and male homosexuality in comparative perspective." Archives of Sexual Behavior 6(July):297-325.

Miller, Brian, and Laud Humphreys. 1980. "Lifestyles and violence: Homosexual victims of assault and murder." Qualitative Sociology 3(Fall):13-25.

Miller, Patricia, and William Simon. 1980. "The development of sexuality in adolescence." In Handbook of Adolescent Psychology, ed. Joseph Adelson, pp. 383-407. New York: Wiley.

Miller, Patricia, and William Simon. 1974. "Adolescent sexual behavior." Social Problems 22(October):58-76.

Money, John. 1976. "Letter to the editor." Science 191 (February 27):872. (Incorrectly referred to by Sagarin (1975) below as appearing in Science, January 4, 1975; this error was repeated in Kessler and McKenna (1978) above).

Money, John, and J. Brennon. 1968. "Sexual dimorphism in the psychology of female transexuals." Journal of Nervous and Mental Disorders 147(November):487-499.

Money, John, and Anke Ehrhardt. 1972. Man and Woman, Boy and Girl. Baltimore: Johns Hopkins University Press.

Money, John, and Eileen Higham. 1976. "Juvenile gender identity: Differentiation and transpositions." In Child Personality and Psychopathology: Current Topics, ed. A. Davids, pp. 115-137. New York: Wiley.

Morin, Stephen. 1977. "Heterosexual bias in psychological research on lesbianism and male homosexuality." The American Psychologist 32(August):629-637.

Morris, Richard, and Raymond Murphy. 1959. "The situs dimension in occupational structures." American Sociological Review 24(April):231-239.

Nemerowicz, Gloria. 1979. Children's Perception of Gender and Work Roles. New York: Praeger.

Newton, Esther. 1979. Mother Camp. Chicago: University of Chicago Press.

Norland, Stephen, Jennifer James, and Neal Shover. 1978. "Gender role expectations of juveniles." Sociological Quarterly 19(Autumn):545-554.

Norland, Stephen, and Pamela Loy. 1981. "Gender convergence and delinquency." Sociological Quarterly 22(Spring):275-283.

O'Donnell, John, Harwin Voss, Richard Clayton, Gerald Slaytin and Robin Room. 1976. Young Men and Drugs: A Nationwide Survey. Washington, D.C.: National Institute on Drug Abuse.

Oppenheimer, Valerie. 1970. _The Female Labor Force in the United States_. Berkeley: Institute of International Studies.

Ovesey, Lionel. 1969. _Homosexuality and Pseudohomosexuality_. New York: Science House.

Ovesey, Lionel, and Sherwyn Woods. 1980. "Pseudohomosexuality and homosexuality in men." In _Homosexual Behavior_, ed. Judd Marmor, pp. 325-341. New York: Basic Books.

Parsons, Talcott, and Edward Shils. 1951. "Values, motives, and systems of action." In _Toward a General Theory of Action_, ed. Talcott Parsons and Edward Shils, pp. 47-243. New York: Harper Torchbooks.

Pauly, Ira. 1969. "Adult manifestations of male transsexualism." In _Transsexualism and Sex Reassignment_, ed. Richard Green and John Money. Baltimore: Johns Hopkins University Press.

Peplau, Anne, and Susan Cochran. 1982. "Value orientations in the intimate relationships of gay men." _Journal of Homosexuality_ (in press).

Pietropinto, Anthony, and Jacqueline Simenauer. 1977. _Beyond the Male Myth_. New York: New York Times Books.

Polk, Kenneth. 1969. "Class, strain, and rebellion among adolescents." _Social Problems_ 17(Fall):214-224.

Polk, Kenneth, and David Halferty. 1972. "School cultures, adolescent commitments and delinquency." In _Schools and Delinquency_, ed. K. Polk and W. Schafer, pp. 70-90. Englewood Cliffs, N.J.: Prentice-Hall.

Raymond, Janice. 1979. _The Transsexual Empire_. Boston: Beacon Press.

Reichert, Reimut, and Martin Dannecker. 1977. "Male homosexuality in West Germany." _Journal of Sex Research_ 13(February):35-53.

Reynolds, H. T. 1977. _Analysis of Nominal Data_. Beverly Hills, Calif.: Sage.

Sagarin, Edward. 1975. "Sex rearing and sexual orientation: The reconciliation of apparently contradicting data." _Journal of Sex Research_ 11(November):329-334.

Saghir, Marcel, and Eli Robins. 1973. _Male and Female Homosexuality_. Baltimore: Williams and Wilkins.

262

Sawhill, Isabel. 1974. "Perspectives on women and work in America." In Work and the Quality of Life: Resource Papers for Work in America, ed. J. O'Toole, pp. 88-105. Cambridge, MA: MIT Press.

Schafer, Walter. 1972. "Participation in interscholastic athletics and delinquency." In Schools and Delinquency, ed. K. Polk and W. Schafer, pp. 91-101. Englewood Cliffs, N.J.: Prentice-Hall.

Schwartz, Pepper, and Philip Blumstein. 1979. "Sampling the gay community." Paper presented at the Meetings of the American Sociological Association, August, Boston. Mimeographed.

Scott, Joseph, and Edmund Vaz. 1967. "A perspective on middle class delinquency." In Middle-Class Delinquency, ed. Edmund Vaz, pp. 207-222. New York: Harper and Row.

Sewell, William, Robert Hauser, and Wendy Wolf. 1980. "Sex, schooling, and occupational status." American Journal of Sociology 86(November):551-583.

Short, James, and F. Ivan Nye. 1958. "Extent of unrecorded juvenile delinquency." Journal of Criminal Law, Criminology and Police Science 49(November-December):296-302.

Short, James, and Frederick Strodtbeck. 1965. Group Process and Gang Delinquency. Chicago: University of Chicago Press.

Siegel, Claire. 1973. "Sex differences in the occupational choices of second graders." Journal of Vocational Behavior 3(January):15-19.

Siegelman, Marvin. 1972. "Adjustment of male homosexuals and heterosexuals." Archives of Sexual Behavior 2(June):9-25.

Simmons, Adele, Ann Freeman, Margaret Dunkle and Francine Blau. 1975. Exploitation from 9 to 5: Report on the 20th Century Fund Task Force on Women and Employment. New York: Twentieth Century Fund.

Simmons, J. L. 1978. "The nature of deviant subcultures." In Deviance: The Interactionist Perspective, 3rd edition, ed. E. Rubington and M. Weinberg, pp. 280-282. New York: MacMillan.

Simmons, J. L. 1965. "Public stereotypes of deviants." Social Problems 13(Fall):223-232.

Simon, Rita. 1975. Women and Crime. Lexington, MA: Heath.

Simon, William. 1973. "The social, the erotic, and the sensual."
In <u>Nebraska Symposium on Motivation</u>, ed. James Cole and
Richard Diensbier, pp. 61-82. Lincoln: University of
Nebraska Press.

Socarides, Charles. 1978. <u>Homosexuality</u>. New York: Aronson.

_____. 1968. <u>The Overt Homosexual</u>. New York: Grune and Stratton.

Spence, J. T., and R. L. Helmreich. 1978. <u>Masculinity and
Femininity</u>. Austin, TX: University of Texas Press.

Spector, Malcolm. 1977. "Legitimizing homosexuality." <u>Society</u>
14(July):52-56.

Stein, A., and J. Smithells. 1969. "Age and sex differences in
children's sex standards about achievement." <u>Developmental
Psychology</u> 1(May):252-259.

Stein, Peter, and Steven Hoffman. 1978. "Sports and male role
strain." <u>Journal of Social Issues</u> 34(1):148-149.

Stephan, Walter. 1973. "Parental relationships and early social
experiences of activist male homosexuals and male
heterosexuals." <u>Journal of Abnormal Psychology</u> 82
(December):506-513.

Stoller, Robert. 1979. <u>Sexual Excitement</u>. New York: Pantheon
Press.

Stoller, Robert. 1968. <u>Sex and Gender</u>. New York: Science House.

Stoller, Robert. 1967. "It's only a phase: Femininity in boys."
<u>Journal of American Medical Association</u> 201(5):314-315.

Stolz, Lois. 1954. <u>Father Relations with Warborn Children</u>. Palo
Alto, CA: Stanford University Press.

Stringer, Peter, and Tadeusz Grygier. 1976. "Male homosexuality,
psychiatric patient status, and psychological masculinity and
femininity." <u>Archives of Sexual Behavior</u> 5(January):15-27.

Sudman, Seymour, and Norman Bradburn. 1974. <u>Response Effects in
Surveys</u>. Chicago: Aldine.

Sutherland, Edwin, and Donald Cressey. 1978. <u>Criminology</u>. New
York: Lippincott.

Sykes, Gresham, and David Matza. 1957. "Techniques of
neutralization." <u>American Sociological Review</u>
22(December):664-670.

Thompson, Norman. 1975. "Gender labels and early sex role development." Child Development 46(June):339-347.

Tittle, Charles. 1980. Sanctions and Social Deviance. New York: Praeger.

Tittle, Charles, and Wayne Villemez. 1977. "Social class and criminality." Social Forces 56(December):474-502.

Tittle, Charles, Wayne Villemez, and Douglas Smith. 1978. "The myth of social class and criminality." American Sociological Review 43(October):643-656.

Toby, Jackson. 1967. "Affluence and adolescent crime." In Task Force Report: Juvenile Delinquency and Youth Crime, pp. 132-144. President's Commission on Law Enforcement and Administration of Justice. Washington, D.C.: U. S. Government Printing Office.

Tripp, C. A. 1975. The Homosexual Matrix. New York: McGraw-Hill.

U. S. Bureau of the Census. 1978. Statistical abstract of the United States. Washington, D.C.: Government Printing Office.

Vaz, Edmund. 1967. "Juvenile delinquency in the middle-class youth culture." In Middle-Class Delinquency, ed. E. Vaz, pp. 131-147. New York: Harper and Row.

Vener, Arthur, and Clinton Snyder. 1966 "The pre-school child's awareness and anticipation of adult sex-roles." Sociometry 29(June):159-168.

Warren, Carol. 1974. Identity and Community in the Gay World. New York: Wiley.

Webb, Allen. 1963. "Sex-role preferences and adjustments in early adolescents." Child Development 34(September):609-618.

Weinberg, Martin, and Colin Williams. 1974. Male Homosexuals. New York: Oxford Press.

Weinberg, Martin. 1970. "The male homosexual: Age-related variations in social and psychological characteristics." Social Problems 17(Spring):527-538.

Weissbach, Theodore and Gary Zagon. 1975. "The effect of deviant group membership upon impressions of personality." Journal of Social Psychology 95(April):263-266.

West, D. J. 1977. _Homosexuality_ _Re-examined_. Minneapolis: University of Minnesota Press.

———. 1967. _Homosexuality_. Chicago: Aldine.

Westwood, Gordon. 1960. _A_ _Minority:_ _A_ _Report_ _on_ _the_ _Life_ _of_ _the_ _Male_ _Homosexual_ _in_ _Great_ _Britain_. London: Longmans.

Whitam, Frederick. 1980. "The prehomosexual male child in three societies: The United States, Guatamala, Brazil." _Archives_ _of_ _Sexual_ _Behavior_ 9(April):87-99.

———. 1977. "Childhood indicators of male homosexuality." _Archives_ _of_ _Sexual_ _Behavior_ 6(March):89-96.

Whitam, Frederick, and Mary Jo Dizon. 1979. "Occupational choice and sexual orientation in cross-cultural perspective." _International_ _Review_ _of_ _Modern_ _Sociology_ 9(July-December):137-149.

Whiting, B. 1979. "Contributions of anthropology to the study of gender, identity, gender role, and sexual behavior." In _Human_ _Sexuality_, ed. H. Katchadourian, pp. 320-331. Berkeley: University of California Press.

Whiting, B., and C. Edwards. 1973. "A cross-cultural analysis of sex differences in the behavior of children aged three through eleven." _Journal_ _of_ _Social_ _Psychology_ 91(December):171-188.

Whiting, J., and B. Whiting. 1975. "Aloofness and intimacy: A cross-cultural study." _Ethos_ 3(Summer):183-207.

Wolfgang, Marvin. 1958. _Patterns_ _in_ _Criminal_ _Homicide_. Philadelphia: University of Pennsylvania Press.

Yando, Regina, Victoria Seitz, and Edward Zigler. 1978. _Imitation:_ _A_ _Developmental_ _Perspective_. Hillsdale, N.J.: Lawrence Elbaum Associates, Publishers.

Zuger, B. 1970. "The role of familial factors in persistent effeminate behavior in boys." _American_ _Journal_ _of_ _Psychiatry_ 126(February):1167-1170.

Zuger, B. 1966. "Effeminate behavior present in boys from early childhood." _Journal_ _of_ _Pediatrics_ 69(December):1098-1107.

INDEX

ABOUT THE AUTHOR

JOSEPH HARRY is Associate Professor of Sociology at Northern Illinois University. He holds a B.A. from Reed College and an M.A. and Ph.D. from the University of Oregon.

His principal areas of interest are deviance and criminology with principal emphasis on the study of gay men. He has published numerous articles on gay men, including the book (with William DeVall), The Social Organization of Gay Males (Praeger 1978).

For the 1982/1983 academic year he will be at the Alfred C. Kinsey Institute for Sex Research at Indiana University.